ILLINOIS MUNICIPAL FINANCE

UNIVERSITY OF ILLINOIS PRESS URBANA · CHICAGO · LONDON 1968

ILLINOIS MUNICIPAL FINANCE
A POLITICAL AND ECONOMIC ANALYSIS

GLENN W. FISHER AND ROBERT P. FAIRBANKS

Manufactured in the United States of America
Library of Congress Catalog Card No. 67-21852

252 72373 2

to Marvel and Nancy

ACKNOWLEDGMENTS

Local government is often defended on the grounds that it is close to the people, yet the experience of the authors in writing this book suggests that less is known about the operation of local government than about the operation of state and federal government.

This book grew out of a request from the Illinois Cities and Villages Municipal Problems Commission that the Institute of Government and Public Affairs of the University of Illinois study the financial problems of Illinois municipalities. In the course of the study, the authors soon discovered that much basic information about local financial processes in Illinois is known only to a few specialists. Furthermore, it became apparent that local government decision-making is not the simple process that is sometimes described in textbooks. The usual descriptions of an elected municipal council making decisions which are then implemented by administrative departments reveal little of the complex interactions among the various branches of the state government, other units of local government, and the numerous experts that are involved in financial decisions.

The effort to unwind these complexities required the help of a great many persons and any attempt to name all who made major contributions runs the risk of omitting some who should be included. Nevertheless, it would be ungracious not to make the attempt.

The Illinois Cities and Villages Municipal Problems Commission provided the opportunity and the funds to gather much of the information contained in the volume, although the book is not an official report to the commission nor is the commission responsible for any of the views expressed. Senator A. L. Cronin was chairman of the commission during the 1963-65 biennium and Senator Everett R. Peters was chairman during 1965-67.

Colleagues at the University of Illinois and at Northern Illinois University provided encouragement, information, and criticism. The computer facilities at both universities added in compiling data and made possible the statistical analysis reported in Appendix A.

Thanks is due to Northern Illinois University for providing released time for one of the authors during the 1964-65 academic year.

The Illinois Municipal League provided much information about municipalities, mailed questionnaires, and answered numerous questions. Also, several municipal officials contributed many hours explaining their operations and discussing problems with the authors. Many also filled out questionnaires, answered letters, and sent copies of municipal reports and records.

Several persons who have no official connection with local government but who have special knowledge of some phase of municipal finance granted interviews and provided information. Special thanks is due to Mr. Louis Ancel for the many hours he devoted to discussing municipal finance and for answering innumerable questions about municipal law.

The following persons have read and commented on one or more chapters: H. K. Allen, Wayne Anderson, Thomas Anton, James M. Banovetz, Leo Cohen, Eugene Maynard, Phillip Monypenny, Thomas Page, Gilbert Y. Steiner, and Amos Watts.

James McBrearty and V. Russell Whitesel did much of the field work involved in collecting data from county clerks. Other students who worked on the project at some stage include Roderick Bricksin, Leslie Dean, Ann H. Elder, Gerald Gulley, Alfred Svancarek, and Richard K. Swenson.

Mrs. Jean Baker, Mrs. Janet Cullison, Mrs. Lorena McClain, and Mrs. Loretta Ward McKeighen typed several versions of the manuscript.

Probably not all of the persons interviewed will agree with the authors' interpretations. Not all of the suggestions made by readers have been accepted. Nevertheless, a great deal of effort has been expended to insure that facts are accurate and interpretations reasonable.

CONTENTS

LIST OF TABLES

LIST OF APPENDIX TABLES

LIST OF FIGURES

APPENDIX FIGURE

LIST OF EXHIBITS

INTRODUCTION

This book is about the finances of Illinois municipal government. It contains much numerical data which show where municipalities get their revenue and the purposes for which they spend it. Beyond this, however, an attempt has been made to provide insights into the factors which determine the level and pattern of revenue and expenditure.

According to a popular theory of democracy, public policy is determined by elected officials who compete for the voters' favor by attempting to determine and carry out their will. In fact, of course, the situation is considerably more complicated than this simple theory would suggest. It is true that municipal officials are subject to pressures by various members of the electorate and that there is competition for the voters' favor. On the other hand, it is clear that few voters have a clear understanding of the complexities of municipal finance and that demands made upon municipal officials are apt to be demands for a specific government service or opposition to a particular tax increase.

The municipal official not only finds that he must translate many specific demands into financial policy but that there are many constraints upon the decisions which can be made. Municipalities are created by the state, and many of the financial procedures prescribed by the state are closely tied to property tax procedures established when Illinois was primarily an agricultural state. Furthermore, the municipal official finds that the past is a powerful determinant of the future — even with regard to matters which are legally within his control. Once programs are established, vested interests often oppose change. Once tax rates are established, they arouse little opposition but new taxes or substantial increases in rates are a different matter. The net result of these constraints is that decision-making rarely involves a methodical balancing of all the alternatives. Decisions are incremental responses to particular pressures which are shaped by a variety of political and environmental constraints. Often, in fact, the constraints are so pervasive that few changes are made. In this case, indecision, rather than decision, characterizes the politics of finance.

The first seven chapters of this volume include statistical and descriptive data which indicate where Illinois cities get their money and how they spend it. Although a large quantity of municipal financial information is available, much of the data compiled by municipalities is intended primarily for purposes of internal control or to meet legal requirements which are sometimes archaic. Some municipalities publish financial reports which are well designed to inform residents of the sources of revenue and the purposes for which funds are spent; but, because of variation from city to city, it is seldom possible to use these data in a statewide study. For these reasons it was necessary to rely heavily on data collected by the U.S. Census Bureau for the year 1962. Fortunately, general patterns of municipal revenue and expenditure change rather slowly so that comparisons among municipalities remain valid for several years even though magnitudes have increased. Census data were supplemented by data from various published reports and by information gathered personally by the authors. Appendix B contains additional information about data sources and statistical procedures.

Presenting revenue and expenditure data for so many municipalities in a meaningful fashion also proved to be difficult. To depend upon statewide totals or averages would obscure the great variation among municipalities. Attempts to make the data more meaningful by classifying cities by population or by geographic area were successful for some kinds of expenditure and for certain types of revenue, but no method of classification was useful in all cases. Attempts were made to correlate expenditure and revenue with variables such as population size, population density, income, and level of education. Again there was no single variable which was significant for more than a few types of expenditure or revenue. In the course of experimentation with various methods of classifying or correlating city data, it appeared that the larger cities show a higher degree of regularity than the smaller ones. As a result, it was decided to concentrate upon the 41 cities which had a 1960 population of more than 25,000 persons. For this reason much statistical data are presented for these 41 cities and most of the interviews with municipal officials were with officials of these cities. However, data from other groups of cities are utilized whenever such data are available and seem to make a useful contribution to the purposes of the study.

Even within the 41 cities some problems result because of the unique position of Chicago. Not only are its fiscal variables of a different order of magnitude, but many state statutes contain special provisions which, in effect, apply only to Chicago. For these reasons some of the data provided for the other 40 cities are not available for Chicago on a strictly comparable basis, and some of the descriptions of financial practices and procedures do not apply to Chicago.

To accompany the statistical data a good deal of nonnumerical information has been provided. For example, Chapter 2 contains descriptions of the services provided by municipalities and some of the problems faced by cities in connection with particular services. Chapters 3 through 6 include descriptions of the history and administration of the various revenue sources and indicate some of the problems involved in using these revenue sources. The amount of material of this type which could be included is voluminous; therefore, it was necessary to choose the material which seemed to be most relevant.

Some of the descriptive material concerns units of governments other than municipalities. This reflects the authors' conviction that intergovernmental relationships pervade every aspect of municipal government finance in Illinois. The tax, revenue, and grant-in-aid policies of other units of government are important external conditions that affect municipal finance decisions, and the decision-making system itself is largely created by the state government. Other units of government become deeply involved in the decision-making process as negotiators, as pressure groups, and, in the case of state government, as creator and rule-maker. Finally, even the statistics which indicate the results of past decisions may be affected since there is some confusion as to whether certain boards and agencies constitute departments of municipal government or whether they are independent units.

Appendix A is a report upon an attempt to utilize multiple correlation analysis to study the relationship among various external conditions and the levels of expenditure of municipalities. This technique is a powerful tool for measuring the relationships among variables and contributes considerably to our understanding of the factors which affect government finance. Unfortunately, however, it does not specify the cause-effect relationships or explain the mechanism whereby external conditions influence financial decisions. It is the conviction of the authors that the many recent statistical studies of the determinants of governmental expenditure and revenue have made important contributions to understanding but that the information about Illinois municipal finance in Chapters 1 through 7 illustrates how much detail is obscured by numerical totals. Knowledge of these details not only permits the development of more meaningful totals, it also aids in the interpretation of statistical results.

Chapters 8 and 9 distill the most significant findings of statistical and nonstatistical analysis of Illinois municipal finance into a statement of the factors which affect municipal finance decisions and the effect which such decisions have upon the urban areas. Hopefully, the result is a concise statement which draws upon scholarship without being scholastic.

Both the statistical and nonstatistical analyses of decision-making largely exclude the city of Chicago. This omission is certainly not the result of any feeling that Chicago is unimportant. Not only does Chicago contain 35 per cent of the state's population, but the quality of its government services and the nature of its politics have an impact upon every city in the state. The omission results, rather, from the different nature of the problem to be analyzed and the necessity of keeping the size of the research problem within limits.

Chicago is subject to a different set of state laws and is governed by a system which is vastly more complex than is the government of smaller cities. Politics in Chicago is of a different style than in most downstate cities and the relationship of the mayor of Chicago to the governor and the state legislature is far different from that of a downstate mayor. Undoubtedly, a complete analysis would reveal that a number of the conclusions about decision-making in the smaller cities would have to be modified for Chicago.

1 THE ENVIRONMENT FOR FINANCIAL DECISION-MAKING

A large and growing number of Americans live within the limits of an incorporated municipality. Many of these persons, as well as a good proportion of those who live in unincorporated areas, regularly spend a portion of their time within the boundaries of a municipality. As a result, municipal government has a direct and vital effect upon the lives of most Americans.

Municipal government has important regulatory and leadership functions. City zoning laws and licensing provisions affect the physical growth and appearance of the city. Many civic organizations, private firms, and nonmunicipal governments look to city government for leadership. Further, the city government occupies a symbolic role which is unique among local governments. The mayor is usually an indispensable participant in ground breakings and ribbon cuttings, whether the project is sponsored by private business, religious and philanthropic organizations, or the municipal government itself.[1]

It is municipal service activities, however, which account for most municipal expenditures and thus for the financial problems which plague many American cities. Within most municipalities the principal responsibility for providing police and fire protection, streets, sidewalks, sewerage, and sanitation, as well as public parks and recreation facilities, falls upon municipal government. The public's conception of what con-

[1] The role of the mayor as the community's leading official has its disadvantages as well as its advantages. Every city official can recount instances in which the city has received the credit or the blame for projects over which it had no control or influence. One downstate Illinois mayor recounts that a telephone caller became very indignant when he could do nothing about a stray dog problem in the caller's neighborhood, several miles from the city limits.

stitutes an acceptable level of such services has been rising. At the same time, the changing character of the urban community has created problems for many cities. Central cities and the older suburbs find that the flight of high income residents to the suburbs leaves them with rising expenditures in declining neighborhoods, increasing police and street costs occasioned by increased commuting through or into their city, and a stable or declining tax base. The problem of the newer, rapidly growing suburbs, on the other hand, comes from the need to expand rapidly capital facilities and services.

The level and pattern of the expenditures[2] which are made in an effort to meet the service needs of Illinois municipalities are the result of a complicated series of interrelated decisions which have extended over a long period of time and which have involved millions of people. It is impossible to describe the entire process in detail, but it is possible to highlight some of the major factors which influence the results.

The principal actors in the process are municipal officials who are chosen by election or appointment and given authority to make certain financial decisions. This authority is limited by a number of legal constraints, and, in practice, decision-makers are subject to a great many influences and pressures. The decision-making process is essentially a political process in which widely divergent views and interests come into conflict. Interested parties make their desires known by bringing various kinds of influences to bear upon municipal officials. These pressures vary in intensity from casual comments during chance meetings with aldermen to intensive, well-organized campaigns to bring about the defeat of a member of the city council who voted "wrong" on a particular issue. The groups that attempt to influence financial decision-making may include organizations whose major purpose is far removed from matters of municipal finance or politics, but which may have an interest in a particular program. At the other end of the spectrum are well-financed organizations which have as a major function the influencing of tax and expenditure policies of local governments.

The political process — the pressures and counterpressures, the compromises, and the logrolling — takes place within the framework of a political system which determines the "rules of the game." Such matters as the number of municipal officials, how they are chosen, and the power of each official are part of the political system. The details of procedure, such as the form in which appropriation or tax levy ordinances are drawn and the number of votes required for adoption, are

---

[2] "Level" refers to the *amount* of expenditure and is usually measured on a per capita basis. "Pattern" refers to the *distribution* of total expenditure by function or object.

also aspects of the political system. Since municipal governments are not sovereign but are created by and subject to the state government, many aspects of the municipal political system are determined by state constitutional and statutory provisions. Other features of the system are established by customs, some of which are well established and universal while others are unique to a single Illinois city.

Decisions about municipal finance are also affected by conditions external to the municipal political system. These conditions may be demographic, geographic, economic, governmental, or socio-political.

Demographic conditions are important in that the number, distribution, and age of the population have an effect upon the need for particular types of governmental services. In a thinly populated area, for example, the provision of sewerage and sanitation services might easily be left to the individual householder; but, as the area becomes urbanized and the population density increases, considerations of health and aesthetics dictate that these services become matters of public concern.

Geographic factors include those physical characteristics of the city such as topography, which affects the cost of construction and maintenance of municipal facilities, and the availability and purity of water supplies.

The economic character of the community affects both the need for and the ability to pay for governmental services. A high income residential community may require less fire protection expenditure than a slum or industrial area. However, a given fire protection tax rate in this community will produce a far higher per capita revenue than the same rate in a slum community but a much lower per capita revenue than it would in an industrial area.

As noted above, an important part of the municipal decision-making environment is provided by other governments. The state not only plays the major role in establishing the political system through which local decisions are made but also takes an active part in the decision-making process. The state limits the kind and rate of taxation which may be imposed and provides a few direct cash grants. The federal government also makes grants either directly or through the state government and imposes certain conditions on their use. Both federal and state governments may remove property from tax rolls by purchase or condemnation, and both may issue orders which result in sizable municipal expenditures.[3] The action of other local governmental units may also have an important effect upon the municipal decision-making

[3] Federal orders of this type are less common but in such fields as water and air pollution the federal government can and does take such action.

process. In Illinois, where there are more local governments than in any other state, municipalities are overlapped by several other units of government which provide services and levy taxes in the municipality.[4] Obviously, the quantity and quality of services provided and the tax burdens imposed by the overlying governments have an important effect upon the demand for municipal services and upon the ability of municipalities to finance these services.

In addition there are a number of socio-political characteristics of the residents of a municipality which may affect the results of the decision-making process. Included are such factors as the level of education, general attitude toward government and political participation, and social class. Some of these factors are very difficult to measure but are nonetheless important. The effects of the factors which influence expenditure and revenue decisions are difficult to analyze with precision because many of the variables cannot be measured.

Other obstacles to the precise analysis of financial decision-making are provided by the twin phenomena, *interaction* and *feedback*. Interaction refers to the fact that the variables which affect municipal finance decisions also affect each other. For example, the growth of a slum area may create pressures for certain types of expenditure and, at the same time, affect the assessed value of property in the area which, in turn, may influence the expenditure decision. Feedback refers to the fact that decisions about municipal finance affect the entire character of the community and thus alter variables which in turn influence financial decisions. For example, a decision to improve the sewerage system or to provide better fire protection may make the community more attractive for business and residential use and thus be a factor in the economic growth of the city. This, in turn, creates additional tax revenues and additional demands for municipal improvements. At the same time, the higher taxes imposed to pay for the original improvements may have feedback effects in the opposite direction. The higher taxes may make the municipality less attractive for certain uses and may have an adverse effect upon the tax base. A financial decision may also alter relationships within the political process and may even cause a change in the political system itself. It is not uncommon, for example, for unpopular financial policies to be an important element leading to change in the form of municipal government.

---

[4] The term "overlapping" is used to include three distinguishable cases: (1) the territory of the other unit of government extends over part of the municipality but also includes area outside the municipality; (2) the territory of the other unit of government is coterminous with the municipality; (3) the territory of the other government is smaller than the municipality and lies entirely within the municipality.

FORMS AND POWERS OF ILLINOIS MUNICIPALITIES

Illinois municipalities come into being primarily for the purpose of meeting local needs, but they have no inherent or constitutional powers of self-government. The form of government, its powers, and the duties and responsibilities of its officials are determined by the General Assembly. The Constitution prohibits special municipal charters, and the General Assembly has provided general procedures for incorporation of cities and villages, although there are 19 incorporated towns which still retain special charters issued before 1870.[5]

Because the primary functions of municipal government involve the rendering of services, rather than legislating or administering those state laws which regulate fundamental relations among people, the form of government differs from that of other units of local government. There is generally more separation between the legislative and administrative functions of municipal government than of township or county government. The offices contested in a municipal election are apt to be policy-formulating rather than administrative positions. This is in sharp contrast with county and township governments where such technical or administrative positions as highway commissioner (engineer), assessor, and sheriff (police chief) are elected.[6]

The governing body of villages in Illinois is a board consisting of a president (mayor) and six trustees. Generally, the trustees are elected at large, but a village with a population of more than 25,000 may elect trustees from wards. The president and trustees appoint a treasurer, street commissioner, village marshal, and such other officers as they deem necessary. A village clerk is elected.

The most widely used form of city government in Illinois is the mayor-council or aldermanic form. Cities using this form of government are divided into wards for the purpose of electing members of the city council. The mayor presides over council meetings and votes to break ties. His veto power over ordinances may be overridden by a two-thirds vote. Illinois mayors are not "strong" in terms of statutory powers granted to them, but a forceful mayor is often able to dominate the city governmental process by virtue of his own personality and the prestige of his office.

Cities may vote to adopt the commission form of government. Under this plan a mayor and four other commissioners are elected at large in

---

[5] Based upon *Official List of Counties and Incorporated Municipalities of Illinois,* issued by the Secretary of State in 1965.

[6] Samuel K. Gove, *The Illinois Municipal Electoral Process,* Commission Papers of the Institute of Government and Public Affairs, University of Illinois, November, 1964.

a nonpartisan election.[7] The five commissioners constitute the city council and perform much the same functions as do aldermen in mayor-council cities, but each one also serves as administrative head of a city department as well.

Approximately 60 Illinois municipalities have the managerial form of government. A mayor and council, usually elected at large, but occasionally from wards, carry out legislative functions. The administrative function is the responsibility of an appointed municipal manager who need not be chosen from residents of the municipality and who is usually a person with formal training for the position. In a few cities, the mayor has an administrative assistant who performs many of the functions of a manager even though the municipality operates under a mayor-council or trustee form of organization.

The ten[8] articles of the Illinois Municipal Code contain many direct or indirect references to the powers and functions of municipalities. Article 11 of Chapter 24, entitled "Corporate Powers and Functions," deals specifically and in considerable detail with this subject. This article is composed of 149 divisions which, in turn, are grouped under 40 headings. These headings, listed below, indicate the wide scope of the functions performed by Illinois municipalities.

PUBLIC HEALTH, SAFETY AND WELFARE

- Police protection and public order
- Fire protection
- Planning, zoning and urban rehabilitation
- Health regulations
- Hospitals and sanitariums
- Control over buildings and construction
- Vehicles
- Powers over certain businesses
- General assistance
- Boats and harbors
- Cultural activities
- Cemeteries
- Weights and measures
- Athletic contests
- Coin operated devices
- Oil and gas
- Railroad safety
- Continuity of government
- General powers — Licensing and nuisances

---

[7] For a recent analysis of the role of national and local parties in Illinois municipal elections see: *Ibid.*

[8] There is no article numbered 10. The last article is numbered 11. See: George Platt, "The Illinois Municipal Code," *Smith-Hurd Illinois Annotated Statutes*, pp. 74-76.

PUBLIC WORKS, BUILDINGS AND PROPERTY

Eminent domain and public works — general
Public buildings
Parking facilities
Trees and forestry
Procurement of industrial buildings
Lease, sale and transfer of public property
Streets and public ways
Recreational facilities
Airports
Harbors and watercourses
Public land dedications
Exhibitions on public property
Bridges, viaducts, tunnels, ferries
Drains, culverts, cesspools, sewers
Flood control and drainage
Monuments and memorials
Municipal utilities
Heat, power and light services
Transportation systems
Harbors and terminals
Water supply and sewerage systems

The divisions which fall under each of these headings differ considerably in length and detail. The shortest division, entitled "Oil and Gas," reads: "The corporate authorities of each municipality may grant permits to mine oil or gas, under such restrictions as will protect public and private property and insure proper remuneration for such grants."[9]

More commonly, a division contains several articles which spell out powers and duties in some detail and often provides for a special tax levy to support the activity. For example, the first of five divisions which fall under the heading "Police Protection and Public Order" authorizes corporate authorities to pass and enforce police ordinances and to prescribe the duties and powers of police officers. A special police protection tax is authorized but must be approved in a public referendum. The second division prohibits the transportation of prisoners in uncovered patrol wagons. The third division, a very short one, permits municipalities to establish penal institutions or use the county jail with the consent of county officials. Division 4 deals in considerable detail with houses of correction and farm colonies. Rules for the appointment of a board of inspectors, for compensating the board members and employees, and for keeping of books and statements are provided. The final division gives municipalities specific authority to suppress gambling and prostitution and to prevent disturbances such as

[9] *Ill. Rev. Stat.*, ch. 24, sec. 11-56-1 (1965).

riots, intoxication, fights, and cockfights. Authority is also granted to prohibit the parking of motor vehicles on private property without the consent of the owner and to prevent cruelty to animals. An unusual feature of this last division is that municipalities are given authority to suppress disorderly houses within an area three miles *outside* the boundaries of the municipality.

As this book is concerned with municipal finance, much attention will be devoted to the amounts spent for various functions. It should not be assumed, however, that the amount expended is a measure of the importance of the function to the community. Some powers, such as the power to control building construction, can be utilized in such a way as to have a tremendous impact upon the economic, social, and political character of the community even though relatively small sums are spent in performing the function. On the other hand, a municipality in which gross expenditures for the operation of a utility or municipal hospital are large may differ little from a similar city in which these services are privately provided.

LOCATION AND SIZE OF ILLINOIS MUNICIPALITIES

It is to be expected that both the size of a municipality and its location in relation to other municipalities will affect the services performed by the municipal government, the resources available for financing services, and the process through which financial decisions are made. It is well known, for example, that large central cities must provide levels of governmental services which are far more costly, per person, than the levels provided by smaller, noncentral cities. On the other hand, a central city has some advantages in its quest for revenue. Its larger size makes possible the administration of some revenue sources which smaller cities could not utilize feasibly, and a central location in the metropolitan complex makes it the only suitable location for some economic activities.

In a similar fashion, isolated municipalities would be expected to have different patterns of service needs and revenue availability than would either a central city or a municipality lying within, but not at the center of, a metropolitan complex.

In 1960, over 35 per cent of the population of Illinois lived in Chicago. All the other cities in the state are very much smaller.[10] There are, for example, only two cities other than Chicago which have a pop-

[10] Unless otherwise indicated, all population data in this chapter are 1960 Census of Population figures. Estimates of population of larger cities in more recent years have been made by the authors and are utilized for analytical purposes in later chapters. See Appendix B for details of estimation methods.

ulation greater than 100,000. This contrast in size can perhaps be made even clearer by noting that Chicago contains 28 times as many people as Rockford, the second largest city in the state. Other municipalities range downward in size to Central City (Grundy County) with a population of 30. The large number of small municipalities is emphasized by noting that 56 per cent of Illinois municipalities have populations of less than 1,000 persons. As indicated in Table 1, these small municipalities contain only 3 per cent of the state population.

TABLE 1

NUMBER OF ILLINOIS MUNICIPALITIES, BY SIZE GROUP

Population Group	Number of Municipalities	Population (in thousands)	Population as Per Cent of State Total (cumulative)
200,000 or more	1	3,550.4	35.2
100,000 to 199,999	2	229.9	37.5
50,000 to 99,999	12	804.2	45.5
25,000 to 49,999	26	890.4	54.3
10,000 to 24,999	74	1,145.2	65.7
5,000 to 9,999	86	621.4	71.9
2,500 to 4,999	118	409.2	76.0
1,000 to 2,499	229	353.7	79.5
Less than 1,000	703	300.7	82.5
All Municipalities	1,251	8,304.9	

SOURCE U.S. Bureau of the Census, *Census of Governments: 1962,* I, 32, 33. Population data are 1960 Census data except that estimates or special census data are used for cities incorporated between 1960 and 1962.

The character of a municipality is strongly influenced not only by its size but also by its location in relation to other municipalities. More than two-thirds of the municipal population of the state is located in the six-county area which has been designated as the Chicago Standard Metropolitan Statistical Area (SMSA). This area contains 246 municipalities of which 59 have a population of less than 1,000 persons.

Downstate Illinois is characterized by the cornbelt pattern of many small agricultural shopping and marketing centers interspersed among which are a number of larger cities which serve as regional trade centers and as centers of agriculturally oriented industry. Seven areas in downstate Illinois have been designated as Standard Metropolitan Statistical Areas. Two of these are partly in other states.

The St. Louis SMSA consists of the City of St. Louis, three counties in Missouri, and Madison and St. Clair counties in Illinois. Within the Illinois portion of the area lie 52 municipalities containing a total population of 352,535. The Davenport–Rock Island–Moline SMSA consists of Rock Island County, Illinois, and one county in Iowa. Rock Island County contains 15 cities with a total population of 125,545.

The five downstate SMSA's which lie wholly in Illinois are all centered around a single dominant city except for the Champaign-Urbana area which has a "twin city" nucleus. These five areas contain 97 cities.

The location of all SMSA's (shaded areas) and of all cities of more than 25,000 population is shown in Figures I and II, while Table 2 provides more details concerning the distribution of cities in relation to Standard Metropolitan Statistical Areas.

TABLE 2

NUMBER AND POPULATION OF MUNICIPALITIES, BY STANDARD METROPOLITAN STATISTICAL AREAS

	Number of Municipalities, 1962		Population, 1960	
Area	Population over 25,000	Population under 25,000	Municipalities over 25,000	Municipalities under 25,000
Chicago SMSA	22	224	4,468,569	1,236,009
Cook County	16	103	4,170,385	778,601
Outside Cook County	6	121	298,184	457,408
St. Louis SMSA[a]	4	48	202,096	150,439
Davenport–Rock Island–Moline SMSA[a]	2	13	94,568	30,977
Champaign-Urbana SMSA	2	20	76,877	34,617
Decatur SMSA	1	9	78,004	7,485
Peoria SMSA	2	29	131,308	71,883
Rockford SMSA	1	8	126,706	19,492
Springfield SMSA	1	24	83,271	21,235
Total in SMSA's	35	375	5,261,399	1,572,137
Outside SMSA's	6	835	213,457	1,257,930

[a] Illinois portion only.

SOURCE U.S. Bureau of the Census, *Census of Governments: 1962,* I, 76, 127.

ECONOMIC CHARACTERISTICS OF ILLINOIS MUNICIPALITIES

Illinois municipalities also differ greatly in economic and social characteristics. Some are primarily residential suburbs; others are manufacturing or retailing centers. Many have a balanced economic base in which several kinds of economic activities are important. Some cities are growing rapidly, but others have a stable or declining population.

FIGURE I

MUNICIPALITIES OF OVER 25,000 POPULATION

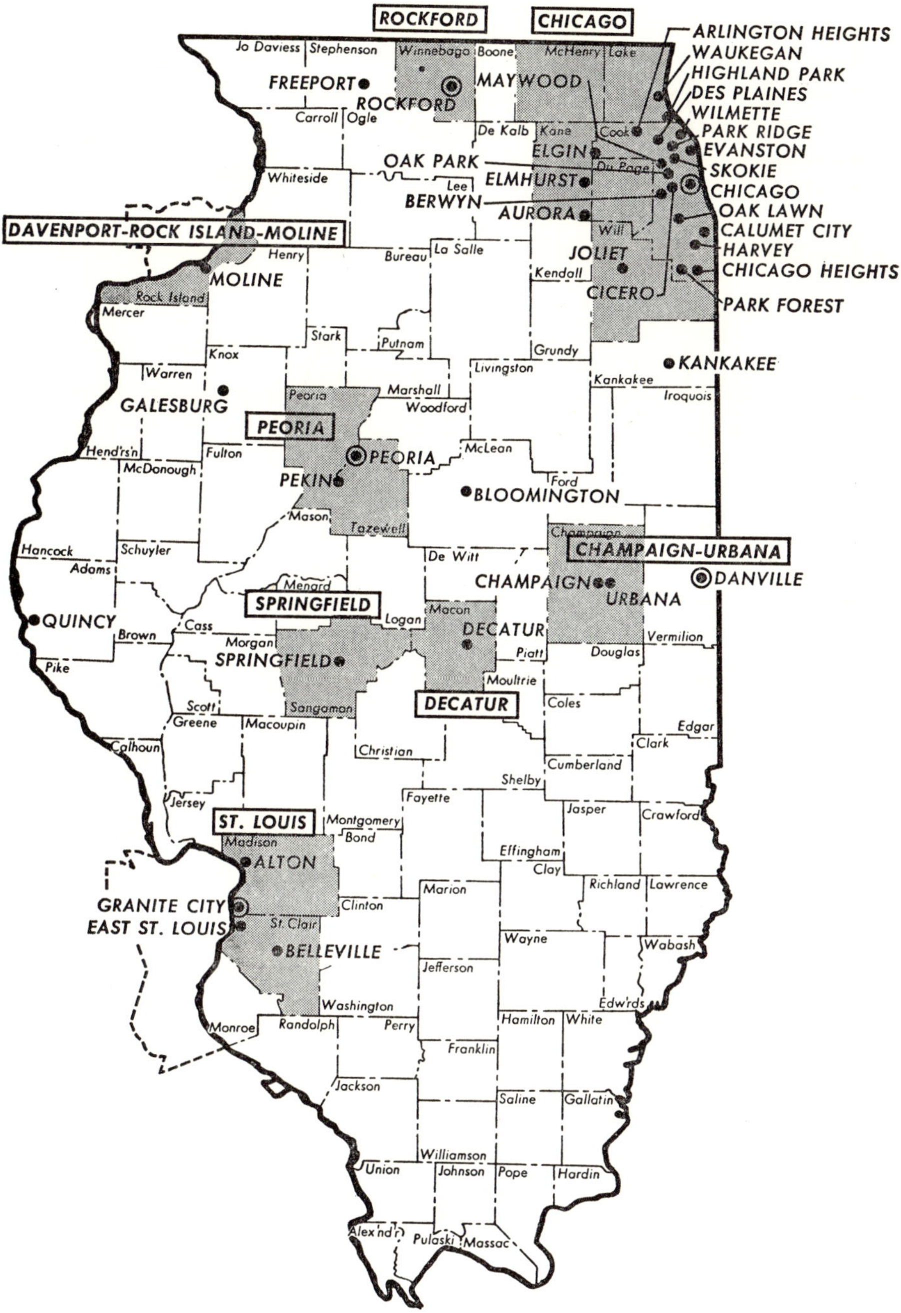

FIGURE II

MUNICIPALITIES OF OVER 25,000 POPULATION IN CHICAGO SMSA

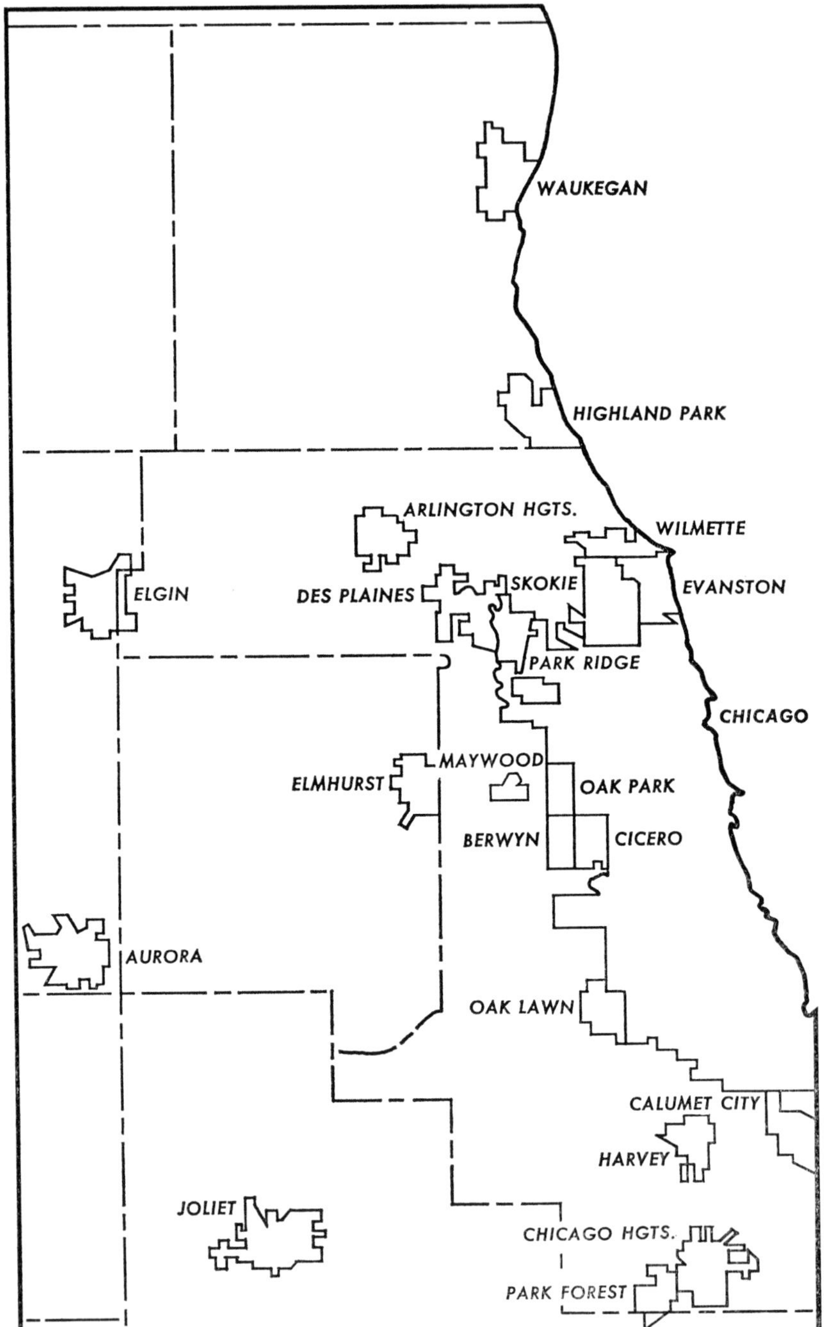

There are significant differences in the income level and the age composition of these cities.

The age composition of a city, its growth rate, the level of income of the population, and the place of employment of residents impinge upon the finances of the community in many ways; primarily they affect the needs and demands for municipal services. Also, the economic character of the city affects both the level of income and the amount of taxable property within the city and thus the financial resources available to meet public needs. Finally, the economic and social characteristics of the population may influence the political process. An older, wealthier population may be less sympathetic to city recreational and welfare programs than a younger, less economically secure population but may demand higher standards of street cleaning and sidewalk repair. The political power structure of a city whose residents are largely employed by a few locally owned industries may be very different from that of a city in which the owners and managers of the principal industry live outside the municipality. Still a different political situation may exist when the majority of male citizens spend their workdays in another city.

In general, the greatest extremes in economic and related characteristics are found among smaller cities, but even within the 41 cities of over 25,000 there are marked differences. For example, the employment-residence ratio, a measure of net commuting into the municipality, ranges from 27 in Park Forest to 149 in Skokie[11] and the median income of families ranges from $4,842 in East St. Louis to $13,661 in Wilmette.[12]

Ten-year growth rates vary from —7.8 per cent in Peoria to 300.2 in Skokie. The varying growth rates, of course, result from different causes. In the case of smaller cities a declining population is often a symptom of the economic decline of the area. In other cases, slight declines in population are the result of movement from central cities to suburbs or from older suburbs to newer ones. In mature suburbs such as Oak Park and Evanston, there is little available land for the construction of additional residential units so that population can increase only as older buildings are replaced by residential units which utilize land more intensively.

The maturity of a suburban city is often reflected in the age composition of its population. Berwyn, Evanston, and Oak Park have much

---

[11] Victor Jones, Richard L. Farstall, and Andrew Collver, "Economic and Social Characteristics of Urban Places," *The Municipal Yearbook, 1963* (Chicago: The International City Managers' Association, 1963), pp. 85-157.

[12] U.S. Bureau of the Census, *1960 Census of Population.*

smaller percentages of children than do the rapidly growing suburbs of Arlington Heights, Oak Lawn, and Park Forest. This undoubtedly results from the fact that younger families tend to move into the new areas, leaving an unusually large proportion of older persons in the older suburbs and creating "new" suburbs with a high percentage of young persons. Central cities such as Chicago and the cities which are not part of a metropolitan complex such as Bloomington, Danville, Freeport, Galesburg, Kankakee, and Quincy tend to have a percentage of young people which falls in between the suburban extremes.

OTHER UNITS OF LOCAL GOVERNMENT

As noted earlier, Illinois has more local governments than any other state. These governments overlap each other in a bewildering fashion so that residents of Illinois are often unaware which governmental unit provides a given service and may not know how their tax payments are divided among the various units.

The multiplicity of governments is a very important part of the environment in which municipal finance decisions are made. The provision of a particular service by an overlapping or neighboring governmental unit may reduce the demands upon the municipality or, occasionally, may increase demand as the result of a "demonstration" effect. Many projects, such as street and sewer projects, need physical coordination with the projects of other units of government. Neighboring areas often compete with each other for new industrial, commercial, or residential developments on the basis of low tax burdens, and officials of overlapping units must take into account the effects which the tax levies of their units have upon the total tax bill. Municipal officials are especially sensitive on this latter point since many city residents tend to hold the municipal officials responsible for the entire property tax levy even though the municipal levies are typically a minor portion of the total.

Table 3 shows the total number of local governments which existed in 1962 according to U.S. Census Bureau count. At that time there were 102 counties, 1,433 townships, 1,540 school districts, and 2,126 special districts.

Counties, municipalities, and townships are units of general government in the sense that they supply varied public services. All areas in Illinois lie within a county and, except for territory within Chicago and the 17 commission counties, also lie within a township.

School districts and special districts ordinarily perform only a single function, although a few dual-purpose special districts exist. These units have been created in response to a variety of problems. Prior to

TABLE 3

NUMBER OF LOCAL GOVERNMENTS IN ILLINOIS, 1962

Type of Government	Number
Counties	102
Municipalities	1,251
Townships	1,433
School Districts	1,540
Special Districts	2,126
Fire Protection	620
Highways	13
Health	18
Hospitals	37
Housing and Urban Renewal	107
Libraries	16
Drainage	852
Flood Control	18
Irrigation, Water Conservation	4
Soil Conservation	99
Parks and Recreation	179
Sewerage	76
Water Supply	34
Utilities Other than Water	1
Cemeteries	19
Sewerage and Water Supply	4
Other	29
Total	6,452

SOURCE U.S. Bureau of the Census, *Census of Governments: 1962,* I, 29, 66.

1870 more than 11,000 school districts were organized. Later the demands for high school education caused the creation of secondary school districts. These secondary districts were not integrated with elementary school districts due, in part, to statutory limitations on the taxing power and constitutional limitations on bonding power.[13] In the last 20 years the number of school districts has been substantially reduced, largely as the result of state-aid policies which provide inducements for consolidation of districts. The total number of school districts fell from about 12,000 in 1944 to 1,540 in 1962.

In contrast, the number of special districts has been rising. From 1952 to 1962 the number of special districts rose from 1,546 to 2,126. Special districts are sometimes formed when the area of need for a particular function does not coincide with the boundaries of any existing unit or when the area over which the function can be performed most

[13] Clyde F. Snider, Gilbert Y. Steiner, and Lois Langdon, *Local Taxing Units: The Illinois Experience* (Urbana: The Institute of Government and Public Affairs, University of Illinois, and Property Tax Division, Illinois Department of Revenue, 1954), pp. 5-18.

efficiently is larger than existing units. In other cases, special districts are formed with boundaries essentially coterminous with those of a municipality or another existing unit which is legally empowered to perform the function. In these cases the motive for forming the special district is to avoid tax or debt limitations or to minimize adverse reaction to increased taxes.[14]

Counties[15] In counties having township government, the county board of supervisors is composed of an elected supervisor from each township plus one or more elected assistant supervisors from the more populous townships. In commission counties a board of commissioners is elected at large. In Cook County special provisions provide that 10 of the 15 commissioners are to be elected from Chicago.

Counties perform a wide range of governmental services including a number of activities in which the county or a county official acts as an administrative or fiscal agent of state government. In this latter role, the county serves as the principal agent for the enforcement of state laws. Counties play a prominent role in the administration of the property taxes levied by all units of local government. Other functions which the county may perform include maintaining workhouses, constructing airports, constructing and maintaining roads and bridges, supervising of schools, zoning and regulating structures outside municipalities, and licensing entertainment outside of municipalities.

Townships The Illinois Constitution provides for an optional system of township organization. If township organization is not adopted, the county is divided into road districts. Of the 102 counties in Illinois 85 have adopted the township form. The township supervisor serves as a member of the county board of supervisors and, along with other elected township officials, administers the affairs of the township. The electors present at the annual town meeting constitute the corporate authorities.

The township, like the county, serves as a political and administrative agent of the state and, in addition, performs certain local services. As an administrative agent of the state, the major functions are to provide welfare (general assistance), build and maintain roads, and assess prop-

---

[14] Actually very few special districts in Illinois are exactly coterminous with other governmental units, but quite a number of park and sanitary districts have boundaries which are approximately the same as that of a municipality. Since it is possible for property to be annexed to special districts and municipalities separately, the exact relationship between city lines and special district lines changes almost constantly in many municipalities.

[15] For more detailed information see Clyde F. Snider and Irving Howards, *County Government in Illinois* (Carbondale: Southern Illinois University, Public Affairs Research Bureau, 1960).

erty. Discretionary powers include such things as preventing the growth of noxious weeds, regulating fences, prohibiting cattle from running at large, establishing parks, licensing various trades, and establishing and maintaining cemeteries. Townships which lie wholly within the limit of an incorporated city or village may transfer money to the city or village to be used for the construction and repair of roads and bridges.

Nineteen Illinois municipalities, including several with populations in excess of 25,000, have boundaries coterminous with the township. In these city-townships the powers of the township are vested in the city council and the council is given authority to provide for the consolidation or discontinuation of certain township offices.

School Districts According to U.S. Census classification, there are 12 types of school districts in Illinois,[16] which may be grouped into three classes: (1) elementary schools providing an eighth grade education, (2) combination or consolidated districts providing elementary and high school education, and (3) high and non–high school districts which provide education in grades nine through twelve.[17] These districts are governed by an elected board except for the Chicago School District and a few special charter districts which have appointed heads.

Prior to the adoption of the Master Plan for Higher Education by the 1965 legislature, some Illinois school districts played a substantial rolc in providing facilities for higher education. The Chicago School Board operated the Chicago Teachers' College, and a number of school districts operated junior colleges. The master plan provides for the transfer of the Chicago Teachers' College to the Board of Governors for State Colleges and Universities and provides methods whereby an existing junior college may become a "Class I" junior college with its own board. As this is written, a large number of new Class I junior colleges are being established, and it seems likely that much of the area of the state will be incorporated within junior college districts.

School districts are rarely coterminous with municipal boundaries, and a number of municipalities, especially in Chicago suburban areas, have parts of several school districts within their boundaries. All school districts have power to levy taxes and borrow money. They are limited to performing the single function of providing education, but the boards do have a considerable amount of discretion with regard to the scope of the educational program.

---

[16] U.S. Bureau of the Census, *Census of Governments: 1962,* I, 279.

[17] Snider, Steiner, and Langdon, *op. cit.,* p. 38. Non–high school districts do not operate a high school, but levy taxes to pay the tuition of pupils in nearby schools.

Special Districts Most special districts in Illinois have been created as a result of an election called upon petition by voters or landowners in the area of the proposed district. A few have been created directly by the legislature. The governing boards of some types of special districts are elected while other types have boards appointed by the county judge or some other official. Often there is no provision in the statutes for the dissolution of the district. Where provisions for consolidating or abolishing districts do exist, procedures required are often onerous.[18]

The types of special districts described below are those which are of special importance to a study of municipal finance because they commonly overlap municipalities and thus affect municipal service needs and revenue availability.

The 620 fire protection districts in Illinois are largely in rural areas, although they often include a small incorporated community. Fire protection districts are relatively easy to form. Fifty voters, or a majority of the voters in the proposed district if there are less than 100 voters, may petition the county judge to call an election. Approval requires a majority vote within each incorporated place and in the unincorporated area.

Fire protection districts are governed by a board of three trustees appointed by the county judge for staggered three-year terms. Typically, the proceeds of the tax levy are used largely for the purchase of equipment. Firemen are usually volunteers who receive a small fee for each fire call which they answer. A new fire district may not divide an existing municipality, but many Illinois municipalities have annexed territory already part of a fire protection district.

Only general park districts may now be formed under Illinois law although township park districts and pleasure drive park districts created under prior law may retain their identity. Park districts are established by the county judge on petition of resident voters and approval of the proposal by referendum. Park district trustees are elected. Most of the larger municipalities lie within a park district although boundaries are seldom coterminous.

The Chicago Park District was created in 1934 as the result of a legislative direction that a referendum be held upon the question of consolidating the numerous park districts existing within the city.[19]

---

[18] Snider, Steiner, and Langdon, *op. cit.*, includes tables which summarize the statutory requirements for the formation, annexation, and dissolution of various types of special districts and indicates the composition and method of selection of the governing boards.

[19] John C. Bollens, *Special District Governments in the United States* (Berkeley and Los Angeles: University of California Press, 1957), pp. 132-38.

Parts of the consolidated district which were outside the city were disconnected by subsequent legislation so that the district is now coterminous with the city. It is governed by a board of commissioners appointed by the mayor with the approval of the city council.

The Metropolitan Sanitary District of Greater Chicago, organized in 1889, was the first sanitary district in Illinois and is now the oldest independent metropolitan sewerage district operating in the United States.[20] It covers about 50 per cent of the land area and about 95 per cent of the population and assessed value in Cook County. It operates sewerage disposal plants and interceptor sewers in more than 70 incorporated places in the county and carries on a number of related activities such as fertilizer manufacture and the operation of dock and navigation facilities in its channels. It is governed by a board of trustees elected from the district at large.

Acts passed in 1907 and 1911 permitted the incorporation of the East Side Levee and Sanitary District in Madison and St. Clair counties and the North Shore Sanitary District in Lake County. Later, more general legislation was passed under which other sanitary districts in the state have been organized. These districts have a three-member board of trustees appointed by the county judge. Districts may be created by referenda after petition and may contain all or part of one or more municipalities. No territory more than three miles from a municipality may be included. Most of the larger municipalities in the state are overlaid by a sanitary district which, typically, operates the sewerage disposal plant and provides the main or interceptor sewers. The municipality installs and maintains the collector sewers.

SUMMARY

Municipal governments exercise, or fail to exercise, control and leadership functions which play a significant role in determining the character of an urban community, but municipal service activities account for most municipal expenditure and for the financial problems which plague Illinois municipalities.

The decisions which determine what services will be performed and how the costs will be met are made by municipal officials within an environment which places certain pressures and constraints upon their actions. First of all, they operate within the framework of a political system established by state law. The state prescribes the conditions of incorporation, the forms of government which may be used, and the powers and duties of municipal government. It specifies the revenue

---

20 *Ibid.*, p. 74.

sources which may be utilized and regulates many aspects of the administrative process. Except for some differences in powers which are based upon population or other systematic methods of classification, the powers and duties delegated to all municipalities in the state are identical. Thus, local decisions with regard to the kind of municipal services to be rendered and the method of finance to be utilized are made within the context of similar political systems.

Municipal officials also face pressures and constraints which are related to factors external to the local political system. Many of these factors, such as the economic and demographic characteristics of the community, influence both the demands for municipal services and the financial resources available to satisfy the demands. Unlike the political system, these external factors vary widely from city to city within the state.

Finally, an important part of the environment for financial decisionmaking is the existence of other units of local government which overlap and neighbor the municipality. Many of these units provide municipal-type services and thus influence the demands for municipal services. All of them collect revenue and, presumably, compete with the municipality for available revenue. Their existence complicates the problem of communication and understanding since many taxpayers and voters do not clearly differentiate among the several units of government which serve them.

2 MUNICIPAL EXPENDITURES

Economic statisticians commonly measure the output of the private or business sector of the economy by summing the prices paid for the products by the ultimate consumer. It is assumed that the consumer's willingness to pay a given amount for a product indicates its value. If the price paid exceeds the cost of inputs utilized by the producer, the difference is profit or compensation for the risk borne by the producer.

Few of the goods and services produced in the governmental sector are sold in the open market; therefore, this measure of output is not available for government services. Only input data in the form of expenditure and employment figures are available, although there are occasional indirect evidences of the efficiency with which inputs are being utilized and of the extent to which services actually performed satisfy the needs and desires of the residents of a municipality.

GENERAL OVERVIEW

A general overview of state and local government expenditure in Illinois is provided by Table 4. In fiscal year 1962, Illinois state and local governments expended $3.25 billion for general governmental purposes.[1] This sum is broken down as follows: school districts ex-

[1] Municipal expenditure items are classified by the U.S. Census Bureau into three main classes — general expenditure, utility expenditure, and employee-retirement expenditure.

Utility expenditure consists of capital outlay, interest paid, and current operation expenditure for water supply, electric power, gas, or transit systems owned and operated by the municipality. Identifiable costs for providing services to parent governments are treated as general expenditure for the function served.

Employee-retirement expenditure consists of cash payments to beneficiaries

pended 31.7 per cent, the state 29.2 per cent, and municipalities 20.0 per cent.[2]

The wide range of services provided by municipalities is emphasized by the fact that Illinois municipalities made expenditures for all functions listed in Table 4 except education, natural resources, and employment security. Six government functions (police, fire, sanitation, airports, parking facilities, and libraries) might well be classified as "municipal functions" since municipal governments spent more than 85 per cent of the total.

The two most costly functions performed by cities are provision of streets and highways and police protection. In 1962, over 40 per cent of Illinois municipal expenditure was for these two functions. Fire protection and sewerage and sanitation accounted for another 21 per cent of municipal expenditure.

Although Illinois is far more urban than is the United States as a whole, municipalities in Illinois spend a slightly smaller percentage of state and local funds than do municipalities nationwide. The figures are 20.0 per cent in Illinois and 22.1 per cent nationwide. Similar comparisons on a function-by-function basis, presented in Table 5, show that Illinois municipalities make a considerably higher proportion of the state and local police expenditure than do municipalities in other states. The importance of special districts in Illinois reduces the municipal share of expenditure for such functions as sewerage, local parks and recreation, and housing and urban renewal.

Aggregative data such as those presented in Tables 4 and 5 are useful as indicators of the total magnitude of municipal government expenditure and of the relative magnitude of expenditure for various functions. In order to compare expenditures among the several cities, however, it is necessary to transform aggregative data into a form which permits meaningful comparison among cities of different sizes. For this purpose per capita data are employed.[3]

(including withdrawals of contributions) of employee-retirement systems administered by the municipal government. Costs of administering a retirement system and employee contributions to state-administered employee-retirement systems are classed as general expenditure.

[2] These are direct expenditures which include payments to employees, suppliers, contractors, and other final recipients, but exclude intergovernmental payments to avoid double counting in the totals. If intergovernmental expenditure were included, state expenditure would be larger than school district expenditure.

[3] This commonly employed basis of comparison has a number of advantages. It is easy to understand and population data is available, or can be estimated, for almost any unit of government for any year. Some types of governmental services may more logically be expressed on a per household basis or on the basis of its relationship to population of a certain age group. In some cases it is desirable to exclude military or institutional population in computing per capita data.

TABLE 4

DIRECT EXPENDITURE OF STATE AND LOCAL UNITS OF GOVERNMENT, 1962 FISCAL YEAR (in thousands)

	Total State and Local	State	Counties	Townships	School Districts	Special Districts	Municipalities
Direct General Expenditure	$3,246,506	$947,408	$302,047	$60,057	$1,029,835	$258,440	$648,719
Education	1,186,884	195,520	802	—	990,561	—	—
Streets and Highways	509,284	263,589	78,646	27,803	—	23	139,223
Public Welfare	316,034	225,478	71,404	18,405	—	—	747
Hospitals	166,319	85,828	45,581	—	—	16,711	18,199
Health	26,791	12,977	3,747	—	—	981	9,086
Police Protection	147,309	11,540	9,000	11	—	—	126,758
Local Fire Protection	62,086	—	—	—	—	4,744	57,342
Sewerage	87,689	—	—	—	—	54,403	33,288
Other Sanitation	48,358	—	70	—	—	—	48,287
Local Parks and Recreation	76,478	—	8,024	—	—	55,874	12,580
Natural Resources	35,217	28,992	534	—	—	5,691	—
Housing and Urban Renewal	116,259	240	9	—	—	97,049	18,961
Airports	35,873	968	166	—	—	2,689	32,050
Water Transportation	3,137	1,528	—	—	—	621	988
Parking Facilities	7,794	—	—	—	—	809	6,986
Correction	30,876	21,563	5,246	—	—	—	4,067
Libraries	18,286	1,385	38	—	—	234	16,629
Employment Security Administration	17,997	17,997	—	—	—	—	—
Financial Administration	44,108	17,731	12,812	2,549	—	—	11,016
General Control	71,647	9,925	30,624	6,699	—	—	24,399
General Public Buildings	27,980	4,257	10,771	—	—	—	12,952
Interest on General Debt	122,301	23,107	9,584	838	39,274	17,221	32,277
Other and Unallocable	87,799	24,783	14,989	3,752	—	1,390	42,884
Utility Expenditure	267,293	—	—	—	—	124,496	142,796
Water Supply	124,342	—	—	—	—	2,736	121,605
Other	142,951	—	—	—	—	121,760	21,191
Insurance Trust Expenditure	269,267	204,620	4,115	—	14,950	11,315	34,267

SOURCE U.S. Bureau of the Census, *Census of Governments: 1962,* Vol. VII, No. 13, pp. 25-26.

TABLE 5

MUNICIPAL DIRECT EXPENDITURE AS PROPORTION OF STATE AND LOCAL EXPENDITURE BY FUNCTION, ILLINOIS AND THE UNITED STATES, 1962

	Illinois (per cent)	United States (per cent)
Direct General Expenditure	20.0	22.1
Education	—	8.7
Streets and Highways	27.3	16.3
Public Welfare	.2	13.5
Hospitals	10.9	18.8
Health	33.9	27.2
Police Protection	86.0	69.1
Local Fire Protection	92.4	87.7
Sewerage	38.0	66.8
Other Sanitation	99.9	91.0
Local Parks and Recreation	16.4	71.7
Housing and Urban Renewal	16.3	55.1
Airports	89.3	51.5
Water Transportation	31.5	26.4
Parking Facilities	89.6	81.9
Correction	13.2	12.1
Libraries	90.9	61.8
Financial Administration	25.0	23.2
General Control	34.1	31.5
General Public Buildings	46.3	34.2
Interest on General Debt	26.4	25.5
Other and Unallocable	48.8	38.1

SOURCE U.S. Bureau of the Census, *Census of Governments: 1962,* Vol. IV, No. 4, p. 32; Vol. VII, No. 13, pp. 25-26.

Data concerning the 188 Illinois cities of more than 5,000 population for which 1962 Census of Government data are available are shown in Table 6. Column 1 shows the number of cities that reported expenditure for the particular function. Average expenditure *of the cities reporting expenditure for the function* is shown in Column 2. Columns 3 and 4 indicate the high and low expenditure among those cities reporting. In some cases great variations between the high and low city result from the timing of capital expenditure and overstate the variation in operating expenditures. Even when allowance is made for this factor, however, it is apparent that there are very large city-to-city variations in expenditure. Some of the reasons for these large variations are suggested in the course of the function-by-function examination of expenditure in this chapter.

TABLE 6

PER CAPITA GENERAL EXPENDITURE, BY FUNCTION, ILLINOIS MUNICIPALITIES OVER 5,000 POPULATION, 1962 FISCAL YEAR

Function	Number of Cities Reporting Expenditures	Average Expenditure	Range	
			High	Low
Streets and Highways	188	$11.05	$55.01	$ .74
Hospitals	15	27.45	72.64	.23
Health	102	.54	5.55	.01
Police	188	7.63	25.08	2.53
Fire	177	4.15	16.45	.04
Sewerage	140	4.84	71.60	.02
Sanitation	156	3.28	10.44	.13
Parks and Recreation	115	2.44	30.10	.02
Housing and Urban Renewal	9	6.68	32.73	.06
Airports	16	2.35	18.92	.07
Parking Facilities	117	1.37	10.69	—[a]
Correction	1	1.15	1.15	1.15
Libraries	129	2.46	16.19	.03
Financial Administration	174	1.04	5.68	.01
General Control	188	2.31	8.16	.30
General Public Buildings	168	1.60	28.14	.05
Interest on General Debt	174	1.79	9.61	.03

[a] Less than .005.

SOURCE U.S. Bureau of the Census, unpublished worksheets for the 1962 Census of Governments.

POLICE AND FIRE PROTECTION

One of the major services performed by municipal governments is the protection of life and property through the activities of police and fire departments. In most Illinois cities police protection and fire protection are provided by different city departments. These services are considered together in this section, since each has a primary purpose the protection of life and property, because many of the problems of organizing and administering the departments are similar, and because intergovernmental aspects are similar.

Police Expenditure Crime and traffic congestion represent serious threats to the life of American cities. Both appear to be growing increasingly serious over time and to increase in severity with the size of the city and the density of the population. The first line of defense against crime in urban areas is the city police department which has primary responsibility for preventive patrol, as well as for the apprehension of criminals after a crime has been committed.[4] Police provide numerous traffic services such as road patrol and investigation of accidents and give various kinds of emergency aid.

The relative importance of the various services performed by police varies from city to city as the result of different local conditions. Municipal officials in some suburban municipalities stress the fact that the large number of commuters who pass through increases the need for police to handle traffic duty. One suburb, with a high percentage of aged population, places special emphasis upon equipping the police department with inhalator units and training officers to administer first aid to victims of heart attack and other seizures. Officials in this city also report that many other, less dramatic, emergency calls to the police department are related to the high proportion of aged population. In some cities the police department answers all emergency ambulance calls. In other cities such services are provided by private ambulance services.

Police in Chicago suburban areas generally cooperate closely with each other and with the Chicago police department. Downstate police departments ordinarily do not answer calls outside the city but they may assist the county sheriff upon request and may operate outside the city in following up a case started in the city. Some cities also provide technical assistance to law enforcement officers in rural areas or smaller localities. For example, Chicago makes the facilities of its police training school available to suburban departments.

Some cities have supplemented their regular police department by organizing auxiliary police units. In Elgin, for example, members of the auxiliary receive police training and are available for hire as special watchmen or for traffic and crowd control duty at special events. Regular police officers may also be employed in off-duty hours through the auxiliary unit. When auxiliary police are called to duty by the city, they are paid from city funds. In some cities civil defense units are closely related to the police department and serve as auxiliary units in times of emergency.

The average per capita expenditure for police and correction in the 188 cities of over 5,000 population was $7.63 in fiscal year 1962.[5] The relationship between urbanization and police expenditure per capita is clearly shown in Table 7 in which per capita police expenditure (cur-

---

[4] A. F. Brandstatter, "Police Administration: Developments in 1963," *The Municipal Yearbook, 1964* (Chicago: The International City Managers' Association, 1964), pp. 405-9.

[5] Separate data for correction are reported only for Chicago.

TABLE 7

AVERAGE PER CAPITA CURRENT POLICE EXPENDITURE, BY METROPOLITAN AREA GROUP AND POPULATION, 1962 FISCAL YEAR

Population	Chicago SMSA	Downstate SMSA's	No SMSA
Over 25,000	$9.11	$6.96	$6.03
10,000-25,000	8.53	5.59	5.57
5,000-10,000	8.82	6.24	4.93
All Sizes	8.75	6.41	5.27

SOURCE U.S. Bureau of the Census, unpublished worksheets for the 1962 Census of Governments.

rent only) is given for cities in the Chicago Metropolitan Statistical Area, for downstate SMSA's, and for cities not in an SMSA. The average expenditure for every size group of cities is highest in the Chicago SMSA and lowest in the non-SMSA cities. The tendency for per capita expenditure to be highest in the large cities is not pronounced in some of the SMSA groups but, when all groups are combined, the large cities have the highest expenditure. It appears from these data that police expenditure rises as the size of the urban complex increases and that the size of the city itself is of lesser importance.

Police expenditure and employment data for the 41 cities of more than 25,000 population are shown in Table 8. Current expenditures are shown separately so that allowance can be made for the distorting effect which major capital expenditures, such as the construction of a new police station, have upon the data in any given year.

The city of Chicago has by far the largest per capita expenditure of any Illinois city, which is to be expected in view of its size and degree of urbanization. The same factors which are responsible for high police expenditure in Chicago may also be responsible for the fact that the highest expenditure among the suburbs is found in the close-in, mature suburbs such as Evanston, Cicero, and Oak Park. There are indications, however, that the crime problem is becoming more serious in other suburban areas. Municipal officials in several suburbs report that the expressway system, the increase in the number of apartment houses and shopping centers, and better law enforcement in Chicago are factors which encourage criminal activity in the suburban areas.[6]

Column 3 of Table 8 shows police employment per 10,000 popula-

[6] Also see: Jon Rowley, "Suburbia's Rising Crime Problem," *Chicago Sun-Times,* May 16, 1965.

TABLE 8

POLICE AND FIRE EXPENDITURE AND EMPLOYMENT, 41 ILLINOIS MUNICIPALITIES, 1962 FISCAL YEAR

	Per Capita Police Expenditure		FTE Police Employment per 10,000 Population	Per Capita Fire Expenditure		FTE Fire Employment per 10,000 Population	Underwriters' Fire Ratings		
	Current	Total		Current	Total		Total	Fire Department	Year
Municipalities Outside Chicago SMSA									
Alton	$6.88	$7.02	12.3	$7.40	$7.46	11.6	5	6	1958
Belleville	5.75	5.93	11.4	5.51	5.53	10.3	6	6	1951
Bloomington	8.53	8.53	16.3	8.72	8.72	12.7	5	6	1958
Champaign	6.72	6.97	10.4	5.38	5.45	9.4	4	6	1960
Danville	4.89	5.11	11.1	6.90	7.06	12.1	6	6	1960
Decatur	6.02	6.13	11.0	6.05	7.49	10.9	4	5	1961
East St. Louis	8.77	9.02	13.1	8.06	8.30	11.1	5	6	1951
Freeport	5.58	5.58	10.0	7.70	7.70	15.9	5	7	1958
Galesburg	5.07	5.26	10.0	4.48	4.93	13.0	5	6	1963
Granite City	5.67	5.86	8.7	6.02	6.02	8.5	6	7	1960
Kankakee	6.31	6.48	12.0	8.65	8.66	13.4	5	6	1963
Moline	6.31	6.42	11.4	8.18	8.40	14.6	4	5	1957
Pekin	5.58	5.70	8.7	7.05	16.45	13.8	6	7	1959
Peoria	10.61	10.67	16.5	8.97	9.13	12.3	4	5	1962
Quincy	5.83	6.05	11.3	6.03	6.83	11.6	5	5	1955
Rockford	7.84	8.10	13.1	7.86	7.90	12.7	3	3	1957
Rock Island	7.30	7.34	14.9	6.97	7.13	11.4	4	4	1958
Springfield	7.76	7.91	14.6	7.65	7.81	13.5	5	7	1960
Urbana	5.30	5.30	9.4	4.77	4.77	8.3	5	8	1956
Average	6.67	6.83	11.9	6.97	7.67	12.0			

TABLE 8 (continued)

POLICE AND FIRE EXPENDITURE AND EMPLOYMENT, 41 ILLINOIS MUNICIPALITIES, 1962 FISCAL YEAR

	Per Capita Police Expenditure		FTE Police Employment per 10,000 Population	Per Capita Fire Expenditure		FTE Fire Employment per 10,000 Population	Underwriters' Fire Ratings		
	Current	Total		Current	Total		Total	Fire Department	Year
Municipalities in Chicago SMSA									
Arlington Hgts.	$ 7.62	$ 7.97	12.7	$2.27	$2.58	3.3	5	6	1960
Aurora	7.58	7.58	14.5	7.38	7.38	12.5	4	5	1964
Berwyn	7.33	10.39	12.8	5.29	5.33	9.3	6	6	1961
Calumet City	7.52	7.72	10.0	4.64	4.66	6.2	7	7	1957
Chicago Hgts.	8.85	8.92	15.8	7.05	7.05	11.1	6	7	1964
Cicero	12.20	12.47	20.2	8.48	8.58	13.0	5	5	1955
Des Plaines	8.33	8.33	11.8	4.55	5.44	6.3	5	5	1964
Elgin	7.70	8.02	15.0	5.63	5.77	10.2	4	6	1957
Elmhurst	7.46	7.74	12.3	3.14	3.15	4.2	6	7	1963
Evanston	12.90	13.21	19.1	8.46	8.52	12.6	3	3	1959
Harvey	6.00	7.31	9.6	5.57	5.65	9.6	5	5	1959
Highland Park	9.00	23.67	15.9	6.76	6.83	10.1	5	5	1958
Joliet	7.64	7.64	12.9	8.17	8.17	13.1	5	7	1960
Maywood	9.29	9.53	NA[a]	6.78	6.78	NA	6	8	1944
Oak Lawn	7.18	7.39	11.5	1.69	2.80	2.4	6	8	1960
Oak Park	10.13	10.52	16.4	8.27	8.50	13.1	3	3	1964
Park Forest	6.07	6.53	9.1	4.58	4.63	4.9	5	5	1960
Park Ridge	6.91	7.09	12.0	2.89	3.02	5.0	5	7	1961
Skokie	9.11	9.54	15.4	7.05	7.27	13.2	5	5	1961
Waukegan	9.96	10.61	13.8	7.60	7.91	10.8	4	5	1957
Wilmette	7.39	7.62	13.0	5.43	8.35	10.3	4	4	1964
Average	8.39	9.51	13.7	5.79	6.11	9.1			
Chicago	24.35	25.08	34.8	9.43	9.65	13.3	2	3	1964

[a] NA indicates data are not available.

SOURCE U.S. Bureau of the Census, unpublished worksheets for 1962 Census of Governments; *Municipal Yearbook*, various years (Chicago: The International City Managers' Association).

tion in full-time equivalent units.[7] There is a fairly high correlation ($r = .61$) between current expenditure and full-time equivalent employment.[8] This is not surprising in view of the fact that a high percentage of police current expenditure is for wages and salaries.[9]

Fire Protection Expenditure The bulk of fire protection expenditure in most municipalities is spent to maintain a force of firefighters properly equipped to extinguish fires. Fire prevention programs range from minimal — "the chief talks to schools" — to rather elaborate inspection and education programs. Evanston, for example, has a seperate fire protection bureau which makes all nonresidential inspections. Residences are inspected on a regular basis by the fire companies. Fire departments in a number of cities also provide other services such as rescue and ambulance services. Commonly, firemen repair parking meters, and in Skokie, they also run a printing shop which does all the municipal printing.

In smaller cities fire departments often consist of volunteers who report for duty upon the sounding of a whistle or other signal and who receive a small payment for each alarm answered. The larger cities have professional firefighters on duty 24 hours a day during an assigned tour of duty.

A number of smaller municipalities lie entirely within a fire protection district and render no fire protection service. In some larger cities a part of the municipality lies within a fire protection district as the result of municipal annexation of territory already in the fire protection district. State law gives jurisdiction over these areas to the fire protection district and prohibits the levy of a municipal fire protection tax, but municipalities actually follow a variety of policies with regard to serving these areas.[10] About one-fourth of one downstate city lies within

---

[7] Part-time workers are converted to "full-time equivalents" on the basis of payroll data. Thus, if the average pay of full-time workers in a given city is $500.00 per month, a part-time worker making $200.00 per month is equivalent to two-fifths of a full-time worker.

[8] Chicago was excluded from the correlation computation.

[9] One estimate is that 89 per cent of the police expenditure of Illinois cities of over 25,000 is for wages and salaries. See: Arlyn J. Larson, *A Price Index for Illinois Municipalities* (Urbana: The Institute of Government and Public Affairs, University of Illinois, 1964), p. 57.

[10] Although amicable solutions to the problem of overlapping responsibilities have been reached in some communities, a considerable amount of friction exists in others. A bill passed by the 1965 legislature provides that if more than 50 per cent of a fire district's territory lies within a municipality, the municipality may file a petition to disconnect that portion from the fire protection district. If the city agrees to assume all bonded indebtedness of the district and to provide fire protection for the remaining portion of the district, the court is to approve the petition. The fire protection district continues in existence and continues to levy

such districts and maintains two fire stations within the territory of fire protection districts. The city manager of this city reports that the municipal department answers all calls and then notifies the fire protection district. He also indicates that many property owners who annex their property to the city do so primarily to obtain municipal fire protection. In other municipalities, city fire departments answer alarms in fire protection districts only when the fire protection district requests assistance. In some communities fire protection districts own no equipment but act as a tax levying agency which pays the proceeds of the tax to the municipality under a fire protection service contract.

Municipalities follow a variety of policies with regard to serving areas outside the municipal boundaries. A number of cities enter into agreements with homeowners or industrial concerns to provide fire service on a fee basis. Quite often the city will not conclude such agreements with respect to property which is eligible for annexation to the city. One city official, however, reported that the fire department of his city will answer calls anywhere in the county.

Cooperative or mutual-aid agreements among fire departments of adjacent cities are common and of special importance in the Chicago suburban area. In some cases cooperation goes beyond assistance at fires to include joint planning of equipment purchases. In Champaign-Urbana there is a three-way agreement among the fire departments of the two cities and the University of Illinois, which maintains its own fire department.

Fire protection is one of the few services provided by municipalities which is subject to systematic grading by an outside agency. Rating engineers of the National Board of Fire Underwriters use the board's rating scale to determine the fire insurance classification of all cities of more than 25,000 population. Smaller cities are rated by engineers from the state rating organization.

Classification is determined by the number of deficiency points which are assessed when conditions are below the standards prescribed by the agency. There are 5,000 possible deficiency points distributed over nine major items: water supply, fire department, fire alarms, police, building laws, hazards, structural conditions, climatic conditions, and a divergence in grading of classes according to the total points of deficiency charged against fire defenses.[11]

---

a tax for operating purposes at the same rate levied prior to annexation. The proceeds of the tax, less overhead expenses, are paid to the municipality. *Laws of Illinois* (1965), pp. 2391-92.

[11] Percy Bugbee, "Fire Administration: Developments in 1963," *The Municipal Yearbook, 1964* (Chicago: The International City Managers' Association, 1964), pp. 375-76.

Column 7 of Table 8 shows the fire insurance class of Illinois cities over 25,000 population. This is the total rating based upon all nine factors. A low number indicates high quality and results in lower insurance rates. Column 8 shows the rating of the fire department alone. Column 9 indicates the year in which the last rating study was made. Neither of these ratings should be considered a measure of the efficiency with which fire protection funds are being used, since varying conditions in different cities affect the cost and difficulty of attaining a given classification. Nevertheless, these ratings are of value as a knowledgeable appraisal of the success which a municipality has had in protecting life and property from fire. The rating system also points up the relationship which may exist between the level of municipal services and private costs. High quality municipal fire protection, as rated by the National Board, means savings in insurance cost for all property owners in the municipality.

The nine-factor rating scale also emphasizes the interrelation among various municipal services. The fire classification depends not only upon the fire department but also upon the adequacy of the water system and the fire alarm system which are maintained by other municipal departments or by private firms. The quality of the police department also enters the rating as do such things as structural conditions and building codes.

The 177 cities of over 5,000 population *which provided fire services* in 1962 spent an average of $4.15 per capita. Although Chicago spent more than any other city, the difference between Chicago and smaller cities is far less than in the case of police expenditure. Most other cities in the Chicago SMSA spend less per capita than do cities in downstate SMSA's which, in turn, often spend less than those cities which are not in SMSA's (see Table 9). The reasons for higher fire expenditure in

TABLE 9

AVERAGE PER CAPITA CURRENT FIRE EXPENDITURE, BY METROPOLITAN AREA GROUP AND POPULATION, 1962 FISCAL YEAR

Population	Chicago SMSA	Downstate SMSA's	No SMSA
Over 25,000	$5.96	$6.91	$7.08
10,000-25,000	2.84	2.71	4.42
5,000-10,000	1.62	2.29	2.12
All Sizes	3.14	4.54	3.44

SOURCE U.S. Bureau of the Census, unpublished worksheets for the 1962 Census of Governments.

the less urbanized areas are not entirely clear but it may be related to the cooperative agreements in metropolitan areas which permit municipalities to depend upon neighboring departments for specialized equipment and for reserve manpower. It is also apparent from Table 8 that many municipalities with extremely low fire expenditures are bedroom suburbs which have a low percentage of older buildings and few complex industrial properties.

Police and Fire Pension Funds All municipalities of more than 5,000 population must maintain a police pension fund and a fire pension fund as provided by state law. The pensions are of the fixed-benefit type and provide pensions of one-half the final year's salary for retired policemen and firemen.[12] Eligibility is earned by 20 years of service and the pension begins at age fifty. Benefits are increased by 1 per cent of final salary for each year of service over 20 with the maximum pension being 60 per cent of final salary for policemen and 65 per cent for firemen. The plans are financed jointly by withholdings from salary and by contributions of the municipality. Firemen contribute 5 per cent of their salary and policemen contribute 7 per cent.

The law does not require full actuarial funding. However, a law which became effective in 1959 provided that within 40 years each municipality must accumulate a full actuarial reserve, or alternately, must accumulate a reserve fund equal to $10,000 for each policeman and beneficiary entitled to protection by the police pension fund. Many municipalities now follow the practice of adding the estimated amount needed yearly to build up the required reserve by 1999 to the estimated expenditure of the fund for that year, then subtract the employees' contributions and other income to determine the required annual tax levy. A few cities maintain a full actuarial reserve.

Firemen's pension funds are required to have a reserve equal to $1,000 for each 1,000 inhabitants of the municipality. A ten-year period beginning on January 1, 1961, is allowed for building the reserve to the required amount. In no case may the reserve be less than it was on January 1, 1948.

The 1963 report of the Illinois Department of Insurance indicates that there were 316 downstate police and fire pension funds in operation. They had aggregate net assets of $26,723,238.98, actuarial liabilities of $137,417,912.00, and aggregate deficiencies of $110,694,673.02. In the words of the report: "In almost all cases the revenue made

[12] This description of the pension funds applies to downstate municipalities. Chicago firemen and policemen are covered by a law with somewhat different provisions.

available to the Pension Funds by the various municipalities has been grossly inadequate to finance the Funds on a systematic basis. The fact of the matter is, such revenue in the great majority of cases has not been sufficient to meet the normal cost needs, let alone provide any amount for past service purposes or to cover interest requirements on the unfunded obligations."[13]

Table 10 shows normal costs as computed by the Department of Insurance and converted to a per capita basis. Adding the annual normal cost to the expenditure data of Table 8 would provide a better estimate of total police and fire costs than does the expenditure data of Table 8 alone.[14]

Table 10 also shows the actual contribution which the municipality made to the pension fund and the accumulated deficiencies in the funds both converted to a per capita basis. The Pension Laws Commission recommends that every city pay into the pension fund a sum at least equal to normal costs plus interest on the accumulated deficiency. Examination of these data reveals that some cities with large deficiencies are not paying normal costs while others have virtually no accumulated deficiencies.

State Regulation of Police and Fire Personnel Policies Personnel costs make up a very large part of the costs of providing police and fire protection, and the quality of personnel employed greatly affects the quality of protection provided. These factors alone would insure a considerable public interest in such matters as selection, tenure, salaries, and hours of work for policemen and firemen. Add to these the intense efforts which Illinois police and fire lobbyists make during each legislative session, and it is apparent that state regulation, potential and actual, is an important part of the environment in which municipal financial decisions are made.

State statutes provide that cities having a population between 5,000 and 250,000 and not having a civil service system shall have a board of police and fire commissioners. This board appoints all members of the

---

[13] State of Illinois, Department of Insurance, *Report of Examination: Public Employees' Pension Funds, 1963* (Springfield: 1963), p. 30.

[14] Under the reporting rules laid down by the U.S. Census Bureau, Illinois police and fire pension costs are omitted from expenditure data. The instructions for reporting municipal expenditure to the U.S. Census Bureau provide that payments to state-operated pension funds should be reported as expenditure, either allocated to the proper function or as other expenditure. In the case of funds operated by the municipality, however, payments into the fund are not to be reported as an expenditure. Payments of benefits and withdrawals from the fund are reported in separate questionnaires and are published in separate reports dealing with retirement funds.

TABLE 10

POLICE AND FIRE PENSION FUNDS, PER CAPITA NORMAL COST, CONTRIBUTIONS AND ACCUMULATED DEFICIENCIES, 41 ILLINOIS MUNICIPALITIES

	Police Pension			Fire Pension		
	Annual Normal Cost	Contributions per Annum	Actuarial Reserve Deficiency	Annual Normal Cost	Contributions per Annum	Actuarial Reserve Deficiency
Municipalities Outside Chicago SMSA						
Alton	$ .47	$ .84	$19.58	$1.08	$ .39	$18.16
Belleville	.74	.07	15.20	.78	.07	18.72
Bloomington	.84	1.01	23.23	1.23	1.54	27.21
Champaign	.69	.40	15.10	.80	.36	14.74
Danville	.59	1.04	12.76	.99	1.08	27.81
Decatur	.70	.50	18.81	1.09	.57	29.77
East St. Louis	.80	.52	22.02	.93	1.03	20.39
Freeport	.60	.51	18.23	1.22	.79	26.84
Galesburg	.53	1.28	15.41	.72	.79	21.69
Granite City	.73	.68	11.22	.91	.72	19.43
Kankakee	.50	.56	11.68	1.08	.80	22.68
Moline	.77	1.26	17.45	1.32	.77	32.18
Pekin	.60	.35	8.40	1.33	.26	13.59
Peoria	1.05	1.35	32.43	1.33	1.26	43.49
Quincy	.61	.54	14.74	.98	.57	28.08
Rockford	.87	1.62	24.00	1.13	1.28	25.06
Rock Island	.83	.66	26.50	1.10	.99	25.59
Springfield	.85	2.12	38.18	1.21	1.36	36.63
Urbana	.57	.37	9.08	.69	.23	12.35
Average	.70	.83	18.63	1.05	.78	24.44
Municipalities in Chicago SMSA						
Arlington Hgts.	.80	.81	3.33	.22	.22	−.27
Aurora	.86	1.05	25.66	1.23	.71	27.06
Berwyn	.76	1.38	22.49	.89	.53	21.49
Calumet City	.56	.56	5.86	.54	.16	8.82
Chicago Hgts.	.97	1.34	19.44	1.13	.86	24.27
Cicero	1.31	2.15	40.03	1.35	.77	37.38
Des Plaines	.83	.17	15.21	.64	.09	6.32
Elgin	.73	.53	17.39	.86	.26	23.68
Elmhurst	.80	.61	5.66	.31	.46	3.10
Evanston	1.15	1.57	31.25	1.28	1.36	38.07
Harvey	.71	1.06	10.08	.84	.63	17.61
Highland Park	.92	1.59	18.93	1.00	1.96	24.45
Joliet	.83	.96	29.43	1.24	.67	28.08
Maywood	.97	1.49	27.41	1.05	1.00	22.54
Oak Lawn	.69	.36	4.19	.19	.01	.18
Oak Park	1.12	1.06	33.66	1.33	1.20	39.15
Park Forest	.58	.08	2.45	.43	.09	3.99
Park Ridge	.82	.65	10.12	.37	.19	1.93

TABLE 10 (continued)

POLICE AND FIRE PENSION FUNDS, PER CAPITA NORMAL COST, CONTRIBUTIONS AND ACCUMULATED DEFICIENCIES, 41 ILLINOIS MUNICIPALITIES

	Police Pension			Fire Pension		
	Annual Normal Cost	Contributions per Annum	Actuarial Reserve Deficiency	Annual Normal Cost	Contributions per Annum	Actuarial Reserve Deficiency
Skokie	$.95	$ .37	$ 9.11	$1.12	$ .02	$ 8.17
Waukegan	.85	1.12	16.74	1.13	.39	23.07
Wilmette	.75	.82	20.54	.94	.17	19.21
Average	.86	.94	17.57	.86	.56	18.01
Chicago	NA[a]	2.38	43.64	NA	2.08	20.70

[a] NA indicates data are not available.

SOURCE State of Illinois, Department of Insurance, *Report of Examination, Public Employees' Pension Funds, 1963* (Springfield, 1963). Chicago data are for fiscal year ending December 31, 1962, and are from the 1965 report.

police and fire departments except that the city council may, by ordinance, provide for other methods of appointing the chief of each department. The system is "closed" in that all appointments to advanced ranks must be made from the members of the department presently in the next lowest rank. The chief may be appointed from any rank or, by ordinance, may be chosen from outside the department. Policemen or firemen who have completed their probationary period may be discharged only for cause and after a hearing.

State statutes have prescribed minimum salaries to be paid policemen and firemen since 1937. The present schedule, which has been in effect since 1953, is as follows:

City Population	Minimum Monthly Salary
5,000-25,000	$300
25,000-75,000	325
75,000-150,000	350

Recent sessions of the Illinois legislature have witnessed intensive efforts by the police and fire lobby to obtain increases in these minima.[15] Lobbying efforts have included the appearance of great numbers of of uniformed policemen and firemen in the galleries and committee rooms of the legislature as well as well-organized letter-writing cam-

[15] The following summary of these efforts is based upon: Gilbert Y. Steiner, "Wages and Hours Legislation for Municipal Policemen and Firemen" (unpublished statement filed with the Cities and Villages Municipal Problems Commission in 1962).

paigns. Police and fire representatives argue that these tactics are necessary because the critical position of policemen and firemen prevents the use of the strike weapon which is available to other classes of organized labor and because budget-minded municipal officials fail to provide adequate wages.

Municipal officials argue that legislative action in imposing minimum wages is a violation of the "home-rule" principle and that the legislature, which restricts the taxing power of municipalities, should not impose additional costs without providing additional revenue. Many municipal officials have also been irritated by the tactics of employing uniformed personnel in lobbying activities. In 1959, the Illinois Municipal League adopted a resolution insisting that lobbying activities by municipal employees be on their own time and without display of official uniform.

In 1961, a bill raising the minimum salaries for policemen and firemen passed both the House and Senate but was vetoed by Governor Kerner. The veto message stressed the importance of home-rule principles and indicated that the levels provided in the bill were above those in comparable communities in other states. At the same time the governor warned that the minima were too low and that municipalities must provide reasonable wages if they expect to avoid state action.

In 1963, legislation to increase minima by amounts ranging from $100 to $150 a month was passed and again vetoed. In this veto message Governor Kerner referred to his message of two years earlier and reported that some municipalities had made progress but warned that, unless more progress was made, approval of similar legislation could be expected in the future.[16] In 1965, legislation which would have increased minima by as much as $200 per month passed the House but died in the Senate[17]

Prior to 1957, state law provided that no fireman in a city of more than 12,000 population should be required to work more than 12 hours per day (figured in the aggregate over the period of one month). Several unsuccessful attempts to get this minimum reduced were made. A bill reducing hours to 56 per week was vetoed by Governor Stratton in 1955. The governor's message emphasized the home-rule principle and pointed to the varying effect which such a uniform law would have upon municipalities. At the same time, the message pointed out that the municipalities had been given additional revenue sources and that if they failed to improve working conditions remedial legislation might

[16] Veto message of Governor Kerner, August 23, 1963.
[17] H.B. 619, 74th General Assembly.

become imperative. In 1957, Governor Stratton signed legislation which reduced the work week for firemen to 56 hours in all cities with a population of more than 12,000. It became effective on January 1, 1958.

Several attempts to legislate maximum hours for police have been made but no such legislation has become law. In 1959, a bill to impose a 40-hour weekly maximum passed both houses of the legislature by overwhelming margins but was vetoed by Governor Stratton.

General Conclusions The provision of police and fire protection is among the most important and costly functions performed by Illinois municipal governments. Although it is not possible to untangle all of the factors which affect the level of expenditure for this service, both statistical analysis and interviews with city officials suggest that external conditions create needs which are apt to be reflected rather clearly in expenditure. For example, the degree of urbanization of the area and, to a lesser extent, the size of the city appear to be major factors in determining police expenditure. Municipal officials interviewed expressed little uncertainty about their ability to judge the adequacy of these services. Answers such as "adequate now, but we will need 3 more patrolmen next year," "We badly need 13 more policemen," or "We need a new fire station in the north part of town" were common. One city official volunteered the statement, "There are objective standards by which we can judge the need for police and fire services, but for many other types of services there are few useful standards." In addition to using rule-of-thumb standards, such as the ratio of employees per 1,000 population, some cities keep and analyze detailed statistics concerning crimes, accidents, and fires which aid them in determining the need for additional personnel or for redeployment of existing personnel.

There was obvious concern among officials interviewed about personnel matters. Many expressed a desire to pay higher salaries to policemen and firemen but were also concerned about the financial consequences which would result from a substantial rise in the state-imposed minima. There is also a strong feeling among city officials that something should be done to utilize more fully the time of firemen. It is in the nature of a fireman's duties that he spend most of his time at the fire station waiting for a call. Further, the present pattern of 24 hours on and 48 hours off duty makes it relatively easy for firemen to hold other jobs. Some city officials suggest that these facts, plus the generally less pleasant nature of police duties, justify a substantially higher pay scale for policemen. A few cities have moved in this direction, but any attempt to break the traditional pattern of equality is strongly resisted by firemen and a number of bills to prohibit integration of police and fire departments have been introduced in the legislature. Other cities have approached the problem through programs designed to utilize firemen's "waiting time." Minimum efforts in this direction involve such things as having firemen repair parking meters. The most comprehensive approach which has been adopted by Evanston, Glencoe, and a few other cities involves creating a combined police-fire department. Peoria has achieved partial integration by training patrolmen for firefighting duties. Smaller crews are then used on fire apparatus and augmented at the fire by patrolmen who temporarily leave patrol duties to answer the fire call. This system has resulted in a substantial financial saving to the city even though the patrolmen receives a salary increment for taking the fire training program.

STREETS AND HIGHWAYS

Anyone who has driven in a number of Illinois cities is well aware of the great variation in the condition of streets within a city as well as between cities. These variations result from the cumulative effect of many decisions made over a long period of time and may show little relationship to the amount of street expenditure in a given year. Streets are long-lived facilities and the benefits of a street improvement are enjoyed over a number of years. Extraordinarily high or low capital expenditure in a single year will have little immediate effect upon the quality of the street network. A city which shifts emphasis from maintaining low quality streets to construction of high quality ones may suffer an immediate decline in the over-all quality of street service even though the long-term effect will be an improved quality.

A second reason for the lack of correlation between recent expenditure and the condition of streets is that a substantial portion of new street construction in some cities is undertaken by private developers rather than by the city itself. This results from the common requirement that the developers of new subdivisions build streets to specifications determined by the city. If these specifications are high and a large portion of the city is newly developed, the city may have excellent streets and low municipal street expenditure.

Still a third reason for the lack of close relationship between yearly expenditure and the quality of the street network is that topography, location in relation to through traffic patterns, soil conditions, and land use patterns greatly affect the cost of constructing and maintaining adequate streets. The variation in population density and land use patterns, for example, is reflected in the ratio of street mileage to population. Among cities of over 5,000 population Benton has 7.66 miles of street for every 1,000 population while Chicago has only 1.02. Generally speaking, the smaller, more rural cities have higher ratios of street mileage to population but construct and maintain them to lower standards.

Decisions concerning street construction and maintenance are characterized by the prominent role which other units of government play in the process and by the large number of methods of finance which can be used. City streets may be part of a state or county highway network which is financed, in part, by federal funds. Streets may be financed by state motor fuel tax funds or entirely by local revenue. Often street construction projects lie partly outside of the municipality and become a joint project involving the township, county, or even another municipality.

Use of Motor Fuel Tax Funds Illinois municipalities receive 32 per cent of the proceeds of the 5 cent gasoline tax after certain statutory deductions. The money is deposited in the State Treasury and allocated among the municipalities on the basis of population. Funds are paid to the city after approval of a project by the State Division of Highways and the passage of a city ordinance appropriating the funds.

The Illinois statutes designate the specific uses for which a municipality may utilize motor fuel tax funds.[18] These are:

1. Construction and maintenance of state highways.
2. Construction and maintenance of county highways.
3. Construction and maintenance of arterial streets.
4. Construction and maintenance of extensions of arterial streets outside corporate limits.
5. Construction and maintenance of extensions of arterial streets within park districts.
6. Construction or maintenance on arterial streets of automatic traffic signals or school crossing guards.
7. Construction or maintenance of street lighting systems on arterial streets or state highways.
8. Construction or maintenance of storm sewers on arterial streets or state highways.
9. Construction and maintenance of pedestrian subways or overhead crossings on arterial streets or state highways.
10. Matching of federal aid funds.
11. Investigations needed to determine the need for any of the work for which motor fuel tax funds might be used.
12. Engineering costs.
13. The payment of any municipal indebtedness incurred in connection with an improvement eligible for the use of motor fuel tax funds.
14. Maintenance and repair of sidewalks located within the right of way of any street within the municipality.
15. Construction or maintenance of nonarterial streets.

---

[18] *Ill. Rev. Stat.*, ch. 121, sec. 7 (1965).

Use on nonarterial streets is subject to the provisions that a municipality may not spend more than 50 per cent of the total motor fuel tax allotments of the preceding year and that not more than one-half of the 50 per cent may be expended for maintenance. The statutes also provide that motor fuel tax funds may, subject to referendum, be turned over to a local mass transit district.

The statutes provide that a specific three-step procedure must be followed in order to use motor fuel tax funds: (1) The city council must adopt a resolution or ordinance stating specifically the purposes for which the funds are to be used and appropriating the funds. (2) After approval of the ordinances or resolutions by the Division of Highways, the municipality must prepare surveys, plans, specifications, and estimates and submit them to the Division of Highways for approval. (3) The municipality must advertise for bids and let contracts. No contract shall be let without the approval of the Division of Highways and bids cannot be advertised prior to approval of surveys, plans, specifications, and estimates.

These statutory requirements, as interpreted by the division, result in a good deal of paperwork and the Division of Highways makes many decisions which seem arbitrary and unrealistic to municipal officials.[19] The statutory requirements and the resulting regulations of the Division of Highways are the source of considerable friction between state and municipal officials. State officials point out that municipal officials often fail to follow all of the procedural steps or submit documents which are incorrect or incomplete.[20] City officials, on the other hand, complain about excessive delays and added costs resulting from state requirements. One knowledgeable municipal official stated flatly that the Division of Public Works slows down projects in his city from six months to one year and adds 20 to 50 per cent to the cost. He further stated that the division did not have people skilled in the design of urban streets and that approved designs were often more suitable for rural highways. This same official also pointed out that the present procedures place the emphasis upon approval of the plans prior to construction, rather than upon checking to see that the approved design has been followed. Most of the officials who commented on this problem during interviews or in testimony before the Municipal Problems

---

[19] For a discussion of legislative and administrative regulation see: D. R. Connor, "Motor Fuel Tax Improvements," *Illinois Municipal Review* (December, 1960); and William M. Dutelle, "Legislative Changes Affecting Municipal M.F.T.," *Illinois Municipal Review* (March, 1962).

[20] Connor, *op. cit.*; William M. Dutelle, "Financing Municipal Street Programs — Motor Fuel Tax," *Illinois Municipal Review* (April, 1960).

Commission were not quite so strong in their criticisms, but there were frequent references to the detailed requirements and delays in approving plans. One official interviewed characterized the department as "a paperwork empire designed to keep civil engineers off the streets." In contrast, a number of municipal officials reported no problems with the state and some indicated that the Division of Highways is very helpful.

Beginning on July 1, 1965, federal funds may not be used on any project in an urbanized area (SMSA) which is not based on a continuing, comprehensive transportation planning process carried on cooperatively by states and local communities. Since most of the money spent on state highways involves federal funds, it is necessary for municipalities in urbanized areas to participate in this process. The Federal Bureau of Public Roads has ruled that the following criteria must be met in order for a project to qualify: (1) that the proposed project must be on a route that is or will become part of the area's highway transportation system; (2) that due consideration be given to anticipated land uses in the area immediately affected by the project; (3) that traffic estimates support the type and size of facility and that provisions for traffic entering or leaving the facility are such that the project will operate efficiently; (4) that any additional terminal facilities necessary for efficient operation of the project can be provided without conflict to anticipated land uses.[21]

It is difficult to appraise the effect of the complicated intergovernmental situation upon municipal street systems. It is the somewhat impressionistic judgment of the authors that the Division of Highways has imposed unnecessarily detailed requirements and that the failure to delegate more authority to field office personnel has resulted in unnecessary delays and much uncertainty about requirements. On the other hand, there seems to be a strong case for some state supervision over local use of motor fuel funds. Because of the intense and highly localized pressures generated by proposals for constructing or reconstructing streets, there is much to be said for having plans reviewed by an agency which is free to consider the wider, longer-term implications of a proposal. One city official points out that there is no area of municipal expenditure policy where local pressure to make "wrong" decisions is greater and that the Division of Highways renders an important service by insisting upon street designs that are safe and adequate for long-run community needs.

Expenditure Levels U.S. Bureau of the Census statistics for the fiscal

---

[21] C. S. Monnier, "Financing Federal-Aid Streets," *Illinois Municipal Review* (April, 1965), p. 17.

year 1962 show that the 41 Illinois cities of over 25,000 population spent an average of $12.81 per capita for street and highway purposes. For reasons already stated, these statistics do not provide a very accurate picture of the normal level of expenditure for streets and highways in a given city. The per capita current and capital expenditures shown in column 1 of Table 11 include capital expenditures which range from zero in Alton to $31.71 in Rock Island. In an attempt to reduce the variation due to the irregular timing of capital expenditure, data for the three fiscal years 1961-63 were obtained from the Division of Highways and averaged. These data are shown in columns 2, 3, and 4 of Table 11. The variation in these data is considerably less than the variation in the single year data, but even so there is no obvious relationship between the level of expenditure and the geographic location or population of the city.[22]

SEWERAGE AND OTHER SANITATION

In a thinly populated area, each inidvidual residence or industrial plant provides its own on-site sewerage disposal plant. As population density increases, on-site disposal plants become dangerous to health and are uneconomical as compared with the cost of a community collection and disposal system. In Illinois, the provision and operation of a community system are often the joint responsibility of the municipality and an overlapping sanitary district. A total of 99 out of 188 municipalities of more than 5,000 population are largely or wholly overlaid by a sanitary district. Thirty of the 41 cities of over 25,000 population lie largely or wholly within a sanitary district. More than 90 municipalities of all sizes in Cook County lie within the Chicago Sanitary District. Most of the districts outside Cook County have boundaries which roughly coincide with the borders of a single city or a small group of adjacent cities.

Since the boundaries of sanitary districts are not usually coterminous with that of the municipality, it is not possible to determine the total expenditure for sewerage within a given municipality. It is possible, however, to approximate this expenditure by determining the tax levy which the sanitary district imposes upon residents of the municipality.[23]

---

[22] These data are not based upon exactly the same definitions as are Census statistics. For example, sidewalks and street lighting are included in the Census classification but excluded from the data which were obtained from the Division of Highways. Toll road expenditures are also excluded from Division of Highways data.

[23] Computed by multiplying the sanitary district tax rates times the assessed value of property in a municipality. See Appendix B.

TABLE 11

PER CAPITA STREET AND HIGHWAY EXPENDITURE, 41 ILLINOIS MUNICIPALITIES

	1962 Expenditure	Three-Year Average, 1961-63 Construction	Maintenance	Total
Municipalities Outside Chicago SMSA				
Alton	$ 5.95	$4.88	$4.30	$ 9.17
Belleville	5.38	1.95	4.92	6.87
Bloomington	15.93	4.53	6.11	10.63
Champaign	8.94	3.68	4.04	7.72
Danville	9.67	4.57	4.58	9.15
Decatur	14.94	9.00	3.12	12.11
East St. Louis	12.18	.76	6.00	6.76
Freeport	10.64	5.08	4.63	9.70
Galesburg	8.75	6.16	4.93	11.09
Granite City	11.34	3.19	6.24	9.43
Kankakee	12.13	3.75	5.54	9.29
Moline	20.03	9.67	4.64	14.31
Pekin	15.96	4.78	4.31	9.09
Peoria	5.78	2.65	5.00	7.65
Quincy	10.73	4.02	4.66	8.68
Rockford	13.85	9.99	4.20	14.19
Rock Island	42.21	10.58	4.77	15.35
Springfield	7.50	4.29	4.67	8.97
Urbana	10.43	17.75	4.57	22.32
Average	12.75	5.86	4.80	10.66
Municipalities in Chicago SMSA				
Arlington Hgts.	15.80	.93	8.84	9.77
Aurora	14.84	5.98	6.66	12.63
Berwyn	10.78	4.67	3.98	8.65
Calumet City	16.37	5.76	6.49	12.25
Chicago Hgts.	7.01	4.48	3.75	8.23
Cicero	8.66	1.87	5.78	7.66
Des Plaines	15.22	2.48	4.81	7.30
Elgin	9.65	2.42	5.23	7.66
Elmhurst	11.42	1.44	5.13	6.57
Evanston	11.21	3.23	5.12	8.35
Harvey	20.58	5.54	3.80	9.34
Highland Park	22.80	13.58	7.90	21.48
Joliet	9.52	1.95	6.18	8.12
Maywood	11.77	2.10	3.72	5.82
Oak Lawn	11.82	4.68	3.90	8.57
Oak Park	8.97	6.31	3.28	9.59
Park Forest	9.87	6.82	5.37	12.18
Park Ridge	13.34	4.49	3.74	8.23
Skokie	8.97	4.40	3.78	8.18
Waukegan	10.47	4.46	6.82	11.27
Wilmette	9.81	4.89	2.48	7.37
Average	12.33	4.40	5.08	9.49
Chicago	23.96	7.61	5.09	12.70

SOURCE U.S. Bureau of the Census, unpublished worksheets for the 1962 Census of Governments; State of Illinois, Department of Public Works.

The amount of these levies, expressed on a per capita basis, are shown for the 41 cities in column 3, Table 12. Comparison of these data with municipal expenditure for sewerage (columns 1 and 2) suggests that the sanitary district typically spends considerably more for sewerage than does the municipality. Thus, data on city expenditure for sewerage by itself provides little useful information concerning the level of sewerage service.

A few cities did not report sewerage expenditure to the U.S. Census Bureau. In the case of Joliet it is known that sewerage expenditure was reported as part of water expenditure. In the other cases it is likely that the zero expenditure results from reporting difficulties rather than from the fact that no expenditures were made.

The cost of providing sewerage collection and disposal varies with the topography, population density, and the standard of services provided. Engineering studies show that the larger systems of collection and treatment are more economical to construct and operate.[24] However, the dense population which makes large systems feasible may also result in the need for higher standards of purification and more expensive disposal systems.

The level of treatment of sewerage which a given city provides may have greater effect upon other areas than upon the city itself. For example, a city located on a sizable river might be able to dump raw sewage into the river with little adverse effect upon its own residents, but with possible serious effects upon the health of downstream residents and upon the aesthetic and recreational conditions in a wide area. For this reason, both state and federal governments take an active interest in problems of stream pollution.

The Sanitary Water Board, an agency of the State of Illinois, has primary responsibility for preventing water pollution in all areas in Illinois except the area covered by the Chicago Sanitary District. This board, which includes among its members the directors of the Departments of Public Health, Conservation, Public Works and Buildings, and Agriculture, has a staff consisting primarily of sanitary engineers employed by the Department of Public Health. The board has the power to order municipalities to discontinue the pollution of streams and to specify the conditions and time within which such discontinuance must be accomplished. It issues permits for all sewerage works in the state and may institute legal proceedings to compel compliance with

---

[24] Advisory Commission on Intergovernmental Relations, *Performance of Urban Functions: Local and Areawide,* Commission Report M-21 (Washington, D.C.: September, 1963), pp. 200-203.

TABLE 12

PER CAPITA MUNICIPAL SEWERAGE AND SANITATION EXPENDITURE AND SANITARY DISTRICT LEVY, 41 ILLINOIS MUNICIPALITIES, 1962 FISCAL YEAR

	Municipal Sewerage Expenditure		Sanitary District Levy	Other Sanitation Expenditure	Total Sewerage and Sanitation
	Current	Total			
Municipalities Outside Chicago SMSA					
Alton	$1.32	$1.32	$ —	$3.34	$ 4.66
Belleville	4.37	4.47	—	3.52	7.99
Bloomington	1.70	1.70	2.71	2.90	7.31
Champaign	1.17	4.58	6.26	.67	11.51
Danville	.80	1.07	4.94	2.81	8.82
Decatur	.45	.45	6.00	.56	7.01
East St. Louis	2.62	4.15	8.91[a]	1.70	14.76
Freeport	2.88	3.15	—	2.00	5.15
Galesburg	—	—	3.77	2.23	6.00
Granite City	1.61	12.37	13.93[a]	4.07	30.37
Kankakee	4.78	17.46	—	4.08	21.54
Moline	2.03	7.01	—	2.73	9.74
Pekin	.88	1.20	—	3.74	4.94
Peoria	.73	.73	4.65	6.07	11.45
Quincy	.33	35.31	—	1.89	37.20
Rockford	1.55	1.55	3.98	3.61	9.14
Rock Island	3.46	6.83	—	2.56	9.39
Springfield	2.86	13.53	4.05	6.32	23.90
Urbana	—	—	4.97	1.14	6.11
Average	1.77	6.15	3.38	2.94	12.47
Municipalities in Chicago SMSA					
Arlington Hgts.	—	—	8.17	—	8.17
Aurora	1.22	1.22	4.92	4.52	10.66
Berwyn	—	—	8.75	2.62	11.37
Calumet City	1.01	1.01	6.90	1.91	9.82
Chicago Hgts.	2.37	2.49	6.48	4.73	13.70
Cicero	2.59	2.59	12.88	9.01	24.48
Des Plaines	1.25	1.40	9.78	4.27	15.45
Elgin	—	—	9.28	2.34	11.62
Elmhurst	4.04	7.69	—	4.18	11.87
Evanston	.71	.71	12.31	6.68	19.70
Harvey	1.46	1.46	8.65	2.60	12.71
Highland Park	.53	3.16	10.04	3.14	16.34
Joliet	—	—	—	2.90	2.90
Maywood	—	—	9.88	3.86	13.74
Oak Lawn	1.16	1.47	8.57	3.70	13.74
Oak Park	.68	.70	11.68	4.62	17.00
Park Forest	.69	.81	4.78	.68	6.27
Park Ridge	1.25	1.25	12.10	2.90	16.25

[a] Levy shown for East St. Louis and Granite City is for East Side Levee and Sanitary District which has been primarily concerned with flood control and surface drainage problems.

TABLE 12 (continued)

PER CAPITA MUNICIPAL SEWERAGE AND SANITATION EXPENDITURE AND SANITARY DISTRICT LEVY, 41 ILLINOIS MUNICIPALITIES, 1962 FISCAL YEAR

	Municipal Sewerage Expenditure		Sanitary District Levy	Other Sanitation Expenditure	Total Sewerage and Sanitation
	Current	Total			
Skokie	$ —	$ .22	$15.10	$4.71	$20.03
Waukegan	1.02	1.02	7.21	3.05	11.28
Wilmette	.74	.74	14.35	8.60	23.69
Average	.99	1.33	8.66	3.86	13.85
Chicago	2.02	4.39	9.99	10.10	24.48

SOURCE U.S. Bureau of the Census, unpublished worksheets for the 1962 Census of Governments; Illinois county clerks' offices.

its orders. Before permits are issued sanitary engineers review construction documents for the proposed sewerage works. They also make special investigations of stream pollution, undertake routine stream surveillance, and sponsor technical conferences for plant operators and municipal officials.

The federal government provides grants for the construction of sewerage works and also takes a direct role in efforts to eliminate pollution of interstate waters. The Department of Health, Education and Welfare has authority to require states and their subdivisions to prevent pollution of such waters. In recent years the federal government and the Sanitary Water Board have ordered a number of cities in Illinois to construct sewerage plants.

The term "other sanitation" is used by the U.S. Census Bureau to refer to the collection and disposal of trash, garbage, and other solid wastes from private property and to the cleaning of streets and other public areas. In 1962 the Illinois Municipal League conducted a survey of garbage disposal and collection methods and financing in approximately 200 Illinois cities.[25] Twenty-eight per cent of the cities surveyed in this study provide collection service using municipal employees and equipment. All but one of these cities levy a garbage collection tax and about 25 per cent of them also charge a service fee. Twenty-four per cent of those surveyed contract with private haulers or other municipalities to provide collection service. Twenty per cent of the cities provide no municipal service but license private scavengers. One city has unlicensed scavengers. Other municipalities reported a combination of

[25] Illinois Municipal League, Information Service, May, 1962.

methods, presumably in different parts of the city or for different types of service.[26]

In the same survey, 43 per cent of the cities replying reported that garbage is disposed of in a sanitary landfill. Twenty-five per cent reported use of an open dump and 6.5 per cent use incineration. Other cities did not answer the question or report the use of a combination of methods. The number of cities using an open dump is probably smaller now than when the survey was conducted since a recently enacted state law prohibiting burning in such dumps has caused a number of cities to switch to other types of disposal.

PARKS AND RECREATION

In the summer of 1966 riots in Chicago were touched off by the fact that police insisted upon closing open fire hydrants on a hot day. Obviously, the causes of such riots involve far more than the lack of adequate recreational facilities in slum areas, but the incident does focus attention upon the fact that providing park and recreational facilities is an essential service in a modern urban community.

Responsibility for providing public park and recreational facilities is often shared with other governmental units and private agencies. Some municipal governments provide such facilities as parks, playgrounds, swimming pools, and golf courses, but such facilities are also provided by overlapping park districts. Residents of many municipalities are also within a short distance of county forest preserves or state parks. Such private agencies as the YMCA, Boy Scouts, country clubs, and private business organizations often supplement governmental programs by providing facilities to members or to particular client groups.

Municipalities which operate a recreational system are permitted to vest the power to operate the system in the school board, park district board, or other existing body or may establish a municipal playground and recreational board with members appointed by the mayor.

Table 13 shows per capita municipal expenditures as reported to the Census Bureau and estimated per capita "within-municipality" levy by overlapping park districts. It is clear from these data that there is some tendency for park district and municipal expenditure to substitute for each other. Municipalities tend to spend more for park and recreation purposes if there is no overlapping park district or if the park district levies relatively moderate taxes. A comparison of assessed values and expenditures for park purposes indicates that residents of the wealthier

[26] Many cities which provide free service in residential areas provide no service or levy charges for service to business places.

TABLE 13

PER CAPITA PARK AND RECREATION EXPENDITURE AND PARK DISTRICT LEVY, 41 ILLINOIS MUNICIPALITIES, 1962 FISCAL YEAR

	Municipal Expenditure		Park District Levy	Municipal Expenditure and Park District Levy
	Current	Total		
Municipalities Outside Chicago SMSA				
Alton	$3.84	$3.84	$ —	$3.84
Belleville	3.05	3.05	—	3.05
Bloomington	3.65	3.65	—	3.65
Champaign	1.56	1.56	3.02	4.58
Danville	3.25	3.54	—	3.54
Decatur	1.35	1.38	4.59	5.97
East St. Louis	—	—	5.04	5.04
Freeport	1.11	1.11	6.02	7.13
Galesburg	2.65	2.72	—	2.72
Granite City	—	—	4.47	4.47
Kankakee	—	—	5.18	5.18
Moline	4.25	4.34	—	4.34
Pekin	.27	.27	2.99	3.26
Peoria	2.61	2.61	5.08	7.69
Quincy	—	—	3.07	3.07
Rockford	3.36	3.36	4.14	7.51
Rock Island	3.41	4.25	—	4.25
Springfield	2.26	2.45	2.31	4.76
Urbana	.01	.01	3.36	3.37
Average	1.93	2.01	2.59	4.60
Municipalities in Chicago SMSA				
Arlington Hgts.	—	—	6.56	6.56
Aurora	3.91	4.38	3.62	8.00
Berwyn	1.97	2.72	—	2.72
Calumet City	—	—	3.25	3.25
Chicago Hgts.	.31	.31	3.09	3.40
Cicero	—	—	5.95	5.95
Des Plaines	—	—	5.64	5.64
Elgin	2.23	2.70	—	2.70
Elmhurst	—	—	4.94	4.94
Evanston	6.55	7.51	.36	7.87
Harvey	—	—	1.88	1.88
Highland Park	3.30	3.34	4.72	8.06
Joliet	.35	.35	—	.35
Maywood	2.09	2.14	.41	2.55
Oak Lawn	—	—	2.52	2.52
Oak Park	4.44	4.75	3.23	7.97
Park Forest	2.59	3.33	—	3.33
Park Ridge	—	—	6.90	6.90

TABLE 13 (continued)

PER CAPITA PARK AND RECREATION EXPENDITURE AND PARK DISTRICT LEVY, 41 ILLINOIS MUNICIPALITIES, 1962 FISCAL YEAR

	Municipal Expenditure		Park District Levy	Municipal Expenditure and Park District Levy
	Current	Total		
Skokie	$ —	$ —	$ 7.55	$ 7.55
Waukegan	1.30	1.35	2.57	3.93
Wilmette	4.34	4.45	5.40	9.85
Average	1.59	1.78	3.27	5.04
Chicago	1.54	1.58	11.33	12.91

SOURCE U.S. Bureau of the Census, unpublished worksheets for the 1962 Census of Governments; Illinois county clerks' offices.

cities receive a much higher quality of service than do residents of low income areas.[27]

OTHER GENERAL EXPENDITURE

All except one of the municipalities of over 25,000 population maintain municipal libraries.[28] The statutes vest authority for managing the library and the expenditure of library funds in the library board, with the exception that the board must obtain the approval of municipal authorities before selling or otherwise disposing of real estate or issuing bonds. The library boards do not have authority to levy taxes, but in their annual report to the municipal council they include a statement of financial requirements for the ensuing fiscal year and indicate the amount of the tax levy which, in their judgment, is necessary.

In practice, the relationships between the library board and the city council vary considerably. In some cities, the council appears to regard itself as an agent for an independent board and to assume that it must levy the amount requested without questioning library operations. In other cities, library funds seem to be fully integrated into the accounting and budgeting system of the city and the city council considers it to be fully within its power to change the amount requested by the board.

Among the 41 larger municipalities average per capita current expenditure for libraries in 1962 was $2.19. Capital expenditure averaged $1.06.

[27] The coefficient of simple correlation between per capita assessed value and per capita "expenditure plus levy" is .66.

[28] Elgin does not operate a library since a township library is located within the city.

Many Illinois cities report little or no expenditure for health purposes. This results from the fact that public health services are often provided by a county health department or by a local health district. The latest available report of the State Department of Public Health lists 21 county health departments, several of which cover more than one county and two of which (Cook and Peoria) exclude one or more cities within the county. The same publication lists 11 full-time city or local health district departments.[29] The State Department of Public Health is working toward the realization of a master plan which calls for coverage of the state by single- or multiple-county health departments and, to this end, carries on promotional and educational work directed toward achieving favorable votes on the establishment of such districts.[30]

In 1962 the largest reported public health expenditure among Illinois cities was $5.55 per capita in Winnetka, but this figure is completely misleading since Winnetka provided services on a contractual basis to several neighboring municipalities. Since that time Winnetka has discontinued its public health department and is served by Evanston on a contractual basis. Among the cities which maintain their own departments, the expenditures of $2.67 by Peoria and $1.86 by Springfield are typical.

Expenditures for the "general overhead" functions such as financial administration, general control, and general public buildings make up a relatively minor portion of expenditure in most municipalities. Nevertheless, such activities are vital to the operation of the municipality. The policies of the city council determine the service activities which will be performed. The quality of top management and the nature of the budgeting, accounting, and purchasing functions have a tremendous impact upon the policies followed by the city and the efficiency with which services are performed.

Expenditure for financial administration in 1962 averaged $1.09 per capita in the 41 larger cities. Analysis of expenditure in the group of 188 cities shows a tendency for financial administration expenditure to be higher in the Chicago SMSA. Expenditure for general control averaged $2.05 per capita in the 41 cities, and there is a tendency for expenditure to be higher in the Chicago SMSA and in smaller cities throughout the state.

---

[29] State of Illinois, Department of Public Health, *44th Annual Report*, pp. 75-76.

[30] *Ibid.*, p. 71.

SEMI-COMMERCIAL GENERAL EXPENDITURES

The governmental services discussed thus far in the chapter are usually financed from general revenue rather than on a self-supporting basis.[31] For convenience, expenditure for these services will be designated as "noncommercial general expenditure."

Another group of municipal services such as hospitals, parking facilities, and airports are partly or entirely self-supporting in many municipalities and are sometimes provided, in whole or part, by private enterprise or other nongovernmental agencies. Expenditure for these services will be referred to as "semi-commercial general expenditures." This term indicates the borderline nature of these activities as compared with utility enterprises which are recognized as being properly self-supporting whether operated as government enterprise or as regulated private enterprise.

It must be emphasized that classification of a function as general or semi-commercial does not reflect a judgment as to whether or not the function is properly a general governmental function. Its sole purpose is to group as nonenterprise general expenditure those functions which are common to a large number of Illinois cities so that meaningful comparisons of the level of expenditure can be made.

Hospitals Few Illinois cities maintain city hospitals. Among the 41 cities of over 25,000 population, only Moline and Champaign do. These are largely self-sustaining so that the large per capita expenditures reported are covered largely by earnings, federal grants, or other nontax sources.

Parking Facilities At one time most cities allowed on-street parking. As traffic congestion increased the parking meter was promoted as a means of forcing the all-day parker to leave space in front of commercial establishments for the "two-hour shopper." Gradually, parking meters have become almost universal on all commercial streets on which parking is permitted. At the same time, street parking has become increasingly inadequate so that parking lots and ramps now provide most of the parking space in all but the smallest cities. As these developments occurred, it became increasingly clear to municipal officials and transportation planners that there is little reason for govern-

---

[31] There are some exceptions. For example, certain recreational services such as golf courses and swimming pools are often on a partly or entirely self-financing basis and there is a growing tendency to regard sewerage as a utility-type operation to be financed from user charges. Garbage collection is privately provided in many Illinois cities.

ment to provide free parking in congested areas.[32] As a result, off-street parking facilities, whether operated by commercial firms or municipal government, are usually on a profit-making or self-liquidating basis. In fact, many municipal parking facilities in Illinois are financed by means of revenue bonds.

In U.S. Census publications all expenditures for off-street parking are classified as parking expenditure as are expenditures for the purchase and maintenance of on-street meters. Construction, maintenance, and cleaning of street surfaces are classified as street or sanitation expenditure, even though part of the street is devoted to parking purposes. On a per capita basis, reported expenditure in the 41 largest cities ranged from a high of $2.86 in Rockford to lows of 19 cents in Springfield and zero in Urbana.

Airports It has been stressed repeatedly that the unit of government which provides a particular kind of governmental service varies from community to community in Illinois, but few examples are as vivid as airports. Consider: Residents of the Chicago metropolitan area are served by airports operated by the City of Chicago. Residents of Champaign-Urbana use an airport operated by the University of Illinois. The Decatur airport is operated by the Decatur Park District. The Bloomington-Normal Airport is operated by an airport authority. Residents of the East St. Louis area have depended upon the St. Louis (Missouri) Municipal Airport but will soon be served also by an airport in Illinois operated by the Bi-State Development Agency, a special district authorized by a compact between Illinois and Missouri.

In 1962 Chicago spent $8.99 per capita for airports, most of which was capital expenditure at O'Hare Airport then under construction. In the same year, Galesburg reported expenditures of $1.01 per capita and four other cities among the 41 reported expenditures of less than $1.00 per capita.

Housing and Urban Renewal Illinois cities have the power to engage in urban renewal activities and to operate public housing projects directly, but only 5 of the 41 cities report expenditure for these purposes in 1962. Actually, most housing and urban renewal activities in Illinois are carried on by housing or land clearance authorities. Twenty-three of the 41 largest cities have city housing authorities or land clearance commissions. These may be established in any city of over 25,000 pop-

---

[32] That this has not become as clear to the average motorist, especially in smaller cities, is evidenced by the furor which commonly greets each new installation of parking meters or restriction on on-street parking.

ulation. They are governed by a board of commissioners appointed by the mayor with the approval of the State Housing Board. They have the power to borrow and spend money and to accept grants but do not have the power to levy taxes. Many cities which do not have city housing authorities or land clearance commissions lie within the jurisdiction of county authorities which have a board appointed by the presiding officer of the county.

Utility Services Municipal ownership of utilities seems to be less common in Illinois than in many other states. Springfield is the only one of the 41 largest cities to operate an electric utility.[33] Pekin is the only one of these cities to operate a bus system.[34]

A few cities, particularly those along the Mississippi River, operate toll bridges. Even municipally owned water supply systems are less universal in Illinois than in many other states. Ten of the 41 largest cities are served by private water companies.

In Illinois, some 60 municipalities west of Chicago purchase treated water from Chicago and distribute it through their own system. Several other cities also sell water to neighboring municipalities. Almost all municipal water supply systems are self-supporting and some make substantial contributions to the support of general government, but it is difficult to determine the exact contribution because of differences in accounting systems. According to 1962 Census of Government figures, net receipts from water utilities exceeded total expenses for 27 of the 31 largest cities with municipal water systems. These expense figures, however, include capital expenditure but do not include depreciation allowances or interest payments.

It is known that some municipalities utilize water charges as a substantial source of revenue for general purposes. For example, in 1963 the Evanston City Council raised water rates substantially. This came about after the council had debated the relative merits of property taxes, utility taxes, and increased water rates as a source of needed additional revenue.[35]

Some cities set up accounting procedures which place the water util-

[33] Bloomington recently sold its municipally owned electric utility.

[34] The Chicago Transit Authority, which operates in Cook County, is a separate unit of government with a board of seven members, four of whom are appointed by the mayor of Chicago.

The Bi-State Development Agency operates transit facilities in the St. Louis area. It is governed by a board of directors, one-half of whom are appointed by the governor of each state.

[35] Since Evanston sells water to Skokie, about 40 per cent of the additional revenue was obtained from residents of Skokie.

ity in a position comparable to that which would be occupied by a privately owned utility. For example, Bloomington's water department pays the general fund amounts comparable to the franchise and property taxes which would be paid by a private firm and also pays an administrative charge to cover the services performed for the department by city officials.

SUMMARY AND CONCLUSIONS

Municipal expenditure data reveal a great deal about the kinds of services which Illinois municipalities provide. Analysis of Table 4 reveals that Illinois municipalities do most of the spending for police, fire, sanitation, airport, parking, and library services and that the most costly municipal services are provision of streets and highways and police protection.

Analysis of data for individual cities reveals that there are substantial differences in expenditure per capita among Illinois cities. The greatest difference occurs in expenditure for public utility and semi-commercial enterprises, but Table 14 and the more detailed breakdown presented in Appendix C reveal that there are substantial variations in nonenterprise general expenditure.

The descriptive material presented in this chapter provides a clue to some of the factors which influence municipal financial decisions. It is clear, for example, that municipal expenditure decisions are affected by the allocation of responsibility among overlapping units of government. This is most marked in the case of sanitary and park expenditures where overlapping special districts often make most of the expenditure for the function. It is also important in the case of fire protection expenditure. Special fire districts provide all fire services in some smaller cities, and there are a number of kinds of working arrangements between municipalities and the fire protection districts which overlap them. There are also differences in the allocation of functions between municipalities and overlapping units of general government such as the county or township. Sometimes these general units provide health service or library service within the municipality and there is considerable difference in policies in regard to the expenditure of county road funds within municipal boundaries.

A somewhat different summary view of nonenterprise general expenditure (including park and sanitary district levies) is provided in Table 15. The first two columns relate to Chicago's expenditure for certain major functions and combinations of functions. Columns 3 and 4 show the same data for 40 other cities of more than 25,000 population and the last two columns provide similar (not identical) informa-

TABLE 14

ESTIMATED PER CAPITA EXPENDITURE, 41 ILLINOIS MUNICIPALITIES, 1962 FISCAL YEAR

	Nonenterprise General Expenditure	Nonenterprise Expenditure, Sanitary and Park District Levies	Semi-Commercial Enterprise Expenditure	Interest on General Debt	Utility Expenditure	Grand Total
Municipalities Outside Chicago SMSA						
Alton	$39.40	$39.40	$ .93	$4.66	$ —	$44.99
Belleville	37.59	37.59	.78	2.67	—	41.04
Bloomington	52.26	54.98	1.96	3.05	14.67	74.66
Champaign	38.41	47.68	36.59	1.99	—	86.26
Danville	37.77	42.71	2.14	.95	—	45.81
Decatur	38.70	49.29	2.79	2.08	8.25	62.42
East St. Louis	43.02	56.98	.39	9.61	—	66.98
Freeport	39.24	45.27	1.01	1.25	8.93	56.45
Galesburg	41.41	45.19	2.76	.80	9.30	58.05
Granite City	47.63	66.02	.66	1.02	—	67.70
Kankakee	56.23	61.41	1.33	3.96	—	66.70
Moline	62.52	62.52	58.44	3.29	15.20	139.45
Pekin	46.78	49.78	.97	1.46	2.86	55.07
Peoria	53.53	63.27	2.60	.49	—	66.36
Quincy	68.09	71.16	1.42	5.85	11.48	89.91
Rockford	63.28	71.41	6.15	1.21	13.49	92.27
Rock Island	58.87	58.87	2.43	5.47	9.59	76.35
Springfield	65.73	72.09	.19	3.99	76.05	152.32
Urbana	42.31	50.64	—	2.70	—	53.34
Average	49.09	55.06	6.50	2.97	8.94	73.48

TABLE 14 (continued)

ESTIMATED PER CAPITA EXPENDITURE, 41 ILLINOIS MUNICIPALITIES, 1962 FISCAL YEAR

	Nonenterprise General Expenditure	Nonenterprise Expenditure, Sanitary and Park District Levies	Semi-Commercial Enterprise Expenditure	Interest on General Debt	Utility Expenditure	Grand Total
Municipalities in Chicago SMSA						
Arlington Hgts.	$34.63	$ 49.36	$ 1.55	$1.20	$13.52	$ 65.63
Aurora	50.02	58.55	1.80	1.34	7.89	69.58
Berwyn	40.82	49.57	.81	.74	11.11	62.23
Calumet City	37.40	47.55	.38	1.14	12.97	62.04
Chicago Hgts.	46.48	56.05	1.79	.70	18.31	76.84
Cicero	53.04	71.87	.95	3.67	20.42	96.91
Des Plaines	36.79	52.21	1.06	.84	13.14	67.24
Elgin	34.06	43.34	2.02	.90	6.37	52.63
Elmhurst	37.53	42.46	.57	.57	7.53	51.14
Evanston	64.19	76.87	1.37	1.71	6.65	86.61
Harvey	34.82	45.36	1.43	2.48	28.62	77.89
Highland Park	94.36	109.12	1.51	6.90	9.60	127.12
Joliet	37.80	37.80	4.04	.26	12.60	54.70
Maywood	39.63	49.91	18.22	.66	14.59	83.39
Oak Lawn	32.00	43.10	—	3.13	12.26	58.49
Oak Park	71.91	86.82	2.55	1.59	21.96	112.94
Park Forest	43.48	48.26	.36	.85	8.90	58.36
Park Ridge	35.93	54.92	1.31	2.67	18.40	77.31
Skokie	49.77	72.40	.25	1.49	11.95	86.08
Waukegan	51.46	61.25	.62	.19	5.93	67.98
Wilmette	52.47	72.22	.62	.71	5.24	78.79
Average	46.60	58.52	2.06	1.61	12.76	74.95
Chicago	84.76	106.13	17.58	6.31	14.23	144.26

SOURCE U.S. Bureau of the Census, unpublished worksheets for the 1962 Census of Governments; State of Illinois, Department of Public Works. See Appendix C for more detailed breakdown.

TABLE 15

NONENTERPRISE GENERAL EXPENDITURE AND PARK AND SANITARY LEVY, BY CITY SIZE[a]

	Chicago		Other Cities over 25,000		Cities 5,000-25,000	
	Per Capita	Per Cent of Total	Per Capita	Per Cent of Total	Per Capita	Per Cent of Total
Police	$25.08	23.6	$9.26	15.8	$ 8.10	17.5
Fire	9.65	9.1	8.17	13.9	3.75	8.1
Streets	12.71	12.0	9.92	16.9	10.02	21.6
Sewerage and Sanitary District Levy	14.40	13.6	9.75	16.6	8.96	19.3
Other Sanitation	10.11	9.5	3.66	6.2	2.67	5.8
Libraries	2.03	1.9	3.46	5.9	1.31	2.8
Health	2.04	1.9	.70	1.2	.23	.5
Parks and Recreation and Park District Levy	12.94	12.2	5.15	8.8	3.61	7.8
Financial Administration, General Control, and Public Buildings	7.84	7.4	3.96	6.7	4.89	10.5
Miscellaneous General Expenditure	9.35	8.8	4.71	8.0	2.86	6.2
Total	106.13	100.0	58.75	100.0	46.39	100.0

[a] Per capita figures weighted by city population.

SOURCE U.S. Bureau of the Census, unpublished worksheets for the 1962 Census of Governments.

tion about cities with populations between 5,000 and 25,000.[36] Unlike other "average per capita" data which have been presented in this chapter, these data are weighted by city size. That is, the total expenditures of the cities in the size group are divided by the total population of the cities so that the contribution which each makes to the average is dependent upon its population rather than being equal regardless of size. It is clear from these figures that the smaller cities spend less per capita and that the relative importance of various functional expenditures varies among the different size classes, but it is not possible to specify just how the size of a city affects expenditure decisions. The size of a city is related to many economic and political characteristics which, in turn, may be related to the expenditure decisions which are made.

Not only are the general powers and duties of municipalities derived from the state, but municipalities may also be required to maintain a certain level of services, as in the control of air and water pollution, or to follow a particular personnel policy, as in the case of policemen and firemen.

The state also influences the pattern of expenditure by providing grants for specific purposes and often insists upon overseeing the details of expenditure from these grants.

[36] Data for the smaller cities differs from that for the larger ones in that 1962 Census figures for streets and highways are used for the smaller city. This probably has little effect upon the figures for the group of cities since the main effect of the substitution of three-year average figures is to reduce annual city-to-city variation.

3 HISTORY AND ADMINISTRATION OF THE ILLINOIS PROPERTY TAX

One of the first things that a municipal official learns about municipal finance is that there are certain features or parameters of the local fiscal system which are fixed, at least in the short run. Municipal expenditures, unlike most state and federal expenditures, are related closely to particular revenue sources. For example, property taxes are levied for particular funds which may be expended only for specified purposes; grants from state and federal governments are earmarked for particular programs, while the fees and other charges collected by municipalities are frequently based on cost estimates of the value of the services rendered. Further, the municipality's long-run expenditure and long-run revenue must be equal since local governments do not have monetary powers.

Clearly, a great number of the financial problems which concern a municipal official involve the property tax system. This is not surprising since, traditionally, the property tax has been the major source of local government revenue. In fact, the historical dependence of local governments on this tax has made it a focal point in the financial decision-making process. To cite an example, most municipal finance decisions must take account of fund structures established by property tax statutes and of appropriation procedures which are tied to property tax levies. Both the taxing and borrowing capacities of a municipality are closely related to the property tax base.

The longevity of the tax and some of its unique features have resulted in a very complicated body of law and an elaborate and highly decentralized administrative system. The very close legal connection between property tax administration and municipal budgeting, accounting and appropriation procedures, and the important role which other units of local government play in property tax administration necessitate that a great deal of attention be devoted to the Illinois property tax.

The detailed analysis of the property tax in the next three chapters includes material which is tedious and somewhat difficult to understand but which is of vital importance in understanding significant aspects of municipal finance. The very complexity of these matters and the fact that no single person is likely to be familiar with all of the legal, political, and administrative aspects of property taxation makes the property tax process one of the most important determinants influencing municipal decision-making.

PROPERTY TAX HISTORY

The colonial property tax was not a very sophisticated levy and the forms adopted in the several colonies and territories varied substantially. The objects of taxation differed depending upon the definition of property used.[1] If a common thread linked these early levies, it was the belief that property represented faculty or ability to pay.[2]

Uniform property tax procedures had not developed by the date of Illinois' statehood in 1818. Some states assessed land on the basis of quality, while others assessed it on the basis of quantity or not at all.[3] Most of the earliest assessments were based largely on some constant value per acre, irrespective of market value or productivity. Ad valorem assessment was stipulated in Illinois' first Constitution, but the tax base consisted of only certain enumerated types of property and state and local rates applied to different tax bases.[4] Other states were experimenting with assessments based on the product of the property or the ability of the property to produce an income. In either case, taxes were usually levied against individuals, not their property, and tax liabilities were distributed in the most arbitrary fashion.

While the costs of government remained minimal and property taxation was an occasional levy, objections to the tax were probably few. However, when the levy became an annual tax supporting both state and local governments, widespread concern developed over the equity

---

[1] Sumner Benson, "A History of the General Property Tax," in G. C. S. Benson, S. Benson, H. McClelland, and P. Thomson, *The American Property Tax: Its History, Administration, and Economic Impact* (Claremont, California: College Press, 1965), p. 24. This work contains a more detailed history of the tax and specific examples of colonial taxation in the several colonies.

[2] Richard T. Ely, *Taxation in American States and Cities* (New York: Thomas Y. Crowell & Co., 1888), pp. 109-13.

[3] *Ibid.*, p. 116.

[4] I. M. Labovitz, *The Illinois Revenue System, 1818-1936,* Special Report No. 4 (Springfield: Illinois Tax Commission, 1936), p. 29.

and uniformity of the tax. Government officials, taxpayers, and scholars turned their attention to developing a more general and uniform basis for the tax. The emphasis on assessment led to the adoption of an ad valorem or "at fair value" basis for defining the tax base. Also, the base was extended to include more classes of intangible property as well as all real properties. To aid collection, real property taxes were levied against the property itself rather than against the owner. Efforts to improve the tax seemed self-reenforcing. As more property became subject to assessment, the taxpayers sought even more general tax laws to insure that all property, tangible and intangible, would be treated the same and tax liabilities spread more equitably.

In 1839, the Illinois General Assembly broadened the definition of taxable property to include all property not specifically exempted.[5] This act, like those being enacted in other state legislatures, specified that: (1) both land and personalty were to be assessed on an ad valorem basis, and (2) state and local levies were to be extended over the same base. Many features of this act were incorporated in the 1848 and 1870 constitutions and are distinguishable in current property tax law in Illinois.[6]

Nineteenth-century attempts to achieve generalization of the property tax were manifest in "uniformity" and "universality" clauses in revenue acts and state constitutions. Twenty-nine uniformity requirements appeared in state constitutions between 1819 and 1895,[7] but as Benson notes, they "were a moderate corrective. . . . For they required not that *all* property be taxed, but that whatever property *was* taxed should be taxed at an equal rate."[8] Some 21 state constitutions went further to provide universality, requiring that all property be subject to taxation.[9] Most of the remaining states had statutes or less specific constitutional provisions aimed at providing uniformity and universality.

The two provisions of the 1870 Constitution that set the framework for present-day property taxation in Illinois read as follows:

> Sec. 1. The General Assembly shall provide such revenue as may be needful by levying a tax, by valuation, so that every person and corporation shall pay a tax in proportion to the value of his, her or its property — such value to be ascertained by some person or persons, to be elected or appointed in such a manner as the General Assembly shall direct, and not otherwise; but

[5] Department of Revenue, State of Illinois, *The Revenue Act of 1939: As Amended Through 1963* (Springfield: July, 1964), p. iii.

[6] All property tax law in Illinois was recodified in the Revenue Act of 1939 and is found in this act as amended, to date. See: *Ibid.*

[7] Benson, *op. cit.,* p. 40.

[8] *Ibid.,* p. 37.

[9] *Ibid.,* p. 42.

the General Assembly shall have power to tax peddlers, auctioneers, brokers, hawkers, merchants, commission merchants, showmen, jugglers, inn-keepers, grocery keepers, liquor dealers, toll bridges, ferries, insurance, telegraph and express interests or business, vendors of patents and persons or corporations owning or using franchises and privileges, in such manner as it shall from time to time direct by general law, uniform as to the class upon which it operates.

Sec. 2. The specification of the objects and subjects of taxation shall not deprive the General Assembly of the power to require other subjects or objects to be taxed in such manner as may be consistent with the principles of taxation fixed in this Constitution.[10]

There is some dispute as to whether the Illinois Constitution did or did not provide for uniformity and universality, but subsequent developments make the point rather moot. In fact, the Constitution has been interpreted by the courts and the legislature as requiring uniform and universal property taxation.

Difficulties arose as urbanization and industrialization shifted the balance of property wealth away from real property. Much new wealth was represented by bank accounts, capital stock, patent rights, and the good will of corporations. These classes of property were harder to find or list and more difficult to value equitably. Thus, intangible personal property wealth increased more rapidly than real property wealth after the Civil War, but bore a declining relative share of the tax bill.[11] The conclusion reached by Seligman and a host of others was that the general property tax lacked universality and uniformity since personalty was assessed inversely to its quantity; hence: ". . . the tax becomes an anachronism, personalty escapes, until finally the general property tax . . . reverts to its original form of the real property tax."[12]

Illinois, like many other states, had statutes requiring that corporate personalty be added to the tax rolls. Local assessors had a hard time finding and listing this type of property and the Revenue Act of 1872 placed the responsibility for assessing corporate (capital) stock with the State Board of Equalization. As evidence of the merit of reform, a 30-year high in assessed values was returned in 1873.[13] Two years later, when much of the assessment of capital stock was returned by statute to local assessors, assessed values of corporate intangibles began declining steadily.

By the turn of the century, discontent with the levy was such that many states sought to classify property according to character and net

---

[10] *Illinois Constitution* (1870), Article IX, Secs. 1, 2.

[11] E. R. A. Seligman, *Essays in Taxation,* 9th ed. (New York: The Macmillan Company, 1923), p. 24.

[12] *Ibid.,* p. 56.

[13] Labovitz, *op. cit.,* pp. 34-36.

income-producing capability. There was a growing belief that not all types of property represent the same ability to pay and that more individuals will list their personalty if it is taxed at lower rates. By 1939 at least 21 states permitted some type of classification,[14] and four states now limit the base to real property. In Illinois, diligent efforts to revise the uniformity provisions to allow for classification of property, especially intangible personalty, have been made. Five referenda aimed at amending the uniformity clause of the Constitution failed in 40 years, despite the fact that three times a majority of those voting on the amendment voted in favor.

As legal classification was not possible in Illinois, de facto or administrative classification systems arose in many counties, most notably and pointedly in Cook County. When J. L. Jacobs was appointed Cook County Assessor by Governor Horner in 1931, he unified the extra-legal system of classification already in existence. In Jacobs' second report to the governor, he noted the substantial improvement made in reaching personalty, especially intangible personalty, but "that no amount of courage, ingenuity and persistence will solve those problems [assessing and taxing personalty] if the State of Illinois adheres to the antiquated and inadequate general property tax with its so-called rule of uniformity."[15]

While agreeing with the State Tax Commission's position that no official recognition could be afforded the general practice of assessing cash at 10 per cent of face value and stocks and bonds at 20 per cent,[16] Jacobs nevertheless allowed classification.[17] His successor reports that Jacobs used a 20 per cent equalization factor on all intangibles, thereby establishing the confidence of the taxpayer and inducing him to file his intangibles for a lower rate of assessment.[18] Despite the depression, Jacobs was able to raise the assessed value of intangibles from approximately $10 million in 1930 to over $93 million in 1941.[19] The court's

---

[14] William H. Avery, Jr., "The Property Tax and Its Administration," *Illinois Tax Problems: Proceedings of an Open Forum,* Special Report No. 5 (Springfield: Illinois Tax Commission, 1939), p. 10.

[15] J. L. Jacobs, *Assessment of Real Estate and Personal Property in Cook County, Illinois for the Tax Years of 1931, 1932, 1933* (Chicago: November, 1934), p. 11.

[16] *Ibid.,* p. 22.

[17] Ray S. Osgood, "Taxing Intangibles: Personal and Corporate," *Illinois Tax Problems: Proceedings of an Open Forum,* Special Report No. 5 (Springfield: Illinois Tax Commission, 1939), pp. 156-57.

[18] John S. Clark, "Taxing Intangibles: Personal and Corporate," *Illinois Tax Problems: Proceedings of an Open Forum,* Special Report No. 5 (Springfield: Illinois Tax Commission, 1939), pp. 152-53.

[19] *Ibid.*

position that money, mortgages, bonds, and securities should be valued just as other personal and real property[20] seemed unrealistic if Chicago was to compete in the financial world with cities in some 36 other states that had abandoned taxation of tangible personality.[21] The board of appeals and the state's attorney in Cook County announced they would not stand in the way of classification and Jacobs' successor, John S. Clark, gave classification official recognition in a 1935 assessment order.[22]

Classification has continued to exist in Cook County and the governor proposed in 1965 that authority to classify personal property and real estate be extended statewide by constitutional amendment. This proposal encountered much opposition, especially from business interests, and several compromise drafts of this part of the proposed amendment were considered. The proposal to amend Article IX which finally passed the 1965 legislature and was submitted to popular vote in November, 1966, contained language purporting to legalize the existing classification system in Cook County but prohibiting classification elsewhere.

It is clear from this brief history that the property tax system is the result of a long evolutionary development and that many features of the complex system can be understood only by referring to historical developments. Exhibit I lists some of the major events in the history of the Illinois system and Chapter 4 is devoted to a detailed examination of the postwar developments in the area of assessment equalization and rate limitation. Before turning to this material, however, it is important to understand the major features of the administrative cycle as it now exists.

PROPERTY TAX ADMINISTRATION

There are five major steps in the property tax administrative cycle. Each step is defined below, after which a separate section is devoted to a more detailed description of each step.

1. Assessment and Review. Property tax liabilities are distributed among taxpayers in a taxing district on the basis of assessed value. It is the duty of an assessing official to find, list, and value all taxable property within his jurisdiction. The values so determined, unless changed by review or equalization, become the tax base against which the tax rate is applied to determine the tax to be paid by a particular

[20] *First National Bank* v. *Holmes,* 246 Ill. 362 (1910).

[21] Clark, *op. cit.,* p. 150.

[22] Osgood, *op. cit.,* p. 157.

taxpayer. The board of review has the responsibility for general verification of the assessor's work and has the authority to hear and decide appeals from taxpayers who are not satisfied with their assessment.

2. Equalization. Although Illinois law specifies that all assessments are to be at 100 per cent of full value, it is common for assessment to be at a lower level. Equalization is the process of adjusting the average level of assessment in different assessment districts to the same level. This is essential to tax equity since many taxing units overlap assessment districts and thus contain areas assessed by different assessors. Also, because assessed value is one component of the formula used to distribute state aid to school districts, inequities would result if assessment levels varied from district to district.

EXHIBIT I

SELECTED EVENTS IN THE HISTORY OF THE PROPERTY TAX IN ILLINOIS, 1792-1965

1792 — Court of Quarter Sessions District levies to be apportioned by population and wealth and further on the basis of fixed values for tangible property.

1795 — "Yearly value and profit" made the proper basis of apportioned levies.

1798 — Unimproved lands subject to taxation for the first time.

1805 — First over-all territorial property tax levy.

1818 — First Illinois Constitution and state to take a share of property revenues collected. Constitutional provisions for the property tax included a rough classification of properties subject to taxation and include intangibles (bank stock and negro slaves) for the first time.

1839 — Revenue Act of 1839. Classification eliminated and provision made for the taxation of both land and personal property as valued according to true value. State and local rates are to be extended against the same tax base.

1848 — Second Illinois Constitution. Includes most of the provisions of the 1839 act and specifically states corporations are to be subject to property taxation. Minimum valuation law superseded, township form of government optional and a mandatory annual levy on property for debt service provided for.

1853 — Revenue Code. Real estate includes both buildings and improvements and personality includes all tangibles and claims (except pensions). Foreign insurance companies are to be taxed on gross yearly receipts.

1867 — State Board of Equalization created.

1869 — Only the net receipts of foreign insurance companies are to be taxable.

1870 — Third Illinois Constitution. Several classes of individuals and businesses added to the enumerated lists of taxable individuals. Specified taxes were to be levied by general law and be uniform as to the classes affected.

1872 — Revenue law revised. Board of Equalization equalized assessments to be the basis of local rates as well as state rates, and the board is given original assessment powers for the rolling stock of railroads and for the capital stock of all corporations.

1875 — Capital stock returned to local assessment primarily.

1885 — First interim Revenue Commission established.

EXHIBIT I (continued)

1898 — Revenue Act of 1898. Only minor revision of 1872 Act.
1899 — General Assembly fixes equalization assessment ratio at 20 per cent.
1901 — Local taxes to be extended on the basis of county equalization rather than state.
1909 — Equalized assessment ratio fixed at 33⅓ per cent.
1910 — Special Tax Investigating Committee reports in favor of constitutional amendment to allow classification of personal property and recommends creation of a tax commission.
1919 — Tax Commission created. Equalized assessment ratio fixed at 50 per cent.
1927 — Equalized assessment ratio fixed at 100 per cent of full, fair, cash value.
1930 — Tax Commission recommends revision of uniformity provision to make possible classification, low-rate taxation of intangibles, and an income tax.
1932 — Last state general property tax levy.
1939 — Revenue Act of 1939. Largely recodification.
1943 — Department of Revenue and Property Tax Division created to replace Tax Commission.
1945 — Full-value program and rate restriction.
1947 — Rate limitation formula revised.
1949 — General Assembly provides for a county supervisor of assessments in all counties except Cook and St. Clair (later declared unconstitutional).
1951 — Rate limit program further revised.
1951 — Assessment placed on a quadrennial basis in counties of less than 500,000 population.
1953 — General Assembly makes possible the appointment of a county assessor or county supervisor of assessments in all counties under 150,000 (extended to all counties except Cook and St. Clair in 1957).
1959 — Equalization of assessments placed on a quadrennial basis with resulting equalization factors to be used for intervening four years. Cook County divided into four assessment districts with staggered quadrennial assessment years.
1961 — Department of Revenue required to publish a statement on equalization methods followed.
1963 — Department of Revenue instructed to continue valuation of the rolling stock of railroads at 100 per cent of full, fair, cash value, but to debase the equalized assessment to the statewide average assessment ratio after equalization.
1965 — General Assembly provides that Cook County shall have one equalization factor for the entire county each year.
1965 — General Assembly provides that counties of 100,000 to 500,000 population may be divided into four assessment districts with different assessment years.

SOURCES Department of Revenue, State of Illinois, *The Revenue Act of 1939: As Amended Through 1963* (Springfield: July, 1964), pp. iii-viii; Illinois Tax Commission, *Illinois Tax Problems: Proceedings of an Open Forum,* Special Report No. 5 (Springfield: 1939); I. M. Labovitz, *The Illinois Revenue System, 1818-1936,* Special Report No. 4 (Springfield: Illinois Tax Commission, 1936), pp. 12-13, 15, 29-43; Robert Murray Haig, *A History of the General Property Tax in Illinois* (Urbana: University of Illinois Studies in the Social Sciences, Vol. III, Nos. 1 and 2 [1914]), pp. 1-236; *Laws of Illinois* (various years).

3. Levy. Levy is the legal process of imposing property taxes. In Illinois levies are made by the governing board of the governmental unit and are usually expressed in dollar amounts.

4. Extension. Assessed values and tax levies are certified to the county clerk who computes the tax rate necessary to produce the amount levied by each governmental unit. The computed rate or, if smaller, the maximum legal rate is multiplied by the assessed value of each parcel of property to determine the amount of tax due.

5. Collection. Real property taxes become a lien against the property as of the assessment date. Collection of real property taxes is seldom a problem except in time of economic depression in the community or when the taxes involved are very high in relation to the current value of the property. Personal property taxes are levied against the owner of the property and present a greater collection problem.

Assessment and Review Illinois property tax law, contained in the Revenue Act of 1939 as amended, regulates the appointment, election, minimum salaries, terms of office, and duties of assessors. Various provisions in the law specify what type of assessors will serve in counties of different populations or governmental forms. Cook County, for example, elects a county assessor and township assessors for areas outside of Chicago every four years. St. Clair County (St. Louis SMSA) elects a five-member board of assessors with staggered six-year terms and township assessors with four-year terms. In the 17 commission counties the county treasurer becomes the ex officio county assessor unless the county board has appointed a supervisor of assessments or county assessor. Township counties may appoint a supervisor of assessments. If no appointment is made, the county treasurer serves ex officio. Township assessors are elected.[23]

Each county, except Cook, has a board of review[24] whose function it is to adjust individual assessments upon complaint. The board may adjust assessments between classes of property and among assessment districts. Board members are subject to oaths as are the assessors. In Cook County, there is a board of appeals with power to hear and act upon taxpayer complaints.

The assessor's job is a difficult one, but there are well-developed techniques of real estate assessment which can produce reasonably complete and accurate assessment of some of the more common types of real estate. These techniques include property numbering systems and the use of aerial mapping to ensure that all property is entered on the rolls, land value maps to systematize the determination of land values, and property record cards to record details about the physical attributes of the property. Formulas have been developed which are based upon

---

[23] *Ill. Rev. Stat.*, ch. 120, secs. 482-87 (1965).

[24] For make-up and duties of the boards, see *ibid.*, ch. 120, secs. 489-92 (1965).

engineering techniques for estimating the value of property, and sales and income information can be utilized to check and revise the formulas in the light of current economic conditions. Assistance in the assessing process can be obtained from the Department of Revenue. The department also conducts annual informational meetings for assessors throughout the state.

In 1949, the General Assembly enacted legislation providing for county supervisors of assessments appointed from lists of qualified persons certified by the Department of Revenue. Local assessors within a county were to be made more responsible to the supervisor, and he was to endeavor to provide *intra-county* equalization of assessment and to coordinate the property tax calendar. The State Supreme Court declared the legislation unconstitutional the following year.[25] Legislation passed in 1953 established the present system of optional supervisors of assessment. Currently, 42 township counties have appointed supervisors of assessment.

Actual assessment practice in Illinois varies tremendously. Some property is assessed by poorly qualified part-time assessors who either are not capable or are insufficiently motivated to do a good assessment job. They rely primarily on a copy of the previous year's tax roll for current assessment values. The Department of Revenue reports that less than one-third of the 1,558 assessors invited to training schools in November, 1965, attended: "The basic reason for this low attendance is the fact that practically all township assessors are part-time and must devote the majority of their time to their regular occupation . . . in some cases the assessors desire to attend but their local town board does not provide the necessary travel and expense money."[26]

On the other hand, there are a number of well-equipped assessor's offices in Illinois which are manned by competent personnel. In Cook County a large staff is employed to man a massive computerized system with an elaborate system of records and a number of appraisal specialists.

Even well-trained and well-equipped assessors have difficulty valuing certain types of property and a large degree of subjectivity must enter the assessment process. The fact that some large, difficult-to-assess properties such as commercial and industrial buildings sell only infrequently may make it difficult to determine value. Very difficult problems also arise in areas where land use is changing rapidly. As farm

[25] *Giebelhausen* v. *Daley,* 407 Ill. 29 (1950).

[26] Eugene Berghoff, "Remarks Before the Commission to Study Full Value Assessments and Tax Rate Limitations," Springfield, Illinois, December 17, 1965.

land changes to residential use and as slum land in the intercity becomes the site of high-rise apartment or office buildings, land speculation is common. If an assessor tries to value all property in such areas at its value in the highest potential use, the property tax may confiscate the income of property which is not utilized for such a purpose. On the other hand, if he ignores actual and potential higher uses, large elements of wealth escape taxation.

Many kinds of personal property are difficult to find and may be even more difficult to evaluate than is real estate, especially when the property is unusual or highly specialized in purpose. How, for example, does an assessor determine the value of expensive machinery which is performing the job for which it was designed but which, if placed on the market, might attract bids only from scrap dealers? Generally, property tax law defines value to be "market" value or the price which a willing buyer would pay a willing seller, but the courts are not likely to support a scrap value assessment when the property is successfully fulfilling the purpose for which it was designed. The Illinois Supreme Court has stated on several occasions that income from property is an element to be considered in assessment but has also warned that "the value of property does not depend upon the business astuteness of the owner."[27]

Illinois law provides that all real property is to be assessed every fourth year. Under special circumstances where physical changes to the property or certain changes in use have occurred, assessment should be annual.[28] In view of the rapidity with which property values change, rigorous compliance with the law in this regard would undoubtedly mean that most assessments would be changed at least quadrennially. However, the costs of such changes and the opposition which every alteration of an assessment figure arouses discourage frequent changes, and the value affixed to a parcel of real estate is apt to remain unchanged for long periods of time.

When property values are rising, the reluctance to make frequent changes in existing assessments results in a progressive lowering of the average assessment level within the assessment district. Such a decline is usually accompanied by a decline in the equality of assessment within the district, but of even more immediate interest to local governments is the effect which such a development has upon the fiscal capacity of the governmental unit. Tax limits are expressed as percentages of assessed value and a decline in the assessment ratio makes a given rate

[27] *People* v. *Marine Trust Co.,* 31 N.E. 2d 922 (1940).

[28] The particular year of assessment depends upon the population, size, and governmental form of a county. See *Ill. Rev. Stat.,* ch. 120, secs. 511, 524-25 (1965).

more restrictive. Thus, there is an intimate and complicated interrelation among tax assessment, equalization, and property tax limitation. In Illinois these interconnections are more complicated than in most states and are clearly one of the most important aspects of the environment in which local government officials make financial decisions.

Equalization When the State Board of Equalization was created by the legislature in 1867, assessment practices were far from uniform. The tax burden of supporting state government was distributed haphazardly and inequitably since the same state rate applied whether property was assessed at 20 or 60 per cent of its true value. Hence, a local assessor could reduce the share of state taxes which his community paid by reducing the assessment ratio. The new board was charged with equalizing, on a county basis, the average assessment ratio of properties subject to state levies.

In 1889, the General Assembly set the legal ratio for valuation at 20 per cent, but this had little effect on local assessment practices. Two years after this ratio was set, local tax extensions were again being spread against county equalized values rather than state equalized values. It was not until 1945 that legislation was passed to correct this situation (See Exhibit I).

Legal assessment ratios were periodically raised from 20 per cent until they reached 100 per cent of full, fair, cash value in 1927. The ratios were largely ignored by local assessors and since equalization applied only for statewide tax levies, the effect of equalization efforts was limited. Adequate sales and appraisal data were lacking, thus further hampering any equalization program. In 1943, the equalization responsibilities of the Tax Commission were transferred to the newly created Department of Revenue, and two years later the department was instructed to equalize property at full value for all extension purposes. As the state had not exercised its authority to levy the property tax after 1932, the equalization program in the state had been virtually dormant for 12 years.

In the 1945 legislation the department was instructed to raise or lower the total assessed value of property in each county until it was assessed at full, fair, cash value.[29] The department was to ascertain the full value of property in each county by the use of information regarding sales of property, through appraisal studies, and by any other means it deemed necessary.

The department was not to equalize assessments among taxing districts within a county, or even among classes of property. Thus, in-

[29] *Ill. Rev. Stat.*, ch. 120, sec. 146 (1965).

equities that existed in assessments within a taxing district, or among taxing districts in the same county, were not to be corrected by the full valuation program. These inequities would be made more obvious since equalization would raise all local assessments in the county by the same percentage. For example, if the total locally assessed value in a county was $20 million and the department determined the full value should be $50 million, the county clerk would raise the assessed value of each parcel of property by multiplying the assessed value by a multiplier of 2.5000.[30] This would mean that if two property owners in the same county were assessed $10,000 and $7,000 on homes with the same market value, say $20,000, their assessed values after equalization would be $25,000 and $17,500, respectively. The degree of inequity would not be changed but the inequity would probably be obvious to the owner of the house now assessed 25 per cent above market value.

Equalization procedures have not changed a great deal since the days of the Illinois Tax Commission. The department ascertains the average assessment level in each county by sales-ratio studies.[31] Field workers for the department collect information on bona fide real estate sales. The information is then compared with the assessed values of the same parcels. The median assessment ratios for several classes of property or areas are weighted to adjust for the amounts of property in each. Final determination of the average assessment level for each county is based on the averaging of sales-ratio studies for the latest two or three years for which such studies are available, and further adjusted for subsequent significant changes in valuation. For example, in determining 1963 ratios, weighted sales-ratio studies for the years 1958, 1959, and 1960 were used by the department.[32] Besides sales-ratio studies, the department receives building cost indexes, copies of instructions given to local assessing officials, and estimates of the value of farm properties by the Department of Agriculture.[33] Appraisals of specific properties may also be undertaken, but are often felt to be less reliable than sales data

---

[30] Note: 2.5 is the reciprocal of the aggregate locally assessed value to the aggregate full, fair, cash value as determined by the department. In this case, the reciprocal of 2/5, or 5/2 which equals 2.5. The multiplier is usually carried to four decimal places.

[31] For a discussion of the statistical procedures, see: Illinois Tax Commission, *Tax-Rate Limits and Assessment Ratios, 1925-1940* ("Survey of Local Finance in Illinois," Vol. 8; Springfield: 1940), pp. 11-13.

[32] Interview, Eugene Maynard and Allen Garber, Property Tax Division, Department of Revenue, Chicago, June 11, 1965.

[33] Statement of the Property Tax Division reproduced in: Economic Development Committee, *Illinois Taxes and Economic Growth, Part III* (Springfield: Illinois State Chamber of Commerce, October, 1964), pp. 18-19.

since appraisers often value according to "normal value" or some "long-time average value" which is less than current market value.[34]

Once the department has determined the assessment ratio for each county, it certifies multipliers to the county clerks which are to be applied to all property assessments within a given county. While the statutes require equalization at 100 per cent of full, fair, cash value, this level has never been attained.[35] Just exactly how the department determines the average level of market value at which it equalizes is not clear. Representative John K. Morris has sponsored two unsuccessful bills in the Illinois House seeking to reduce the equalization goal to 55 per cent of full value.[36]

Equalized values as a per cent of market value have steadily declined since the initial implementation of the Full Valuation Act of 1945. As will be explained in the next chapter, when tax rate limitations are effective, a declining assessment ratio restricts local revenue potential. Table 16 represents ratios of statewide equalized real property values to market values estimated by the department, the U.S. Bureau of the Census, and Rolf A. Weil, former employee of the department.

Department figures show that the ratio has declined from about 75 per cent in 1945 to 48 per cent in 1957. Estimates of the ratio of equalized assessed value to market value appear even lower in the U.S. Bureau of the Census estimates and estimates for specific counties presented in railroad cases before the Illinois Supreme Court. In *People ex rel. Kohorst* v. *Gulf, Mobile, and Ohio Railroad Company* and *People ex rel. Kohorst* v. *Chicago and North Western Railroad Co.*,[37] the court established the Sangamon County equalized ratio at 46.29. Equalized assessed value in Grundy County was estimated at 45.20 per cent of full value.[38]

These and other railroad valuation cases arose because the Department of Revenue has original assessment responsibilities for the operating property of railroads and the capital stock of certain domestic corporations. In evaluating these properties the department has assessed them at "full value" and certified the portion of this value that is to be apportioned to local taxing districts within the county. County

[34] State of Illinois, Property Tax Division, *Assessment Equalization by Boards of Review* (Springfield: Illinois Department of Revenue, June, 1956), p. 5.

[35] Economic Development Committee, *op. cit.*, p. 19; Rolf A. Weil, "Property Tax Equalization in Illinois," *National Tax Journal* (June, 1953), p. 160; Illinois School Problems Commission, *Report No. 3* (Springfield: September, 1954).

[36] H.B. 843, 72nd General Assembly; H.B. 480, 73rd General Assembly.

[37] Consolidated. 22 Ill. 2d 104 (1961).

[38] *People ex rel. Enrietta* v. *Gulf, Mobile, and Ohio Railroad Co.*, 29 Ill. 2d 605 (1963).

TABLE 16

RATIO OF STATEWIDE EQUALIZED ASSESSED REAL PROPERTY VALUES TO FULL, FAIR, CASH VALUE OF REAL PROPERTY IN ILLINOIS, SELECTED YEARS, 1945-61

	Illinois Department of Revenue Ratios (1) (per cent)	Statewide Median Level of Equalized Assessment (2) (per cent)	U.S. Bureau of Census Sales-Based Average Weighted by Type and Size of Property (3) (per cent)
1945		30.90[a]	
1946	74.48	88.40	
1947	64.00	—	
1948	63.20	—	
1949	62.18	—	
1950	56.78	62.70	
1951	52.62		
1952	51.32		
1953	51.28		
1954	49.80		
1955	49.79		
1956	47.74		45.70
1957	48.10		
1961			44.70

[a] Not equalized under current law.

SOURCE (1) James R. Parham, "Taxation of Property in Illinois," *The University of Illinois Law Forum* (1961), p. 649; (2) Rolf A. Weil, "Property Tax Equalization in Illinois," *National Tax Journal* (June, 1953); (3) U.S. Bureau of the Census, *Census of Governments: 1957,* Vol. V, Table 12; U.S. Bureau of the Census, *Census of Governments: 1962,* Vol. II, Table 13.

multipliers are not used to equalize these assessments since they are theoretically at the 100 per cent level. In *People ex rel. Hillison* v. *Chicago B. & Q. R.R.*[39] the county court of Lee County ruled that valuation of railroad property at 100 per cent of full value when local property is equalized at 50 to 55 per cent of full value amounts to constructive fraud. The court ordered a refund of 45 per cent of the taxes extended against the railroad property for the year 1958. The State Supreme Court upheld the findings of constructive fraud in this and several other cases but held that the measure of recovery should be the difference between the amount of taxes extended against the property and the amount which would have been extended had locally assessed property been equalized at 100 per cent of full, fair, cash value. This means that all of the rates extended against the railroad property in each taxing district must be recomputed using an adjusted valuation.[40]

[39] 22 Ill. 2d 88 (1961).

[40] For discussion of the railroad cases see James R. Parham, "Taxation of Property in Illinois," *The University of Illinois Law Forum* (1961), pp. 645-60.

Tax Levy Before a municipality may levy the property tax, it must first enact and publish a detailed appropriation ordinance for those sums of money necessary to meet anticipated expenditures for the coming fiscal year.[41] Levies are made by funds, with the typical city utilizing several funds. All cities utilize the corporate fund, but, as indicated in Table 17, there are several funds which are utilized by only a few cities. Most funds are subject to a maximum rate limit but a few, generally those such as bonds and interest funds, retirement funds, or the judgment funds for which expenditure obligations are fixed, are not subject to rate limits, per se. Some funds have limits and must also be included with the corporate fund for limit purposes while other funds have limits which are outside the corporate limit.

Levies are made in dollar amounts, but governing boards of the local units usually have an accurate knowledge of what the assessed valuation will be and thus can compute what rate will be produced by a given dollar figure. If the unit wishes to levy the maximum permitted, the levy must be set high enough to insure that the maximum rate will result.

Both appropriation and levy ordinance must follow an exact form and must meet exacting legal requirements. Mistakes in the wording of a referendum ballot to authorize a levy for a particular fund, failure to itemize correctly in an appropriation ordinance, failure to publish the appropriation ordinance correctly, and similar mistakes may render a tax levy invalid.

Extension of Taxes Once the county clerk has received all certified tax levy ordinances, it is his duty to extend the taxes on the equalized assessed value of the respective taxing districts.[42] As tax levies are to be made by dollar amounts and by funds, the county clerk must divide the dollar amount levied for each fund plus the estimated loss and cost of collections by the equalized assessed value of the taxing district to determine the rate to extend over all of the taxable property within the respective district. If the rate so determined exceeds the maximum rate authorized for a particular fund, he is to extend the maximum rate.[43] The levies for bonds and interest are adopted and certified to the clerk at the time the bonds are issued and the clerk extends for this purpose whether or not the annual tax levy ordinance includes such sums.

The "loss and cost" allowance covers the fees which must be paid to other governmental units and uncollectible taxes. The amount

[41] *Ill. Rev. Stat.*, ch. 24, sec. 8-2-9 (1965).
[42] *Ill. Rev. Stat.*, ch. 120, sec. 643 (1965).
[43] See Chapter 5 on Rate Limitation.

TABLE 17

MUNICIPAL TAX FUNDS UTILIZED BY ILLINOIS MUNICIPALITIES

Fund	Municipalities with Populations of over 5,000		Municipalities with Populations 2,500-5,000	
	Number	Per Cent	Number	Per Cent
Corporate	200	100.0	118	100.0
Policemen's Pension	170	85.0	4	3.4
Bonds and Interest	155	77.5	74	62.7
Library	150	75.0	65	55.1
Garbage Disposal	141	70.5	50	42.4
I.M.R.F.[a]	120	60.0	17	14.4
Public Benefit	94	47.0	22	18.6
Civil Defense	91	45.5	33	28.0
Street and Bridge	91	45.5	26	22.0
Firemen's Pension	89	44.5	1	.8
Fire Protection	78	39.0	35	29.7
Playground	55	27.5	19	16.1
Park	44	22.0	29	24.6
Band	40	20.0	23	19.5
Social Security	29	14.5	10	8.5
Police Protection	21	10.5	8	6.8
Hospital	12	6.0	—	—
Working Cash	10	5.0	1	.8
Street Lighting	7	3.5	1	.8
Sewerage	6	3.0	5	4.2
Forestry	6	3.0	2	1.7
Cemetery	5	2.5	7	5.9
Judgment	5	2.5	—	—
T.B. Sanitarium	3	1.5	—	—
Community Building	2	1.0	2	1.7
Airport	2	1.0	—	—
Comfort Station	2	1.0	1	.8
General Assistance	2	1.0	—	—
Election	1	.5	—	—
Youth Community Center	1	.5	—	—
Pumping	1	.5	—	—
Levee	1	.5	1	.8
Community Nurse	1	.5	—	—
Harbor	1	.5	1	.8
Coliseum	1	.5	3	2.5
Loss and Cost	1	.5	1	.8
Health	1	.5	—	—
Zoning Commission	1	.5	—	—
Hydrant Rental	1	.5	—	—
Streets and Alleys	—	—	1	.8

[a] Illinois Municipal Retirement Fund.

SOURCE Compiled from *Illinois Municipal Review* (June, 1962). Some of the funds listed are actually special sections of other funds, and have been classified here as listed in the *Illinois Municipal Review*.

allowed varies depending upon local conditions but cannot force the rate extended above any applicable rate limit.[44] For example, in Champaign County where the percentage of uncollectible taxes is very low, the total allowance is 5 per cent. In Chicago, the allowance is usually 8 per cent.[45] East St. Louis, which has a serious problem with uncollected real and personal taxes, allows 20 per cent of the levy.[46]

The county clerk aggregates all rates to be extended against certain properties. Due to the overlapping of taxing districts, tax code areas that include the assessed value subject to the same tax rates are established. As Figure III suggests, any given tax district might be carved up into any number of tax codes depending upon the number of districts that overlap it, and the particular pattern of overlap.

Once the tax codes are established within the county, the clerk aggregates the authorized rates of the respective districts that apply to the particular areas. Except in Cook County, the clerk may extend the tax by either the aggregate rate or the particular rates for each fund.[47] In Cook County the aggregate rate must be extended. The usual practice in other counties is to extend the aggregate rate, but to include with the tax bill a list of the rates for particular funds and taxing districts that make up the total. With the advent of electronic data-processing equipment, some counties now have tax bills with the breakdowns printed on them. Separate bills are sent for personal property taxes and real property taxes. Personal property taxes become delinquent on May 1 in Cook County and June 1 downstate. Real property taxes may be paid in two equal installments, the first of which is due at the same time as personal property. The second installment of real estate taxes becomes delinquent on September 1. In the event the billing date is late, say in July or August as has happened in some counties, the entire tax is due on September 1 or 30 days after the billing date.

Collection Tax bills are collected by county, or in a few cases, township collectors. In commission counties the sheriff acts as the county collector. Fees, based upon the amount collected and number of lines of extensions, are allowed to the offices of the collector and county clerk. In those few cases in which city-townships are located in a county

---

[44] *People ex rel. Gill* v. *Schweitzer,* 366 Ill. 568 (1937). Loss and cost estimates may vary from year to year and, in absence of proof to the contrary, may be established by the city council on the basis of previous levy experiences. The percentage of loss and cost will depend on the circumstances in particular cases. *People ex rel. Schlaeger* v. *Brand,* 59 N.E. 2d 664 (1945).

[45] City of Chicago, *Appropriation Ordinances* (various years).

[46] City of East St. Louis, *1964 Budget.*

[47] *Ill. Rev. Stat.,* ch. 120, sec. 645 (1965).

FIGURE III

HYPOTHETICAL TOWNSHIP TAX CODES IN A MUNICIPALITY

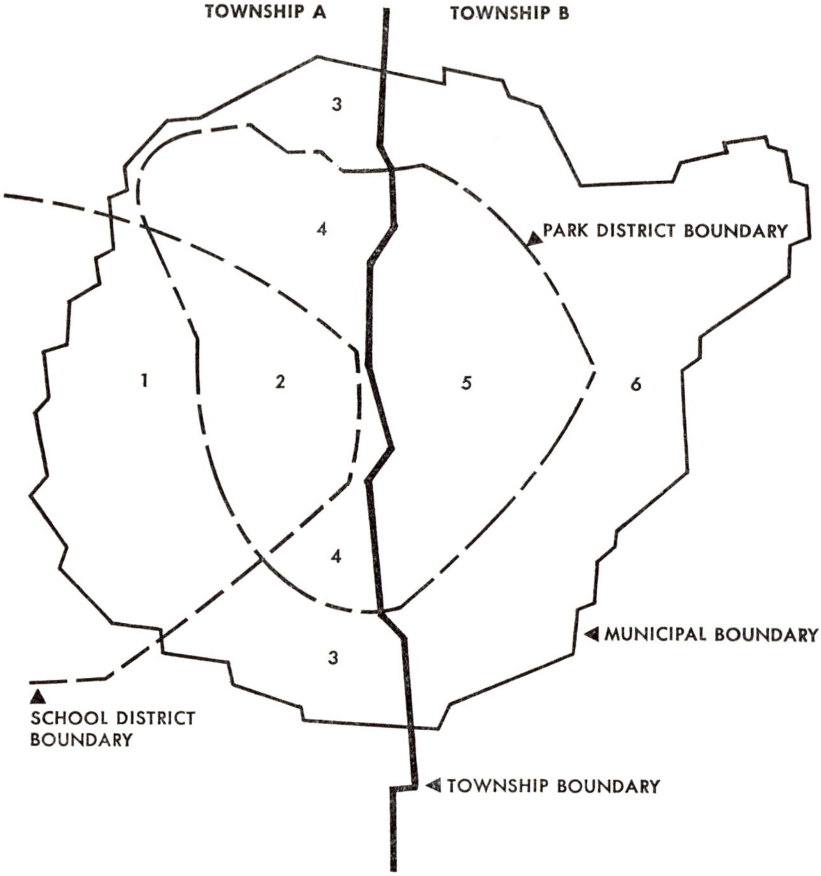

	Township A — Code #				Township B — Code #	
	1	2	3	4	5	6
County rate	.238	.238	.238	.238	.238	.238
Township rate	.151	.151	.151	.151	.272	.272
Municipal rate	.753	.753	.753	.753	.753	.753
School dist. rate	2.016	2.016	2.503	2.503	2.503	2.503
Park district rate	–	.100	–	.100	.100	–
Combined rates	3.158	3.258	3.645	3.745	3.866	3.766

having the township collector system, municipal treasuries receive commissions on collections for other units of government.

Taxes upon real estate automatically become a prior first lien on the property against which they are levied. Procedures for foreclosing the lien when taxes are delinquent and procedures for redeeming property after the tax lien has been sold are spelled out in the statutes. The statutes also provide procedures whereby taxes may be collected from the rents or profits of income-earning property and permit the appointment of a receiver to preserve the property during the foreclosure process.

Collectors in counties with less than 500,000 inhabitants may publish a list of those persons who are delinquent in the payment of personal property taxes. The collector may also provide for the seizure and sale of personal property to satisfy taxes. Provisions also exist whereby real estate taxes may be collected by selling personal property of the owner and personal property taxes can be collected from real estate owned by the same person.

In most areas of the state real estate tax delinquencies are negligible during prosperous times. Delinquencies that exist for an extended period of time are usually in depressed areas or involve property of little value or property with clouded titles.

Personal property tax collection is not as good. Here the collection procedure is not automatic and requires that elected officials assume the initiative in taking unpopular actions such as seizing and selling household goods and personal effects. As a result, taxpayers in some areas of the state have little fear of the consequences of not paying personal property taxes and collections lag badly.

One other feature of the collection process which is important is the method of protesting taxes. A taxpayer who believes that some part of the taxes levied against him are incorrect or illegal may pay his taxes under protest and then file an action to obtain a refund of the illegal portion. Taxes paid under protest are held by the county treasurer and are not available to the governmental unit which levied the tax until the case is settled.

In some counties railroads and other large taxpayers routinely pay their taxes under protest. Grounds for protest range from the allegation that a unit of government has no statutory authority to levy a particular tax to the claim that a tax rate referendum held 20 years before was void because of a missing comma. These cases seldom come to trial but are negotiated at a conference attended by the attorneys for the plaintiff, the state's attorney of the county, and, perhaps, officials of the units of government involved. Then, the judge of the court to which the protest has been submitted accepts the recommendations of the interested parties. Many of the conferences are characterized by an attitude of give and take as both sides are anxious to avoid the publicity, delay, and expense of a trial.

Individuals who do not protest their taxes are not eligible for refunds and most taxpayers are unaware that protesting taxpayers regularly receive a tax refund. In some cases governmental units continue to make the contested levy even though it is always conceded to protesting taxpayers.

CONCLUSIONS

The notion of general property taxation, uniform and universal, reached a pinnacle in the second half of the nineteenth century. Near the middle of that period, Illinois adopted a state Constitution containing a revenue article which appears to have been designed to make uniform property taxation the main source of state and local revenue. Throughout 96 years of social and economic change the wording of the revenue article has remained unchanged. Changes in statute law and Supreme Court interpretation have occurred but both the definition of the tax base in the Constitution and the machinery established to administer the tax seem better adapted to an earlier period than to the present industrialized, urban economy.

Township assessors still exist in much of the state, although appointed county supervisors of assessment have been added in about half of the counties which are organized into townships. County boards of review are charged with equalizing among townships and among classes of property, but in most counties, little equalization occurs. The Department of Revenue was given extensive inter-county equalization powers in 1945 and has carried out a fairly vigorous equalization program since, but the present equalization level is only about one-half that contemplated by the 1945 legislation.

Despite the inequities and complexities of the property tax, it has two characteristics which explain its survival as the major source of local government revenue. One of these is that no other tax is as well adapted to collection by small local governments. Except in the case of some personal property, there is little question as to the location of the property on tax day and thus little question as to which unit has jurisdiction to tax. Further, the almost automatic way in which real property taxes become liens upon the property greatly facilitates local collection of the tax.

The second characteristic which adapts property taxation to local government use is that the complexity of its administrative machinery tends to diffuse responsibility for the unpopular task of levying and collecting taxes. An unhappy property taxpayer finds it difficult to determine whether to blame the assessor, the board of review, the State Department of Revenue, the General Assembly, or the governing body of one of several local government units. Thus, the complexity, which sometimes baffles local government officials, may insulate them from the wrath of neighbors and friends and provide room for ingenious local adaptations that make the property tax less and less akin to the uniform, universal general property tax which was considered to be the last word in taxation a century ago.

To estimate how well adapted property taxation is to local finance, one must be aware of the two types of legal constraints acting on the decision-making process. Procedural requirements, involving the form and timing of appropriation and tax levy ordinances, are spelled out in considerable detail in state law and have been noted in this chapter. The second type of constraint consists of tax rate limits which apply to specific funds. Because of the many interactions between tax limits, assessment, and equalization policy, the 1945 equalization legislation set in motion a long and involved chain of events which greatly affect local government financial policies. These are described in considerable detail in the next chapter.

4 PROPERTY TAX RATE LIMITATION IN ILLINOIS

Property tax rate limits are among the most important constraints which state governments in the United States impose upon the financial powers of local government.[1] In Illinois, as in many other states, these take the form of maximum rates which may be levied for specific local government funds.[2]

An unusual feature of tax rate limitation in Illinois is that in many instances the limit for a particular fund is not the statutory maximum. Instead, a rate computed through the use of a formula is often the controlling maximum limit. Interpreting how the formula is to be used is not an easy matter, and the rate limit program in Illinois has been attended by confusion and frustration.

The abbreviated history of the rate limitation program in Illinois which is presented in the next section of this chapter provides a minimum background for an appraisal of the effects of tax rate limits upon local government finance. A more detailed, technical history of

---

[1] Advisory Commission on Intergovernmental Relations, *State Constitutional and Statutory Restrictions on Local Taxing Powers,* Commission Report A-14 (Washington, D.C.: October, 1962), pp. 27-28. Hereafter cited as ACIR Report A-14.

[2] There are numerous variations in the form of property tax limitations in the United States, but two major types can be distinguished. *Over-all limitations* are maximum rates, usually expressed as a per cent or number of mills per dollar of taxable valuation, which can be levied by all taxing jurisdictions on the taxable value of property within a given area. When this type of limitation is imposed, there must be a method for "rationing" the tax funds among the several overlapping units of government. *Specific limitations* are maximum rates which may be levied by particular types of local governments for specific funds or purposes. Illinois utilizes the specific type of limit, but there is a constitutional provision which limits county rates for all purposes to .75 per cent. Several exceptions have been made to this limit in the Constitution and the limit can be increased by referendum.

the rate limit program is presented in the last half of the chapter. This is detailed and complex and some readers may desire to omit it, but the analysis of the effects of the rate limitation program gains in credibility as knowledge of the program and its history becomes more complete.

THE FULL VALUE PROGRAM OF 1945 AND RATE LIMIT REVISIONS

In 1901, Illinois adopted an over-all 5 per cent rate limit in addition to statutory limits imposed on particular local levies that had been established earlier. The legislation, known as the Juul Law,[3] was adopted at a time when the clamor for reform of the general property tax had grown strong. Proponents of rate limitation insisted their programs would improve the equity of the property tax by encouraging the raising of assessed values to 100 per cent of full value.[4]

The numerous exceptions and amendments to the Juul Law of 1901 had rendered it ineffective as a buffer against further increases in property taxes by the 1930's and the state returned to a system of rate limitations on specific funds.[5] However, as the assessed value of property declined during the depression of the 1930's, it became very clear to local officials that the restrictiveness of rate limitations is associated with the assessed valuation upon which they are applied.[6] A 1927 statute had required that all assessments reflect the full, fair, cash value of all property, yet county boards of review and the courts appeared willing to condone fractional assessment practices of local assessors if the constitutional provision of uniformity was being served.[7] The net result was that specific rate limits restricted municipal property tax receipts much more severely than they would have if assessments had borne a closer relationship to market values.

Increases in property values in the early 1940's led local officials to

---

[3] For a discussion of the Juul Law, see: Illinois Tax Commission, *Tax-Rate Limits and Assessment Ratios, 1925-1940* ("Survey of Local Finance in Illinois," Vol. 8; Springfield, 1940), pp. 94-97; and Irving Howards, "Property Tax Rate Limits," in *Report of the Commission on Revenue*, State of Illinois, 1963 (Springfield: 1963), pp. 524-25.

[4] ACIR Report A-14, p. 35.

[5] For a listing of rate limits on local governments during this period, see: Vernon G. Morrison, "Property Tax Limitations," *Report of the Revenue Laws Commission of the State of Illinois* (Springfield: 1949), pp. 122-23; Illinois Tax Commission, *Tax-Rate Limits of Illinois Local Governments: As of August 1, 1938* (Springfield: 1938); and Illinois Tax Commission, *Tax-Rate Limits and Assessment Ratios, 1925-1940, op. cit.*

[6] Howards, *op. cit.*, p. 526.

[7] The Constitution does not require full valuation. *Illinois Constitution* (1870), Article IX, Sec. 1. See also: *Mobile and O. R. Co., et al.* v. *State Tax Commission,* 28 N.E. 2d 100 (1940); and *People* v. *Commonwealth Edison Co.,* 32 N.E. 2d 902 (1941).

protest low fractional assessments since assessed values did not rise as fast as property values or government costs. The efforts of the Cook County assessor in 1943 to raise all assessed values to full value appear to have prodded the governor and the state legislature into action.[8] This official's action, in turn, seems to have been triggered by a State Supreme Court decision requiring that state assessed property (railroad property) be assessed at the state average ratio.[9] A joint legislative committee was appointed under the chairmanship of Senator Walker Butler to investigate local tax matters. The work of this committee led in 1945 to Senate Bill 229, the full valuation act which amended the Revenue Act of 1939. It became effective January 1, 1946. The avowed purpose of the S.B. 229 was to secure uniformity of assessments among counties via full value equalization by the Illinois Department of Revenue.[10] The average ratio of assessed value to full value of property in each county was to be raised to 100 per cent.

Statewide equalization of assessment at full value would have increased the tax base for all local taxing units. The increase would have been greatest in those counties that had had low assessment ratios before 1946. Had the tax rates in effect prior to full valuation remained in effect after full valuation, individual tax liabilities would have risen proportionately with the percentage increase in the base. However, the purpose of full value legislation was not to provide local taxing units with substantially increased revenue potential but to eliminate nonuniformities among districts.[11] Since it was believed that the total assessed value of the state would be doubled as a result of the full value assessment law, the existing statutory rates were halved. This was not sufficient to protect all taxpayers from large tax increases or to guarantee all taxing units the same property tax potential that had existed under the old rate limits. In many counties full value assessment meant that assessed values would be more than doubled while in other counties smaller increases would occur.

---

[8] Howards, *op. cit.*, p. 527.

[9] *Mobile and Ohio Railroad Co.* v. *State Tax Commission*, 374 Ill. 75 (1940).

[10] Tax Committee of the Illinois State's Attorneys Association, in collaboration with the Illinois Department of Revenue, *The Full-Value Assessment Program: An Analysis of the Butler Program* (February 25, 1946), p. 3. Hereafter cited as Illinois State's Attorneys Association.

[11] The report of the Butler Commission lists three main problems toward which the commission had directed attention. These are: (1) instability and lack of uniformity in the application of statutory limitations on tax rates; (2) rate discrimination within an assessment or taxing district; (3) inequality in the apportionment of state grants-in-aid. State of Illinois, Joint Legislative Committee to Investigate Tax Problems, *Report to Governor Dwight H. Green* (Springfield: March 2, 1945).

To protect both taxpayers and governmental units the legislature devised a transitional formula for determining rate limits for a five-year period. Although the purpose of the formula provisions was to hold effective rate limits close to their pre-1946 levels,[12] confusion immediately arose concerning the interpretation of the formula provisions. When the Illinois Supreme Court issued its interpretation, it became apparent that the results were not acceptable to the General Assembly which was then in session. Thus, in 1947, the legislature provided a set of alternative formulas for rate limit determination and extended the transition period two years. These statutes in turn were subject to confused interpretation and further legislation.

Although designated as transition formulas, neither the 1945 nor the 1947 legislation contained any "transit" provisions. As the end of the seven-year period approached, the legislature still faced the problem of whether to allow the new statutory limits to go into effect, to continue provisions which tended to freeze existing limits, or to establish new limits. The first alternative would have meant severe dislocation as the rate limits for some units of government would have been reduced below existing rates and limits for other funds would have been well above existing rates. The second alternative would have meant perpetuating many of the inequities in the rate limit situation which the full value assessment program was supposed to have eliminated. The third alternative would have added to the confusion surrounding the rate limit program, although it could have been the best alternative. However, as the seven-year transition period progressed, both prices and assessed values had increased and several taxpayer groups feared widespread conversion to the halved statutory limits would permit most districts to increase taxes greatly.

The legislature responded to the situation by passing the Hodge-Downing Amendments of 1951. The amendments provided that prior to December, 1951, the authorities of a taxing unit could establish a maximum rate limit at any level not greater than the limit currently in effect. A corporate fund limit 10 per cent higher than the rate currently in effect could be established for cities and villages by a vote of two-thirds of the governing body. Still higher limits could be established for other funds by a referendum vote in the district. If no action was taken by the governing board before the deadline, the existing limits were to become permanent.

There were several features of the Hodge-Downing Amendments

---

[12] Effective rate refers to the ratio between the tax and the true or full value of the property being taxed.

which created confusion but the most serious question involved the constitutionality of making the formula limits permanent. Many local governments were advised by attorneys that provisions purporting to make these limits permanent by legislative action constituted special legislation and thus violated the state Constitution. These attorneys advised their local governmental clients to take no action to establish permanent limits in the expectation that the Supreme Court would declare that the formula limits could not be made permanent by legislative action. Actually, the State Supreme Court has never ruled the formula limits unconstitutional and those municipalities which followed the advice to take no action are now subject to lower corporate limits than they would be if they had taken action before the December, 1951, deadline.

At the same time that the legislature and the courts were struggling with the problem of writing and interpreting tax limit provisions, county clerks, local government officials, and taxpayers were attempting to understand and adjust to these changes and to rapidly changing social and economic conditions. Most local governments had relatively few financial problems during the war years but this changed rapidly in the postwar years as the demands for public services rapidly outgrew the growth in assessed value.

The formula limits had been developed upon the assumption that full value equalization would be realized. Since it was not, some local units of government began to feel severely restricted by these limits. Most rate limits can be increased by referenda and many local government units went to the voters in an attempt to obtain such increases. For example, in some 67 counties in 1946 and 1947, 1,623 referenda, mostly for school district rate or debt increases, were successful.[13]

Taxpayers and taxpayers' groups were concerned with mounting tax rates, yet municipal officials had cause for concern too. Morrison reported in 1949 that: "The schools are believed to have made such widely successful use of referendum procedure to increase their tax rate limits that the restrictiveness of tax rate maxima for this function remains serious only in scattered counties . . . inasmuch as many school districts had already obtained higher permissible rates through referenda, that similar attempts by other taxing jurisdictions now very likely would be voted down by the electorate."[14]

Certainly, the lot of municipal officials facing increases in service costs and the confusion resulting from the enactment of two tax limit

[13] Morrison, *op. cit.*, p. 128.
[14] *Ibid.*

formulas in as many sessions of the General Assembly was not an easy one. Many municipalities turned to special districts as the solution,[15] and others may have tried referenda seeking the establishment of new municipal funds or sought rate increases for existing funds. But, of the 1,623 successful referenda referred to above, it is interesting to note, less than 50 were for municipal funds. Those other than school referenda were mainly for special districts, county levies, and township levies.

In more recent years there appears to be an increasing tendency for local government officials to supplement these efforts to obtain financial relief by appealing to the legislature to exempt particular funds from the formula provision or to modify its operation with respect to particular funds. Several modifications or exemptions which have been passed by the legislature are listed at the end of the chapter.

It should be noted that the formula provisions of section 162a did not apply to taxing districts of over 500,000 population. Property tax limits for Chicago and overlapping districts with more than 500,000 population were set either by statutory limits or by "pegged levies." Where statutory limits were in force, they were halved in 1945 as were statutory limits of other taxing districts.

Statutes regulating most of the pegged levy funds specify dollar amounts for given years. For example, the statutes dealing with the Chicago Sanitary District corporate fund provide a maximum of $30 million for 1960, $32.75 million for 1961, $35.5 million for 1962 through 1965, and $30 million for 1966 through 1971.[16] Prior to 1955 it had been customary for Chicago city officials to bargain with the leaders of influential taxpayer organizations to obtain support for increases in the pegged levies. In the 1955 legislative session, during the course of some redrafting to make this section conform to changes which had been made elsewhere in the law, the words "and thereafter" were omitted. The taxpayer groups discovered this omission in the last days of the session, but were outmaneuvered in their efforts to get the words reinserted. As a result the Chicago city corporate fund is not subject to a tax limit. Efforts by the taxpayer groups to get a limit reinstated have been made at every legislative session but to date have been unsuccessful.

THE EFFECTS OF RATE LIMITATION

The Illinois system of tax rate limitation affects the level of govern-

---

[15] Clyde F. Snider, Gilbert Y. Steiner, and Lois Langdon, *Local Taxing Units: The Illinois Experience* (Urbana: The Institute of Government and Public Affairs, University of Illinois, and Property Tax Division, Illinois Department of Revenue, 1954).

[16] *Ill. Rev. Stat.*, ch. 42, sec. 332 (1965).

ment spending and even has an impact upon the structure of local government. The unusual complexity of the rate limit legislation and the case law which attempts to interpret this legislation creates confusion and uncertainty which has repercussions throughout the local governing process.

The analysis of the effects of rate limitation which appears in this section is developed in relation to municipalities but much of it applies equally well to other units of local government.

Complexity and Confusion Even the complexity of the technical material which makes up the latter part of this chapter does not fully portray the problems that face a county clerk or municipal official who attempts to make a *de novo* determination of the existing rate limits for any of the many funds subject to formula rate limits. He must first determine the maximum statutory or referendum rate of the fund that was in effect in 1942, the 1942 assessment ratio as certified by the Department of Revenue, the 1945 maximum extension, and the 1946 equalized assessed value. He must make an interpretation of the several disputed points concerning the meaning and application of the formula, and he must search the county records for referenda which may have purported to increase the rate. The clerk must determine the validity of all referenda in the light of a large number of cases which hold that almost every detail of the election procedure must be perfect. He must also search the records of the governing body to determine whether or not permanent limits for the corporate fund were established by timely action in 1951. Finally, he must consult the statutes to determine whether there has been any legislative action to modify or eliminate the application of the formula provision with regard to the particular fund.

Clearly, such a determination of a fund limit is a major piece of legal research which demands extremely specialized knowledge on the part of local officials. Yet, familiarity with the limit statutes and with limit determination is not the "strong suit" of most local government officials. The state is of little aid to perplexed local officials, since it has no agency to help interpret the law. Local citizens seldom press for an interpretation since they generally know little about rate limits or the intricacies of the formula laws. It is not particularly surprising that very few people in the state have any real knowledge of the rate limit program and its effects and that these people have a great deal of influence in local decision-making. The technical nature of the rate limit program not only invites this situation but often masks the way limits are actually determined and local financial decisions made. Frequently it is not the municipal finance officer or the county clerk who is the local authority on rate limitation. Often it is not even a public official. But the individual who purportedly does know something of the determination of the limits wields a considerable amount of influence.

Municipal and railroad attorneys, county clerks, judges, legislative commissions, members of the Department of Revenue staff, and many other students of municipal government have reviewed the rate limit program since its inception in 1945. Their efforts have not cleared up confusion over the law, but have often led to conflicting interpretations of the law. Some of those interested in the program have given up all hope of ever understanding it and accepted interpretations of others. Statewide interviews with interested parties were carried out by the authors during 1964 and 1965. The information obtained from these interviews supports the viewpoint that there are very few individuals who feel comfortable in their knowledge of the rate limit laws.

Evidence of what the rate limits happen to be at a given time is not easy to find, and once found, it is difficult to evaluate. County clerks or their assistants in all counties containing municipalities of 2,500 population or over were asked what the limits were for various municipal funds and whether the limits were statutory or formula. Many finance officers, city managers, mayors, and attorneys were asked similar questions. Responses indicated lack of knowledge of the limits and an even greater lack of knowledge as to how the limit had been determined. Some county clerks keep excellent records and can readily produce rate limits for the various funds they extend; others rely on some individual's memory or on the records of interested private groups.

In Cook County, for example, the task of keeping tax limit records was entrusted to John Crane who had worked in the county clerk's office for more than 40 years prior to his death in 1964. Knowledge of the limits for many funds were stored on rate cards, but not all limits were indicated on the cards. His successors, facing the necessity of reconstructing the missing limits and lacking his long experience, found the task all but impossible.

The fact that limits for many municipal funds in Cook County are unknown presented a serious obstacle to the authors' attempt to study the effects of the property tax limits. Complex tax limit data were available from the county clerk's office for only a few municipalities. Fortunately, an attorney who handles many railroad tax cases was willing to provide limits for the major funds of Cook County municipalities of over 25,000 population.[17] Understandably, some of the limits obtained from this source are below the actual rates levied.

[17] Probably only the authors' reluctance to impose upon the generosity of this individual prevented the obtaining of similar data for smaller municipalities.

In downstate counties, some clerks admitted extending over the legal rate limit for particular districts. In one county this was "because the taxing units had no railroads," hence no contestors and a lower tax base. In another case in which the rate extended exceeded the apparent rate limit the clerk indicated the taxing unit "just needed the money, but the practice has been discontinued since." The clerk of a large metropolitan county could not determine what the limits were supposed to be when he took office, so he scaled all statutory limits down to 80 per cent (a practice followed in some other counties as well). He reported the railroads objected to this practice and beat him, but that no one else had ever protested. An assistant in the clerk's office in a southwestern county pointed out that no one would ever know if excessive rates were extended except the railroads and they would be the only ones to get a rebate.

Industries other than railroads often pay their taxes under protest too. In one Southern Illinois city a group of industries protested five municipal rates and, after negotiating with city officials, managed to get a stipulation submitted to the court allowing about 55 per cent of their protest. The industries then withdrew the remaining 45 per cent of their protest. The municipal officials were willing to negotiate as they needed $100,000 of the total sum that was tied up while awaiting a court decision on the protest.[18] Again, the individual residential taxpayer pays the whole tax since the possibility of paying under protest is not usually a realistic alternative to him. In one city of approximately 50,000 population the dominant industry has recently told city officials it will not protest taxes if the city continues to be run in a businesslike manner. This same industry received a compromise settlement several years ago but the ex-mayor could not remember what it was since "it was largely handled by the lawyers for both sides."

Most of the tax limit data for downstate municipalities were obtained from county clerks' offices at the same time that tax levy information was obtained; therefore the rates extended rarely exceed the reported limits. Examples of some exceptions have been cited above. It is known, of course, that lower limits have sometimes been accepted by local officials as a basis for settling tax protests, but these apply only to the protested taxes.

The Multiplication of Taxing Districts The specific type of rate limitation tends to encourage the proliferation of taxing units. Proponents

[18] The exact percentages which were stipulated to the court as the "correct" rates were determined by computing the rates which would yield $100,000 to the municipality.

of increased spending for a particular purpose often find that it is easier to secure public approval of a new special district than to win a referendum increasing the tax limits of an existing unit of government. In some cases this is true because the boundaries of a special district can be drawn so as to maximize the chances of approval. In addition to this, though, there seems to be a tendency for voters to look more favorably on the creation of a new, special-purpose district than upon an increase in the tax limit of an existing district: "Frequently, the need for referendum approval of a new tax levy is the death knell of a critical service. Special district development has been something of a soporific in that a rejected levy for city park purposes creates no excitement when its appears as a rate for park district purposes."[19]

Table 18 indicates that there has been a rapid increase in the number of special districts in the last quarter of a century. Not all of the new

TABLE 18

PER CENT CHANGE IN NUMBER OF ILLINOIS LOCAL GOVERNMENT UNITS, 1940-62

Unit of Government	1940-62	1950-62
Municipalities	9.5	7.9
Road Districts	−38.0	−39.0
School Districts	−87.6	−67.8
Unit Districts	206.7	22.7
Special Districts	459.6	104.3
Fire Districts	968.3	102.8
Park Districts	130.0	50.8
Sanitary Districts	220.7	200.0

SOURCE Compiled from Property Tax Division Report, Department of Revenue, State of Illinois, 1964, p. 9.

special districts can be attributed to property tax rate limitation since special districts are often created because the area to be served is not coterminous with any existing governmental unit. However, local governmental officials interviewed cited tax and debt limitations as the major reasons for the creation of special districts in their communities.

Table 19 presents a comparison between the average aggregate tax rates for 37 of the 41 largest Illinois municipalities, and the number of major taxing units included in the aggregate, for 1940 to 1962. Clearly the number of taxing units overlapping municipal boundaries has increased, although the aggregate rates themselves have declined as a result of the 1945 rate limit acts. This does not indicate extensions have

[19] Snider, Steiner, and Langdon, *op. cit.*, p. 15.

TABLE 19

OVERLAPPING UNITS AND AGGREGATE TAX RATES, 37 ILLINOIS MUNICIPALITIES, 1940 AND 1962

	Average Number of Overlapping Units	Aggregate Rates: Average (per cent)	Aggregate Rates: Range (per cent)
1940	6.9	6.184	4.600-9.420
1962	9.0	4.155	3.137-5.871

SOURCE Compiled from Illinois Tax Commission, *Property Tax Assessments, Levies, Rates and Extension: 1940,* "Property Tax Statistics for Illinois Local Governments, No. 2" (Springfield: 1941), Table 2; and data collected from county clerks in connection with this project. The 1962 figures are actually average aggregate tax rates as explained in Appendix B.

been reduced, however, since extensions are also dependent on changes in the tax base.

Effects on Tax Levies and Government Spending It is never possible to know with certainty what tax levies or governmental expenditures would be in the absence of tax limits, but available Illinois data do provide considerable evidence of the role which they play. The results of multiple correlation analysis suggest that tax limits are important determinants of the level of municipal expenditure. Appendix Tables A2 and A7 reveal that the second most important variable for "explaining" the level of expenditure is tax limits. Since tax limits are not correlated highly with any other known variable, they appear to be important in their own right and not a mere proxy for some other variable.[20]

The conclusion that tax limits affect expenditure directly by affecting potential property tax extensions is supported by the fact that there is a significant correlation between the limits on the six funds for which data are available and the total tax rates (all funds) of Illinois municipalities.[21]

Having established that tax limits do have an important effect upon the level of municipal expenditure, it is important to look more closely at the determinants of the tax limits themselves. In many states identical statutory-type limits apply to all cities or at least all cities in a similar population-size group.[22] In Illinois similarly situated municipalities may

[20] Appendix Tables A12 and A13 show that there is some correlation among tax limits and some other variables which were utilized in the analysis, but the rather low coefficients of correlation and the fact that the variables which enter the stepwise correlation process in the 39-city case and the 107-city case are completely different suggest that the relationships are neither close nor consistent.

[21] See Appendix Tables A10 and A11.

[22] It is of interest that multiple-correlation analysis would be impossible in this situation since tax limits would be constant.

have a very different limit on the same fund. The reasons for these differences must be sought in local history since tax rates are the result not only of legislative action but of referenda before and after 1945 and of actions taken by municipal officials in 1951 in the face of conflicting legal advice about the effects of these actions. In some cases, the situation is confused by the fact that de facto limits have been established by county clerks unable to obtain all of the information necessary to determine the rates, or have been negotiated by interested parties as an alternative to litigation of a disputed point. Due to these circumstances, it is not surprising to find weak and inconsistent correlations between tax limits and the usual measures of demographic, economic, and social characteristics of the community which are recorded in Appendix Tables A12 and A13.

An alternative analysis of some of the relationships between tax limits and other factors is presented in Table 20. Here rate limits of four of the most widely used funds of 149 Illinois municipalities were ranked from lowest to highest and quartile measurements were related to mean family income and mean per capita assessed value. This shows, for example, that 25 per cent of the 149 municipalities were operating with corporate fund rate limits of less than .183 per cent. The mean family income of these 37 municipalities was $6,976 and the mean per capita assessed value was $3,085. Column 4 provides information about the relationship of extensions and limits. For example, of the 37 cities with corporate limits of .183 per cent or less only two were extending below their limit and one was extending at a rate greater than the reported limit.[23] Similar information is provided for the 75 municipalities with corporate tax limits between .183 per cent and .260 per cent and for the 37 corporate limits above .260 per cent.

Study of this table reveals that both median family income and per capita equalized assessed value tend to be inversely related to rate limits. In other words, the most restrictive rate limits are associated with the highest family incomes and the highest equalized assessed value.[24] Column 4 indicates that municipalities with high tax limits are much more likely to extend rates below the limit than are municipalities with low limits.

Another indication of the importance of tax limits is provided by

---

[23] The data of column 4 must be used with some caution since, as indicated above, many county clerks are uncertain of the limits and data from some Cook County municipalities were obtained from private rather than public records.

[24] This method of grouping municipalities and comparing means is a less rigorous test of relationships than is correlation analysis. Tendencies which are nonlinear or too weak to show up in correlation analysis are revealed in Table 20.

TABLE 20

RATE LIMITS OF SELECTED ILLINOIS MUNICIPALITIES OVER 5,000 POPULATION AND RELATIONSHIP TO SELECTED VARIABLES, 1960

Fund	N	Rate Limit[a] (per cent)	Mean 1959 Median Family Income	Mean 1960 Per Capita Equalized Assessed Valuation	Relationship of Extensions to Limits
Corporate Limit	Q_1 37	.183	$6,976	$3,085	Q_1 1 Extending above limit; 2 Extending below limit
	Q_2 75	.227	6,867	2,872	Q_2 0 Extending above limit; 7 Extending below limit
	Q_3 37	.260	6,339	2,660	Q_3 0 Extending above limit; 11 Extending below limit
Garbage Limit	Q_1 25	.050	7,150	3,220	Q_1 0 Extending above limit; 8 Extending below limit
	Q_2 51	.065	7,337	3,154	Q_2 3 Extending above limit; 7 Extending below limit
	Q_3 25	.078	5,813	2,744	Q_3 0 Extending above limit; 15 Extending below limit
Fire Protection Limit	Q_1 15	.054	6,931	3,339	Q_1 0 Extending above limit; 1 Extending below limit
	Q_2 29	.065	6,569	3,022	Q_2 1 Extending above limit; 8 Extending below limit
	Q_3 15	.100	6,326	2,772	Q_3 0 Extending above limit; 9 Extending below limit
Street and Bridge Limit	Q_1 16	.039	7,162	3,293	Q_1 1 Extending above limit; 5 Extending below limit
	Q_2 31	.051	7,230	3,149	Q_2 0 Extending above limit; 5 Extending below limit
	Q_3 16	.079	6,086	2,933	Q_3 0 Extending above limit; 10 Extending below limit

[a] Q_1 = lowest quarter of cases fall below this limit; Q_2 = median, 50 per cent of cases center around this limit; Q_3 = highest quarter of cases above this limit.

SOURCE Compiled from records in county clerks' offices; *Illinois Municipal Review* and U.S. Bureau of the Census, *1960 Census of Population;* and private records noting that 86 per cent of the 149 cities extended their corporate fund taxes at the limits and that 67 per cent of the garbage, fire protection, and street and bridge funds extensions are at the limit.

Summary It is impossible to say exactly what effect tax rate limits have upon municipal finance, but it is clear that the existence of such limits and the confusion surrounding their meaning are important factors in the municipal finance decision-making process.

The existence of correlation between the level of expenditure and tax limits suggests that tax rates do limit municipal expenditure, although it is not logically possible to rule out the possibility that tax levies sometimes tend to rise to the level of the limits, rather than the reverse. It is also clear that tax rate limits encourage the formation of special districts, but it is impossible to measure the influence which they have.

Perhaps the most striking feature of the tax rate limit situation, however, is the complexity and confusion which results from complicated statutes and conflicting interpretation of them. This has added an element of uncertainty to the process of municipal decision-making which may result in municipalities using incorrect limits. It also opens the door for "negotiations" of tax rate limits by interested parties and sometimes means that a single individual, with or without an official position in municipal government, is able to play a very important role.

The technical history of rate limitations which follows describes, in some detail, the series of events which have led to the present complex situation. A careful reading of that section will make clear the magnitude of the problem faced by a local government official who wishes to determine the limits which apply to the various funds. However, the general reader may wish to proceed to the beginning of Chapter 5.

THE TECHNICAL HISTORY OF RATE LIMITATION SINCE 1945

When the full value program (S.B. 229) was passed in 1945, some revision had to be made in property tax rate limitations to provide a smooth transition from fractional assessment to full value equalization. As things stood in 1945, only 4 of the state's 102 counties had assessment ratios over 50 per cent, while 22 counties had assessment ratios of under 25 per cent.[25] Raising assessments to 100 per cent would have greatly increased the tax extensions possible under existing limits. To prevent this, existing tax rate limits were halved on the assumption that the average assessment ratio was 50 per cent. This meant that taxing units in counties assessing at more than 50 per cent of full value would find their maximum extension under the new limits reduced,

[25] Illinois State's Attorneys Association, *op. cit.*, p. 6.

while districts in counties assessing substantially below 50 per cent would find the new rate limits more permissive when the Butler Program took effect in tax year 1946. The purpose of the full value program was to improve the uniformity of assessments among counties and not to provide general increases in extensions to taxing units. With average county assessment ratios equalized at 100 per cent of full value, the new statutory rate limitations would afford similar treatment to taxing districts of equal valuation regardless of geographic location. However, to ease the transition to the new, halved statutory rate limits, section 162a was added to the Revenue Act of 1939 by Senate Bill 314.[26]

Senate Bill 314 provided for a five-year transition period between the 1945 maximum rate limitations and the halved limits which were to become effective in 1951. During this period both statutory and referendum rate limits were to be determined by a formula contained in the act that would assure some continuity with the effective rate limits prior to January 1, 1946. That is, under pre-1946 fractional assessment, the nominal tax rate limit for city corporate purposes was .66⅔ per cent. If two cities with equal amounts of taxable property and both levying the maximum rate were located in counties with 1945 average assessment ratios of 20 per cent and 80 per cent, their effective corporate rate limits would have been .13⅓ per cent and .53⅓ per cent, respectively.[27] With the halving of the corporate limit to .33⅓ per cent, the city located in the low assessment county would have found the halved corporate limit much less restrictive than it was before the full valuation program while the city in the high assessment county would have found its maximum extensions severely restricted. After the five-year transition period both cities would find their maximum extensions the same if their valuations remained equal. The formula provisions of section 162a were designed to hold maximum rate limits close to their pre-1946 effective rates.

Formula Provisions, 1945 There were five major parts or subsections to section 162a of the Revenue Act. They have generally been inter-

---

[26] *Ill. Rev. Stat.*, ch. 120, sec. 643a (1945).

[27] The nominal tax rate is the rate determined by the county clerk as necessary to raise sufficient revenues to cover the appropriations certified to him (providing the computed rate does not exceed the statutory rate limits). The nominal rate is the effective rate of taxation only if property is assessed at 100 per cent of true value. If assessment is at less than 100 per cent of property value, the effective rate of taxation is less than the nominal rate. If the county clerk extends school taxes at a rate of 1 per cent, it is misleading to say that school taxes run 1 per cent of property value if property is assessed at 25 per cent of its full, fair, cash value. The nominal rate is the 1 per cent indicated on the tax bill, but the effective or true rate of taxation is only .25 per cent.

preted in such a way that the first two paragraphs are applied to rate limitations set by statute prior to the effective date of Senate Bill 314. The next two paragraphs refer to limits set by referendum, and the last paragraph specifies provisions for changing by local referendum the limits otherwise set forth by the act, hence removing them from the formula provisions. The formula provisions did not apply to taxing districts of over 500,000 population, township corporate rates, bond and interest rates, and a few other rates.

The first section provided that during the transition period from January 1, 1946, to December 31, 1950, no rate was to be restricted to a percentage less than sufficient to yield an amount equivalent to the product of:

$$\text{Current year EAV} \times 1942\ \frac{\text{AV}}{\text{FV}} \times 1945 \text{ maximum rate applicable}^{28}$$

where EAV is the equalized assessed value for the taxing districts as determined by Department of Revenue equalization after 1945; AV is the average assessed value for the county in which the particular taxing district lies; and FV is the market value of all property in the county in which the taxing district lies as certified and published by the Department of Revenue. Note that $\frac{\text{AV}}{\text{FV}}$ is the assessment ratio.

This formula, which will be referred to hereafter as 1945-1, assured taxing districts in counties with 1942 assessment ratios of over 50 per cent tax extensions no less than those they might have received in 1942 through extensions of 1945 maximum rate limits.[29] A city operating under the maximum corporate rate limit, in a county with an 80 per cent assessment ratio in 1942, was thus assured of a rate limit no less than its effective pre-1946 rate, or a rate that would produce the same amount of revenue in the transition period as had been received prior to the new law (see Exhibit II). This formula was based on the assumption that equalization would be at 100 per cent of full value. If assessed value was not raised to 100 per cent, the potential extension would be less than the 1942 extension, since multiplying the new EAV times the assessment ratio $\left(\frac{\text{AV}}{\text{FV}}\right)$ would reduce the base over which the 1945 maximum rate was spread.[30] Thus, in effect, the formula was

---

[28] *Ill. Rev. Stat.,* ch. 120, sec, 643a (1) (1945).

[29] Providing the district had been extending the maximum statutory limit prior to the effective date of section 162a.

[30] If the base were $100 at full value in 1942 and were assessed at 80 per cent, the taxable base would equal $80. Assuming a tax limit af 1 per cent, the maximum extension in 1942 would have been $80 × .01 = $.80. If the full

providing a *floor* rate for high assessment districts on the assumption that equalization would be at 100 per cent.

Subsection (2) provides that no rate may exceed the product of the 1942 assessment ratio and the maximum 1945 rate applicable by more than 15 per cent. Further, in no one year during the transition period could the tax extension be increased by more than 5 per cent of the maximum extendible in 1942.[31] This subsection provided rate limit ceilings and one provision of the subsection further provided: "the provisions of this paragraph shall not modify any other restrictions upon maximum extendible tax rates."[32] This proviso raised the question of whether the minimum rates established in subsection (1) were not also the maximum rates that could be extended.[33] Did not subsection (1) apply equally as well to taxing units in counties with low assessment ratios and provide a ceiling rate for them?

Subsections (3) and (4) halved referendum rate limits authorized prior to the effective date of the act (though not if this produced less than it would have in the referendum year), and provided that during the transition period extensions must not exceed by more than 15 per cent the extension for 1942 or the referendum year, whichever was later.[34] The proviso limiting effective statutory rate limit increases to 5 per cent in any one year applied to referendum rates, although the proviso was not qualified by a statement regarding modification of other ceiling rates

Subsection (5) specified referendum procedures for increasing rate limits otherwise applicable by as much as 25 per cent of the statutory limit in question, if the limit provided in this act was at the maximum secured by any referendum provided elsewhere by law. No limit could be reduced by more than one-third of the limit otherwise provided by law.[35]

---

value of the base had not changed from 1942, the full value would be \$100 in 1946, and the formula would guarantee $\$100 \times \frac{\$80}{\$100} \times .01 = \$.80$, or the same extension. However, if equalization was at 80 per cent of full value, then the formula would produce only $\$80 \times \frac{\$80}{\$100} \times .01 = \$.64$.

[31] The pre-1946 rate limit was not necessarily the only limit that could be used in computing the ceiling rate. Any authorized referendum rate effective in 1942 could be substituted in the formula for the maximum statutory rate. Also, the subsection was inapplicable to limits expressed in dollars (the pegged levies in Cook County) and to qualifying levies for state aid.

[32] *Ill. Rev. Stat.,* ch. 120, sec. 643a (2) (1945).

[33] Illinois State's Attorneys Association, *op. cit.,* pp. 10-13.

[34] *Ill. Rev. Stat.,* ch. 120, sec. 643a (3) (4) (1945).

[35] *Ibid.,* ch. 120, sec. 643a (5) (1945). Galesburg is the only city known to have reduced its corporate limit by referendum as provided in this section.

Exhibit II presents a list of corporate rate limits that might have been computed by county clerks during the transition period for the two cities previously used as an example. The exhibit illustrates how the rates were computed under the various provisions of the act and shows how different tax bases and interpretations of the formula affect the results.

Irving Howards relates how immediate controversy centered around the provisions of subsection (2) of the act regulating increased extension in any one year by restricting it to 5 per cent of the maximum extendible in 1942.[36] "Strict" interpretation held the maximum extendible in any one year of the transition period to 5 per cent more than the 1942 rate times the 1942 assessed value, with a maximum increase over the period of 15 per cent.[37] This interpretation restricted the effective 1942 limit to a 5 per cent increase, or 105 per cent of the maximum extension for 1942. Hence, the provisions of subsection (2) would have nullified the formula of subsection (1) since it was based on the effective 1942 rate times the equalized assessed value of the *current* year (post-1945), not the 1942 assessed valuation.

EXHIBIT II

INTERPRETATION OF MAXIMUM EXTENSIONS AND MAXIMUM FORMULA RATES FOR 1946, BASED ON SECTION 162a OF THE REVENUE ACT, 1945

This exhibit will illustrate how the provisions of Senate Bill 314 affected potential property tax extensions. Rate limits and potential tax extensions are computed for three hypothetical cities, in separate counties, with assessment ratios equal to their respective county's average assessment ratio. Different, and more complex, examples could be developed showing the effects of the formula on cities assessed at more or less than the county average, but the principles remain the same. Alternative interpretations of the law are allowed for and assumptions regarding changes in valuation stipulated. No attempt has been made to include the effects of price changes on the valuation of the base or on the cost of governmental services. It is thereby assumed prices remain constant in the exhibit and all increases in assessed value are the result of: (1) equalization, (2) additions to the tax base, or (3) increases in local assessment ratios.

Assume three Illinois municipalities extending the maximum corporate rates (statutory) in 1942 and the following valuation data:

	1942 Assessed Valuation	1942 Full Value	1942 Assessment Ratio
City A	$800,000	$1,000,000	80%
City B	200,000	1,000,000	20
City C	200,000	400,000	50

[36] Howards, *op. cit.*, p. 529.

[37] "Strict" is used in the sense of "restrictive." See Exhibit II, 6.

EXHIBIT II (continued)

INTERPRETATION OF MAXIMUM EXTENSIONS AND MAXIMUM FORMULA RATES FOR 1946, BASED ON SECTION 162a OF THE REVENUE ACT, 1945

The maximum 1945 corporate rate was .66⅔ per cent. Based on 1942 assessment ratios, the maximum effective corporate rates for the three cities in 1942 were: A = .66⅔% × 80% = .53⅓%; B = .66⅔% × 20% = .13⅓%; and C = .66⅔% × 50% = .33⅓%. Note that the assessment ratio for City C is equal to the average state assessment ratio assumed by the legislature in devising the formula.

1. Maximum extensions for 1942 were:

	1942 Assessed Value		1942 Maximum Statutory Rate		Maximum Extension	Effective Rate
City A	$800,000	×	.66⅔%	=	$5,333.33	.53⅓%
City B	200,000	×	.66⅔	=	1,333.33	.13⅓
City C	200,000	×	.66⅔	=	1,333.33	.33⅓

2. Maximum extension and rates in 1946 produced by *section 162a (1)*, assuming no increase in valuation from 1942 to 1946:

	1942 or 1946 Full Value		1942 Assessed Ratio		1945 Maximum Rate		1946 Maximum Extension	1946 Nominal Rate Limit	1946 Effective Rate Limit
City A	$1,000,000	×	80%	×	.66⅔%	=	$5,333.33	.53⅓%	.53⅓%
City B	1,000,000	×	20	×	.66⅔	=	1,333.33	.13⅓	.13⅓
City C	400,000	×	50	×	.66⅔	=	1,333.33	.33⅓	.33⅓

making the effective 1942 rates the controlling nominal limits for 1946.

3. The Department of Revenue equalized assessments at approximately 75 per cent in 1946 rather than at 100 per cent.[a] Assuming equalization was at 75 per cent of full value and there were no increases in full value from 1942 to 1946:

	1946 75 Per Cent Equalized Value		1946 Nominal Rate Limit		1946 Maximum Extension	1946 Effective Rate Limit
City A	$750,000.00	×	.53⅓%	=	$4,000.00	.40%
City B	750,000.00	×	.13⅓	=	1,000.00	.10
City C	300,000.00	×	.33⅓	=	1,000.00	.25

yielding 1946 extensions less than 1942 extensions with lower effective limits.

4. Assuming a 40 per cent increase in the full value of the base from 1942 to 1946, equalization at 100 per cent would have produced with 1942 effective rates:

	1946 100 Per Cent Equalized Value		1946 Nominal Rate Limit		1946 Maximum Extension	1946 Effective Rate Limit
City A	$1,400,000	×	.53⅓%	=	$7,466.67	.53⅓%
City B	1,400,000	×	.13⅓	=	1,866.67	.13⅓
City C	560,000	×	.33⅓	=	1,866.67	.33⅓

or an increase in extensions, but not effective rates.

5. With equalization at 75 per cent, maximum extensions would have been (still assuming 40 per cent increase in valuation):

[a] The equalization figure reported by James R. Parham was 74.48 per cent of full value in 1946. "Taxation of Property in Illinois," *The University of Illinois Law Forum* (1961), p. 649, Exhibit 21.

EXHIBIT II (continued)

INTERPRETATION OF MAXIMUM EXTENSIONS AND MAXIMUM FORMULA RATES FOR 1946, BASED ON SECTION 162a OF THE REVENUE ACT, 1945

	1946 75 Per Cent Equalized Value		1946 Nominal Rate Limit		1946 Maximum Extension	1946 Effective Rate Limit
City A	$1,050,000	×	.53⅓%	=	$5,600.00	.40%
City B	1,050,000	×	.13⅓	=	1,400.00	.10
City C	420,000	×	.33⅓	=	1,400.00	.25

That is, to offset the less than 100 per cent equalization by the Department of Revenue, property values would have had to increase approximately 40 per cent to provide the same extension available in 1942. The effective rates would be the same as for the debased equalization given constant property values — see 3 above.

6. *Section 162a (2)* restricted increases in 1942 extensions during the interim period. Assuming a 5 per cent increase in the maximum 1942 extension was permissible in 1946, maximum extensions and nominal and effective rate limits would have (under the assumptions of 2 above) been:

	1942 Maximum Extension				1946 Maximum Extension	1946 Nominal Rate Limit	1946 Effective Rate Limit
City A	$5,333.33	+	(5% × $5,333.33)	=	$5,600.00	.56%	.56%
City B	1,333.33	+	(5 × 1,333.33)	=	1,400.00	.14	.14
City C	1,333.33	+	(5 × 1,333.33)	=	1,400.00	.35	.35

This is the so-called "strict" interpretation of the statute, allowing a 5 per cent increase in 1942 extensions and slightly higher rate limits.

7. With the assumptions of 2 above, the "liberal" interpretation would produce the same as the "strict" interpretation. But given the assumptions of 4 above, the "liberal" interpretation would provide for extensions and rates to be based on the current year equalized value times the 1942 effective rate plus 5 per cent of the 1942 extension, which would yield:

	1946 100 Per Cent Equalized Value		1942 Effective Rate		1942 Maximum Extension		1946 Maximum Extension	1946 Nominal	1946 Effective
City A	$1,400,000	×	.53⅓%	+	(5% × $5,333.33)	=	$7,333.33	.552%	.552%
City B	1,400,000	×	.13⅓	+	(5 × 1,333.33)	=	1,933.33	.138	.138
City C	560,000	×	.33⅓	+	(5 × 1,333.33)	=	1,933.33	.345	.345

Hence, the "liberal" interpretation would have yielded greater extensions, but at lower effective rates than the "strict" interpretation. If value had remained constant with 75 per cent equalization, extensions would have been less under the "liberal" interpretation than under the "strict" interpretation.

8. Repeating 7 above with 75 per cent equalization:

	1946 75 Per Cent Equalized Value		1942 Effective Rate		1942 Maximum Extension		1946 Maximum Extension	1946 Nominal	1946 Effective
City A	$1,050,000	×	.53⅓%	+	(5% × $5,333.33)	=	$5,866.67	.559%	.419%
City B	1,050,000	×	.13⅓	+	(5 × 1,333.33)	=	1,466.67	.140	.105
City C	420,000	×	.33⅓	+	(5 × 1,333.33)	=	1,466.67	.349	.262

Extensions remain more "liberal" yet effective rates have been substantially reduced through the less than 100 per cent equalization.

9. *Section 162a (3) and (4)* related specifically to referenda rates enacted

EXHIBIT II (continued)

INTERPRETATION OF MAXIMUM EXTENSIONS AND MAXIMUM FORMULA RATES FOR 1946, BASED ON SECTION 162a OF THE REVENUE ACT, 1945

prior to January 1, 1946. Assuming 1944 was the referendum year and the referendum rate of .20 per cent was voted in each of the three cities, this rate would have been halved beginning 1946 with some exceptions. Assuming assessed value was the same in 1944 as in 1942, and full value remained constant through 1946, maximum extensions in 1944 under the referendum rate would have been:

	1944 Assessed Value		Referendum Rate Limit		1944 Maximum Extension	1944 Effective Referendum Rate
City A	$800,000	×	.20%	=	$1,600.00	.16%
City B	200,000	×	.20	=	400.00	.04
City C	200,000	×	.20	=	400.00	.10

In 1946, with full value constant and equalization at 100 per cent, extensions would have been:

	1946 100 Per Cent Equalized Value		1946 Referendum Rate Limit		1946 Maximum Extension	1946 Effective Referendum Rate
City A	$1,000,000	×	.10%	=	$1,000	.10%
City B	1,000,000	×	.10	=	1,000	.10
City C	400,000	×	.10	=	400	.10

Only in the case of City C would the same extension be produced; for City A it would be substantially decreased and for City B substantially increased. *Section 162a (3)* also provided for a 5 per cent single year increase in the referendum year (or 1942, whichever was later) extension, which amounts to $80.00 for A, $20.00 for B, and $20.00 for C. However, *section 162a (4)* insured the referendum year extension so that City A's rate limit in the above example would have been reduced only to .16 per cent and not halved. Did the 5 per cent increase apply here also, making the maximum referendum limit for 1946 in City A .168 per cent? City B would have been restricted by *section 162a (3b)* to 105 per cent of the referendum year extensions, or a rate limit of .042 per cent. As the same is true for City C, in the case of referendum limits, then, the effective rates are increased in all cases.

The more "liberal" interpretation was that subsection (2) modified only the provisions of that subsection, and not the formula of subsection (1). For any one year in the transition period the maximum extension could then be determined by adding 5 per cent of the 1942 maximum extension to the product of the transition year equalized assessed value times the 1942 effective limit. The difference in the two points of view centered on the increased extensions made permissible by the increases in the value of the tax base.[38] If there had been no increase in full value since 1942, the question would have been moot. Had property values been declining the provisions of subsection (2)

[38] Note that these increased values need not reflect full value equalization on the part of the Department of Revenue.

would have been meaningless as the formula of subsection (1) would have indeed become the ceiling rate.

The Illinois Supreme Court ruled in favor of the "liberal" interpretation in *Anderson* v. *City of Park Ridge,*[39] holding the intentions of the legislature had not been to restrict the revenues of a taxing district to 1942 amounts when the taxable value of the district might have increased since then. Exhibit II illustrates with examples the contentions of the two groups in the case. The court's decision was handed down in March, 1947, while the legislature was in session, and it became immediately apparent that the court's interpretation differed from that of the members of the 1947 legislature. Whether the 1945 General Assembly had intended the "liberal" interpretation of section 162a, or merely failed to realize its implications, is unclear. However, the sentiments of the 65th General Assembly were apparent.

Several amendments were offered for section 162a. One would have granted legislative sanction of the "liberal" interpretation of the Butler formula, restricting the effective rate limit by computing it with the lowest 1942-44 county equalization factor,[40] and eliminating the 5 per cent increase of subsection (2) of the 1945 formula. This amendment was vetoed by the governor.[41] The other proposed amendments[42] were more restrictive as was the one finally enacted.[43]

Formula Provisions, 1947 The 1947 enactment, sponsored by Representative Orville Hodge and others, repealed the first four paragraphs of the 1945 law and eliminated the restriction against lowering any rate limitation by more than one-third. Also, the act eliminated the provision requiring that maximum rates otherwise obtainable had to be reached before a referendum could be held under 162a (5) to increase a rate. The new formula for computing rates during the transition period, which was extended two years, was the lesser amount of:

$$\text{(a)}\quad 1942\ \frac{AV}{FV} \times \text{Maximum rate 12-31-45, whether referendum or statutory} \times 105\% \qquad (1947\text{-}1)$$

or

$$\text{(b)}\quad \frac{\text{1945 Maximum extension}}{\text{1946 100\% EAV}} \times 105\% \qquad (1947\text{-}2)$$

[39] 72 N.E. 2d 210 (1947). Note in Exhibit II, depending upon circumstances, the "liberal" interpretation could produce less than the "strict" interpretation.

[40] If 1942 had been the year of the lowest equalization factor, the computed effective limit could have been increased by 5 per cent.

[41] *Final Legislative Synopsis and Digest of the Sixty-Fifth General Assembly* (1947), S.B. 224. Hereafter cited as *Legislative Synopsis.*

[42] *Ibid.,* S.B. 234, H.B. 432, H.B. 493, H.B. 441.

[43] *Ibid.,* H.B. 513.

The Hodge Act also excepted from the formula provisions taxing districts, levies, and limits created after the effective date of the full value program.[44]

While the 1947 act eased the restrictions against increasing or decreasing formula limits by local referendum, the new formula provisions had the effect of holding maximum permissible tax extensions to 5 per cent over what they were in 1942. Assuming the 1945 assessed values of all taxing units within a county were at approximately the same per cent of full value, about the only way the (1947-2) formula provision could have produced larger rates than the (1947-1) formula provision, would have been if 1946 full value was less than it had been in 1942. This rarely occurred since property values increased between 1942 and 1946. Exhibit III presents several examples of how the new formula restricted rates.

The formula provisions of the 1947 legislation were much clearer than were the 1945 provisions which they replaced and there was relatively little disagreement about their meaning. Morrison appears to have summarized the feelings of many property taxpayers and municipal officials when he stated in 1949: ". . . perhaps the worst is over for the interim period in Illinois, now that both the taxing jurisdictions and county clerks have actually operated under the new legislation, and that any further change during the interim period would only result in the confusion and irritation of a new set of adjustments."[45] Yet, the legislature then in session was already enacting bills that would complicate interpretation of the existing rate limitation statutes. One bill restored the fire protection limit to its pre-1946 maximum statutory rate, thus apparently liberalizing extensions for fire protection purposes.[46] Another bill was passed which appeared to further restrict municipal extensions for library purposes.[47] Another measure sought to repeal the formula and return to the limits that had been applicable prior to the effective date of the Butler bills.[48] This bill was tabled and the two which were enacted were soon subjected to court interpretation.

Part of the difficulty in interpreting these two acts stemmed from uncertainty as to the effect of the equalization program and formula provisions on municipal fiscal programs. With most of the formula

---

[44] *Laws of Illinois* (1947), p. 1434.
[45] Morrison, *op. cit.*, p. 139.
[46] *Laws of Illinois* (1949), p. 473.
[47] *Ibid.*, p. 1076.
[48] *Legislative Synopsis* (1949), H.B. 469.

limits tied to 1942 assessed and full value figures, it made little difference, at least for formula restricted funds, whether the Department of Revenue was equalizing at full value or not. The 1947 formula generally froze extensions at a little more than they had been in 1942. As assessed value rose, county clerks had to recompute the rate that could be extended for specific funds. Thus, if the 1947 formula was constitutional, the department could do little after 1946 to affect the revenues produced by formula restricted rates, and for these funds, the whole full value program was meaningless.[49] There was considerable doubt,

EXHIBIT III

MAXIMUM EXTENSION AND RATE RESTRICTIONS UNDER THE 1947 FORMULA

In this exhibit, the effects of the 1947 formulas will be illustrated using the same three hypothetical cities and data referred to in Exhibit II. The 1947 formula restricted rates to the lesser of the two formulas given in the text. The (a) portion of the formula would produce the following results:

	1942 AV/FV		1945 Maximum Rate				1947 Formula (a) Minimum Rate
City A	80%	×	.66⅔%	×	105%	=	.56%
City B	20	×	.66⅔	×	105	=	.14
City C	50	×	.66⅔	×	105	=	.35

The same rate is produced as in the "strict" interpretation of section 162a (2) for 1945 (see Exhibit II, 6); however, the rate would apply to current year equalized values as in the "liberal" interpretation of the 1945 formula. Assuming valuation remained constant for the three cities from 1942 to 1948, we have:

	Constant Full Value 1942-48		1947 Formula (a) Maximum Rate		1948 Maximum Extension
City A	$1,000,000	×	.56%	=	$5,600.00
City B	1,000,000	×	.14	=	1,400.00
City C	400,000	×	.35	=	1,400.00

Given the same assumptions, the 1947 (b) formula produces the following rate limits:

	1945 Maximum Extension												
	1945 AV		1945 Maximum Rate		1945 Maximum Extension		1946 100 Per Cent Equalized Value						1947 Formula Limit
City A	($800,000	×	.66⅔%	=	$5,333.33)	÷	$1,000,000	=	.53⅓%	×	105%	=	.56%
City B	(200,000	×	.66⅔	=	1,333.33)	÷	1,000,000	=	.13⅓	×	105	=	.14
City C	(200,000	×	.66⅔	=	1,333.33)	÷	400,000	=	.33⅓	×	105	=	.35

which are identical with the formula (a) limits.

If the assumption is made that full value increased 40 per cent from 1942 to 1946 and 50 per cent from 1942 to 1948, and a 75 per cent equalization ratio is

[49] Actually, the department had not been fully allowing for price changes and in some instances did not change county multipliers despite evidence of value changes and fluctuations in county assessment ratios. Rolf A. Weil, "Property Tax Equalization in Illinois," *National Tax Journal* (June, 1953), pp. 157-67.

EXHIBIT III (continued)

MAXIMUM EXTENSION AND RATE RESTRICTIONS UNDER THE 1947 FORMULA

assumed for 1946 and 65 per cent equalization for 1948,[a] the formula limits would produce:

	1947 Formula (a) Limit (1)		1948 65 Per Cent Equalized Value[b] (2)		1948 Formula (a) Maximum Extension (3)
City A	.56%	×	$975,000	=	$5,460.00
City B	.14	×	975,000	=	1,365.00
City C	.35	×	390,000	=	1,365.00

1945 Maximum Extension (4)		1946 100 Per Cent Value (5)		1947 Formula (b) Maximum (6)					1948 Maximum Formula (b) Extension (6) × (2)
$5,333.33	÷	$1,400,000	=	.3809%	×	105%	=	.40%	$3,900.00
1,333.33	÷	1,400,000	=	.0952	×	105	=	.10	975.00
1,333.33	÷	560,000	=	.2381	×	105	=	.25	975.00

The formula (b) limit is less, hence controlling, yet producing less than before 1946. The 1947 statute (643a) especially states 1946 100 per cent full, fair, cash value will be used in computing formula (b). Since equalization was not at 100 per cent in 1946, but rather around 75 per cent the equalized value for 1946 would have been used in the formula and would produce:

	1945 Maximum Extension		1946 75 Per Cent Equalized Value						1947 Formula (b) Maximum Limit		1948 65 Per Cent Equalized Value		1948 Maximum Extension
City A	$5,333.33	÷	$1,050,000	=	.508%	×	105%	=	.53⅓%	×	$975,000	=	$5,200.00
City B	1,333.33	÷	1,050,000	=	.127	×	105	=	.13⅓	×	975,000	=	1,300.00
City C	1,333.33	÷	420,000	=	.317	×	105	=	.33⅓	×	390,000	=	1,300.00

or under the stated assumptions, the same as the 1942 effective rate. Formula (a) limits would control only if the 1945 maximum extensions had been slightly higher or 1946 equalization at slightly less than 75 per cent. The greater the increase in full value between 1942 and 1946, the more likely formula (b) limits would apply. Conversely, if value increased but little over the period or remained constant, formula (a) rates might have controlled, depending upon the level at which the Department of Revenue equalized specific counties for 1946. In either case, extensions were held fairly close to pre-1946 levels.

[a] James R. Parham reports 74.48 per cent in 1946 and 63.20 per cent in 1948. "Taxation of Property in Illinois," *The University of Illinois Law Forum* (1961), Exhibit 21.
[b] 1942 value + 50% × 65%.

however, as to whether the Hodge formulas (H.B. 513, 1947) were constitutional.[50] The question of constitutionality centered on the non-uniform application of formula rates to taxing units in similar situations and whether this constituted special legislation, as expressly forbidden in the Illinois Constitution.[51]

[50] Morrison, *op. cit.*, p. 139.
[51] Article IV, Sec. 22.

Adjudication of the 1949 legislative enactments helped stem some immediate controversy over the rate limit laws, but left many questions unanswered. In the first instance, the court ruled the library rate restriction imposed by 1949 legislation constituted special legislation since it was not a general law.[52] Library rates were already subject to the transitional provisions of section 162a of the Revenue Act, but the amendment to the Library Act restricted the transitional rate otherwise provided in 162a. Thus, in effect, the 1949 legislation made permanent the halved 1945 statutory limit prior to the expiration of the transition period, provided it did not produce extensions in excess of 110 per cent of 1945 maximum extension.[53] Had the library amendment been allowed to stand, it would have, in most cases, not only restricted the new halved limits before they became permanent, but further restricted formula rate limits of the transition period as they did in the case in point. In striking down the amendment the court stated that it established "dissimilarity in the powers and modes of different municipalities in the levy and collection of taxes . . ." and "a statute authorizing and prescribing tax rates so variant in amount constitutes a flagrant violation of . . . section 22 of Article IV of our constitution."[54] While the court addressed itself to the constitutionality of the amendment of the Library Act and not the 1947 formula, there was obviously heightened interest in the constitutionality of the formula provisions since the formula clearly provided rates "variant in amount" for municipalities in similar circumstances.

The second case the court ruled upon that year concerned statutory construction of the 1949 legislation which restored the pre-1946 statutory limit for fire protection purposes. The question that arose was whether the 1949 amendment to the Fire Protection Act, as the latest expression of the legislature's will, preempted the formula provisions of the General Revenue Act. In *Krimmel* v. *Eielson*,[55] the court held that amendments are to be construed together with the original act to which they relate and that the legislature clearly intended the new statutory limit should remain subject to section 162a of the Revenue

---

[52] *Kremers* v. *City of West Chicago*, 94 N.E. 2d 337 (1950).

[53] *Ill. Rev. Stat.*, ch. 81, sec. 13 (1949). In 1945 the rate limit for library building purposes was .166⅔ per cent. The Butler bills reduced this to a permanent rate limitation of .0833 per cent after the transition period, and to .0833 per cent subject to the provisions of section 162a during the transition period. The amendment to the Library Act provided a permanent limit of .0833 per cent provided it did not produce more than 110 per cent × 1945 maximum rate (.166⅔ per cent) × 1945 assessment ratio.

[54] *Kremers* v. *City of West Chicago, op. cit.*

[55] 92 N.E. 2d 767 (1950).

Act. Such an interpretation meant that the increased statutory limit affected only districts created after 1945 or taxing units that had increased rate limits by referendum after 1945. Otherwise, the provisions of 162a controlled and the formula rates were unaffected by the new legislation. Thus, funds established after the effective date of the full value program were to be far less restrictive than those in existence prior to the program. The court acknowledged this construction was discriminatory in favor of new districts or funds, but noted that the expenses of new taxing units would be higher.[56]

Hodge-Downing Amendment In 1951, one year before the end of the interim period, the legislature passed House Bill 650 known as the Hodge-Downing Amendment.[57] This bill added sections 162b and 162c and extended the interim period through 1953 for all taxing districts except school districts. Purportedly, the amendment was to provide municipalities with an opportunity to fix their own tax rate limits and to abrogate the formula provisions of 162a.[58] Section 162b provided that corporate authorities of taxing districts (except townships) could establish by ordinance or resolution prior to December 31, 1951, the maximum permissible tax rate limit for each of its funds subject to the act. The following procedures could be followed:

(1) A maximum rate could be established that was no greater than the limit in effect as of the date of adoption of the ordinance or resolution.[59]

(2) A maximum rate could be established for the corporate fund not more than 10 per cent greater than the limit in effect as of the date of adoption of the ordinance or resolution, provided two-thirds of the members of the corporate authority voted affirmatively and provided the corporate fund had not been increased by referendum since 1946.[60]

(3) A maximum rate limit could be established greater than the one in effect at the date of adoption of the ordinance for any limited fund other than the corporate, provided it was submitted to the voters of the taxing district at a referendum.[61]

Adoption of present limits as in (1) above, or inaction on the part of corporate authorities, made permanent the maximum limit in effect on the date of ordinance or resolution, or on December 31, 1951. Increased limits were not to become effective until 1952.[62] The maximum limits in effect on the ordinance date or prior to 1952 were:

---

[56] *Ibid.*
[57] *Ill. Rev. Stat.,* ch. 120, secs. 643(b), 643(c) (1951).
[58] Howards, *op. cit.,* p. 531.
[59] *Ill. Rev. Stat.,* ch. 120, sec. 643b (3) (1951).
[60] *Ibid.,* ch. 120, sec, 643b (4) (1951).
[61] *Ibid.,* ch. 120, sec. 643b (5) (1951).
[62] State of Illinois, *Attorney General's Opinion* (1951), p. 177.

(1) statutory rate limit — for districts or funds created after January 1, 1946;

(2) referendum rate limit — authorized by referendum after January 1, 1946;

(3) formula rate limit — for funds in existence prior to January 1, 1946, and scaled down by the provisions of the 1947 formula of 162a.[63]

The provisions of 162b were not to allow an increase in any tax rate limit in excess of statutory or referendum limits, though they could exceed the formula limits of 162a and the new reduced rates of 162c.[64] Section 162c reduced all statutory rates to 80 per cent of the previous statutory rate effective January 1, 1952, and reduced all pre-1946 referendum rates to 40 per cent, as long as they did not affect limits created under section 162a or 162b.[65]

The Hodge-Downing Amendment added further confusion to the already complicated process of tax rate limit determination. Many formula rates were made permanent before the expiration of the interim period, when they were to have been replaced by the permanent, halved statutory rates. Also, in some instances, the new statutory rates themselves were reduced further than they had been in 1945. This restriction must have been aimed directly at funds created after 1945 since they were not subject to the formula provisions of 162a.

The Aftermath of the Hodge-Downing Amendment Municipal officials perplexed by the rate limit morass and complicated formula procedures had little hope of removing funds from formula limits except by referendum. Considering the hazards of sponsoring nonschool referenda and the many technicalities surrounding the proper referendum procedures,[66] the possibility of expanding local government programs to keep pace with population and income growth seemed difficult unless bond financing or alternative revenues could be utilized. In fact, many municipalities did not adopt higher corporate limits by ordinance or resolution since they were advised by attorneys, considered to be experts in the field, against freezing their tax rates. Communities that heeded this advice are operating under more restrictive corporate rates today. Another solution, followed in some downstate metropolitan counties, was to ignore the formula rates and merely scale all statutory rates down to 80 per cent of the rates listed in the statutes.

The intent of the full value program had been to provide uniformity

---

[63] *Ill. Rev. Stat.*, ch. 120, sec. 643b (9) (1951).

[64] *Ibid.*, ch. 120, sec. 632b (6) (10) (1951).

[65] *Ibid.*, ch. 120, sec. 643c (1951).

[66] *People ex rel. Ross* v. *Chicago, Burlington and Quincy R.R. Co.*, 103 N.E. 2d 79 (1951); *People ex rel. Ruchty* v. *Chicago and Northwestern Ry. Co.*, 1 Ill. 2d 574 (1953).

among counties in assessment ratios and rate limits, hence equal revenue powers for municipalities with the same equalized assessment value. The fact that the Department of Revenue was not equalizing property at full value, and that the percentage of full value at which they were equalizing was declining, provided further restrictions for some local fiscal programs. Coupling this with the fact that the Hodge-Downing Amendment had made many of the formula rates permanent, it hardly appears that the original purpose of the full value program was being carried out. Municipalities with similar equalized tax bases, populations, and geographic locations found their fiscal programs restricted in nonuniform ways. This was true of municipalities in different counties as well as municipalities in the same county since the equalization program did not extend to equalizing intra-county assessments.

The question of whether the formula rates did, in fact, provide special legislation had not been satisfactorily answered in the *Kremers* case and it was only a matter of time before the question came up again. When it did in *People ex rel. Carter* v. *Touchette*,[67] the St. Clair County state's attorney, as appellant, based much of his argument on the decision in the *Kremers* case. The court held that "the sole argument being in the form of isolated quotations from a decision holding an entirely different statute invalid . . ."[68] was not sufficient to raise the question of validity of the present statute (162b). Carter had maintained that section 162a had become ineffective December 31, 1952, and the provision of the 1951 Hodge-Downing Amendment extending the formula provisions to December 31, 1953, was unconstitutional. The court also criticized the case presented by the state's attorney on the grounds that there was no analysis of the statute under attack and that there was no proof as to the effect of its enforcement.[69] Whether this indicated the court might consider declaring the 1951 amendment unconstitutional on the basis of further evidence was not clear, but sidestepping the constitutional issue kept alive the whole question of the validity of the Hodge-Downing provisions. Interestingly enough, in contending the law making formula rates permanent was special legislation in violation of the constitution, the state's attorney stated that the county clerk's action, in extending a rate lower than that certified to him, "was tantamount to levying the tax and of determining its legality."[70] This statement will be commented on below.

Other cases ruled on specific rates for specific funds in attempting to

[67] 5 Ill. 2d 300 (1955).
[68] *Ibid.*
[69] *Ibid.*
[70] *Ibid.*

clarify what the proper limit might be. One county clerk in a northern county declared, "the only way to be sure you have the right limit is to take it through the courts." Evidently, many local officials did just that. An opinion handed down in 1956 stated that the provisions of 162b (2) superseded the debased rate under 162a since corporate authorities had acted to adopt the statutory limit as a permanent rate prior to 1952.[71] Strict interpretation of 162b (2) and 162b (3) led most to believe that the phrase ". . . tax rate limit in effect for said fund as of the date of adoption of the ordinance . . ."[72] meant: (a) the formula rate for funds in existence prior to 1946 and not increased after 1945 by referendum, and (b) the statutory rate or referendum rate for funds created after 1945 or increased by referendum after 1945. Section 162b (9) would certainly give this impression, but the court ruled on the basis of section 162b (10) which stated: "Any tax rate limit for any fund established as provided in this Section 162b shall supersede any other tax rate limit for such fund established by any other applicable statute including Sec. 162a. . . ."[73] That is, section 162b (10) supersedes section 162a since the court held that the intentions of the legislature had been to have rate limits established locally on the basis of local needs. The county corporate authorities were acting correctly by adopting the statutory rate limit for the fund and this "limit became effective immediately and without referendum."[74] This decision would not have been particularly surprising if the fund had been created after 1945 or was being adopted for the first time in 1951. The decision would have a significant effect on revenue availability for local officials only where a fund had been in existence prior to 1946.

In other decisions, the court ruled that additional taxes or temporary rates enacted between 1946 and 1950 could have been made permanent in 1951 under the provisions of section 162b.[75] Nothing in that section excluded temporary rates (those voted for a five-year period) and one act can modify another by implication without reenacting every act modified. Again the court appeared to favor local prerogative in setting rate limitations. Rulings were handed down declaring that the tuberculosis sanitarium tax and special charter school taxes were not subject to scaling under section 162a, but that the sanitarium tax was

[71] *People ex rel. Kramer* v. *Chicago, Burlington and Quincy Railroad,* 8 Ill. 2d 382 (1956).

[72] *Ill. Rev. Stat.,* ch. 120, sec. 643b (3) (1951).

[73] *Ibid.,* ch. 120, sec. 643b (10) (1951).

[74] *People ex rel. Kramer, op. cit., passim.*

[75] *People ex rel. Nordstrom* v. *Chicago and North Western Railway Co.,* 16 Ill. 2d 264 (1959).

not in addition to the over-all county limit.[76] But the burning issue that still remained was whether the Hodge-Downing Amendment was constitutional and whether formula limits were still in effect.

Three queries as to the validity of section 162b and 162c were dismissed by the Illinois Supreme Court in 1961. The decision in *People ex rel. Rose* v. *New York Central R.R. Co.*[77] also reviewed rate limit legislation since 1945 and interpreted sections currently applicable. In 1955, sections 162a, 162b, and 162c had been amended to combine two forms of the section and to repeal the formula provisions of 162a which had expired December 31, 1953.[78] Other inconsequential amendments were also made in the sections both in 1955 and 1957, and the maximum permissible rate for each fund was stated to be "the maximum rate applicable on the effective date of this 1955 amendatory Act until changed under the provisions of subsection (3) of Section 162a of this Act."[79] The Champaign county collector contended 162b was "an unconstitutional attempt to revive a repealed statute by its title . . ."[80] (the 1947 formula provisions of 162a) and that 162a and 162b had the effect of special legislation. The court held that 162b made it clear enough that the rate limits for funds in existence prior to 1946 — and not changed since by referenda — *were the formula limits.* As the formula provisions expired, there was no longer need for them in the statutes, but the rates they established were the maximum rates available whether the formula existed or not. Repeal of the formula was not repeal of all of the rate limits computed under the formula, since they became the permanent rates at the end of 1951. Also, the fact that more taxing districts had not availed themselves of the opportunity to increase their rate limits prior to the end of 1951 left the legislature with little alternative other than to continue the temporary formula until local rates were established. The legislature can make laws to regulate township and county affairs, and taxation is one of the regulations. Formula provisions were designed to avoid inequities arising from the full value program and thus cannot be construed as special legislation.

The *Rose* decision also struck down the attempt to have section 162a declared invalid. The collector's contention was that 162c amended

---

[76] *People ex rel. Nordstrom* v. *Chicago and North Western Railway Co.*, 11 Ill. 2d 99 (1957), and *People ex rel. Bell* v. *NYC Railroad Co.*, 10 Ill. 2d 612 (1957).

[77] 22 Ill. 2d 266 (1961).

[78] *Ill. Rev. Stat.*, ch. 120, secs. 643a, 643b, 643c (1955).

[79] *Ibid.*

[80] *People ex rel. Rose* v. *New York Central R.R. Co.*, *op. cit.*

other laws by reference only in violation of section 13, Article IV of the Constitution. That is, it held that the 20 per cent reduction, which commenced in 1953, in the funds created after 1946 did not allow the revenues for which local citizens had voted. As defendant, the railroad filed a cross appeal which alleged that voters should have been informed of the reduced rate on the ballots employed for the referenda, and since they were not, the rates could not be legally levied. The court held 162c valid in that it is part of the General Revenue Law which governs all aspects of property taxation. It was also permissible to vote a rate greater than that which could actually be extended since 162c was also a temporary measure to help offset the effects of full valuation, and when it was repealed, the voted rate would again be controlling.[81]

Commenting specifically on the *Kramer* v. *Chicago, Burlington and Quincy Railroad* case, the decision indicated that the formula rate was not the permanent rate in that case since local officials had acted to adopt the statutory limit. However, in the *Rose* case, no action had been taken by local officials so the formula rates controlled. Any other interpretation, the court held, would have distorted the express purpose of the legislature to return determination of rate limits to local control.[82]

Without doubt, not everyone has been satisfied with the court's ruling in the *Rose* case. Many people still find the laws arbitrary and confusing. Others feel the full value program has never lived up to expectations since the Department of Revenue has not equalized at 100 per cent of full, fair, cash value, and formula limits have only succeeded in tying local fiscal programs to pre-1945 variation in assessment practices.[83] With some transition rates still in effect 20 years after the beginning of the transition period, "maximum permissible rates" are bound to fall unevenly on like communities and the question of the validity of formula limits is still heard despite the court's rulings. As changes have been made in limits and methods for determining them, little effort has been put forth to reexamine the question of tax limits in terms of the effectiveness of the full value program,[84] but there have

---

[81] *Ibid.; People ex rel. Gaston* v. *Southern Ry. Co.,* 21 Ill. 2d. 272 (1961).

[82] *People ex rel, Rose* v. *New York Central R.R. Co., op. cit.*

[83] See: Weil, *op. cit.;* Howards, *op. cit.;* and *Statement of John J. Bresee* (former state's attorney, Champaign County, Illinois), appearing before the Supreme Court on behalf of the City of Champaign and the Policy Committee of the Illinois Municipal League (mimeo), undated, p. 3.

[84] The 1965 General Assembly created a commission to examine tax rate limits and assessment practices. As this is written, it appears that this commission will propose legislation which will raise the limits of major funds in cities where the present limit is below a rate to be stated in the statute. All limits higher than the stated amount will be protected by a "grandfather" clause.

been a number of piecemeal modifications of rates for particular funds. Some of these are discussed in the following section.

Other Modifications of Sections 162a, 162b, and 162c In 1951, section 162c of the Revenue Code[85] reduced rates subject to the General Revenue Law on January 1, 1952, to 80 per cent of the statutory rates. Pre-1946 referendum rates, which had already been reduced by 50 per cent by section 162a (2), were thus further reduced to 40 per cent of the referendum limit. This section was not to interfere with limits set by section 162a or 162b, but was to provide for limitation of funds not otherwise restricted or funds that had been removed from formula restrictions by referenda after 1946. In recognition of the temporary nature of section 162c, the legislature in 1959 amended the section making it applicable only to taxing districts created after January 1, 1952.[86] In effect, the amendment provided restriction for all funds of taxing districts created after 1951 that were not otherwise restricted by section 162b, as amended. Hence, taxing districts created before that date, if not otherwise subject to section 162a or 162b, were now free to extend either statutory limits or their pre-1946 referendum limits for all funds. The legislature appeared to be reversing the court's intepretation in *Krimmel* v. *Eielson* that the expenses of new taxing districts were higher than those of established districts.

Another legislative enactment that eases rate limit restrictiveness was passed in 1963. By exempting referendum general corporate rates from the scaling provisions of section 162c, local voters were allowed to vote a temporary rate increase upon themselves that would not then be reduced to 80 per cent of the amount they had voted. This addition to the Municipal Code indicates simply that the rate limit provisions of the General Revenue Law are not to supersede the referendum provisions for the general corporate fund in the Municipal Code.[87]

Separate amendments have freed specific funds from the Hodge-Downing formulas by exempting them from, or by modifying the operation of, the provisions of one or all three sections of 162. No attempt is made to list all such exemptions or modifications but an account of those affecting municipalities which were passed by the 1965 session of the General Assembly is provided in the following paragraphs.

House Bill 956, passed by the 1965 General Assembly, rewrote and simplified the statutes dealing with the establishment and operation of local libraries in Illinois. This law provides a statutory library rate of

---

[85] *Ill. Rev. Stat.*, ch. 120, sec. 643c (1951).
[86] H.B. 365, 71st General Assembly.
[87] *Laws of Illinois* (1963), pp. 2633-35.

.12 per cent for cities, villages, incorporated towns, and townships and further provides that the rate can be increased to .20 by referendum. The section dealing with city libraries contains no reference to the application of the revenue laws, although such a provision does appear in the section dealing with libraries operated by villages, towns, or townships. The attorney general has ruled that discrimination on the basis of the form of municipal organization is unconstitutional and that the effect of the act is to remove the formula provisions from village and town levies as well as city levies.[88]

Other legislation permitted municipalities whose garbage rate limit on January 1, 1965, was less than .10 per cent to increase such limit by as much as .04 percentage points by action of the corporate authorities taken before December 31, 1965.[89]

The playground and recreation tax levy limit was increased by .12 per cent in 1965, but it was provided that the increase could not exceed .01 per cent in a single year.[90]

---

[88] Opinion of the Attorney General, F 1520, *Libraries, Referendum Required for Increased Tax.*

[89] S.B. 325, 74th General Assembly.

[90] H.B. 1813, H.B. 1814. 74th General Assembly.

5 THE PROPERTY TAX AS A SOURCE OF MUNICIPAL REVENUE

The city official may not be aware of the complex history of the property tax, but he is certainly aware of the close connection between the property tax system and the day-to-day fiscal operations of his municipality. This chapter examines a number of the most important features of the system as seen by the municipal official who is struggling with the problem of financing city government.

PROPERTY TAX FUNDS

Property tax levies are made for particular funds which, in most cases, can be spent only for specified purposes. Transfers within agencies or between sums of money appropriated for specific objects or purposes can be made during the second half of each fiscal year and only by a two-thirds vote of the corporate authorities. The fund structure provides the basic framework within which most municipalities make and report financial decisions.[1]

Data from 188 Illinois cities with 1960 populations of more than 5,000 reveal that the average city levies for eight different funds, although the number runs as high as 16 for a few cities. These are in addition to levies by other governmental units. Table 21 shows the rates levied for ten widely used funds by the 41 largest municipalities in Illinois. An asterisk before a rate indicates that it equals or exceeds the reported rate limits.

---

[1] Municipal budgets, where they exist, are separate and distinct from the appropriation ordinance and have no legal significance insofar as the levy and collection of taxes are concerned. See: Thomas A. Matthews, *How to Levy Taxes for Cities and Villages in Illinois* (Springfield: Illinois Municipal League, 1962), p. 4, and Thomas J. Anton, "Budgeting in Three Illinois Cities" (Urbana: The Institute of Government and Public Affairs, University of Illinois, 1964), p. 5.

The corporate fund is almost always the largest fund and might be called the "general fund" of Illinois municipalities. Expenditures for a number of functions are financed from the corporate fund, and expenditure from the corporate fund often supplements expenditure for a particular function even though a separate fund for that function exists. For example, fire department expenditures may be made from both the corporate fund and the fire protection fund.

The present statutory limit of the corporate fund, established by the Butler Act in 1945, is .333 per cent. This may be increased to .4375 per cent for a period not to exceed five years upon a majority vote in a referendum.[2] However, municipalities incorporated under a special charter are subject to different limitations[3] and the Chicago corporate fund has no limit.

The statutory limit is rarely the limit which actually applies since the corporate fund is subject to the General Revenue Law, as explained in the last chapter. The formula rates established in 1947 as modified by referenda or by appropriate action of corporate authorities in 1951 are the current limits. Corporate funds, as well as others, created after 1952 are scaled to 80 per cent of the statutory limit.

The average corporate limit for the largest 40 cities (Chicago excluded) is .256 per cent. Several municipalities have limits higher than .333 per cent either because the municipality is a special charter municipality (e.g., the town of Cicero) or because higher limits have been approved by referenda. The lowest limit is .102 per cent in Elmhurst. Twenty-seven of the 40 cities subject to corporate fund limit levied the limit in 1960. In addition, three cities had extensions which exceeded the reported limit. All three were in Cook County and involved municipalities for which limit data were obtained from private records.

The public benefit fund is used to pay the portion of the cost of special assessment projects which is assessed against the municipality as a whole. The statutory rate limit is .05 per cent except in certain cities emptying sewerage into Lake Michigan where a larger limit is applicable. The public benefit fund limit is also subject to the General Revenue Law, and thus, to the formula provisions. It is outside the corporate fund limit and may be established by the corporate authorities without a referendum.[4]

The statutory library rate is .12 per cent. Legislation passed in 1965 appears to have freed all municipal library tax levies from the formula

[2] *Ill. Rev. Stat.,* ch. 24, sec. 8-3-1 (1965).
[3] *Ibid.,* ch. 24, sec. 8-3-7 (1965).
[4] *Ill. Rev. Stat.,* ch. 24, secs. 9-2-39, 9-3-49 (1965).

TABLE 21

MUNICIPAL TAX RATES, 1960 LEVY YEAR, 41 ILLINOIS MUNICIPALITIES (in per cent)

	Corporate	Public Benefit	Library	Garbage Disposal	Fire Protection	Street and Bridge	Bonds and Interest	Police Pension	Fire Pension	Illinois Mun. Retirement Fund	All Other Funds	Total Municipal
Municipalities Outside Chicago SMSA												
Alton	*.265[a]	—	.058	*.080	—	.081	—	.031	.015	.043	.196	.769
Belleville	*.206	—	.063	.062	*.062	*.063	.095	.050	.024	.038	.070	.733
Bloomington	*.195	.050	.066	*.053	*.100	*.054	.075	.032	.048	.074	.051	.798
Champaign	.122	.008	.053	.013	.145	.078	.012	.015	.009	.073	.187	.715
Danville	*.438	—	.106	*.081	.030	—	.135	.048	.042	.042	.138	1.060
Decatur	.164	.019	.110	—	*.049	*.008	—	.017	.019	.038	.048	.472
East St. Louis	*.246	—	.045	*.067	*.067	*.068	.355	.029	.043	—	.011	.931
Freeport	*.260	*.036	*.120	.071	—	.071	.103	.018	.020	.027	.057	.783
Galesburg	*.204	—	.083	*.078	—	*.079	.258	.050	.031	.047	.089	.919
Granite City	.258	—	.052	*.080	.131	.058	—	.020	.022	.025	.024	.670
Kankakee	*.188	*.025	.042	*.051	*.051	—	.054	.019	.027	.038	.027	.522
Moline	.332	*.029	.105	*.080	*.056	.049	.025	.035	.015	.040	.093	.859
Pekin	.189	*.027	.119	.065	.200	.071	.071	.013	.009	.038	.065	.867
Peoria	*.169	.018	.116	.067	*.064	*.051	.009	.033	.030	.031	.217	.805
Quincy	*.296	—	*.054	*.045	—	*.091	.359	.016	.008	.028	—	.897
Rockford	*.180	*.025	.082	.048	—	.010	.044	.044	.030	.099	.039	.601
Rock Island	*.212	*.030	.090	*.059	*.059	.057	.014	.022	.033	.053	.179	.808
Springfield	*.213	*.029	.133	.059	*.059	*.059	.089	.075	.047	.050	.063	.876
Urbana	.173	.009	.078	.018	.097	.060	.283	.017	.010	.052	.098	.895
Average	.227	.016	.083	.057	.062	.053	.104	.031	.025	.044	.087	.788
Municipalities in Chicago SMSA												
Arlington Hgts.	*.233	.031	.064	—	—	—	.048	.018	—	.024	—	.418
Aurora	*.166	.010	.085	*.050	*.050	.009	.029	.032	.021	.042	.159	.653
Berwyn	*.238	—	.041	.063	—	.064	.019	.047	.021	.035	.070	.598
Calumet City	.176	—	.049	*.065	—	.024	.171	.015	.002	.049	.009	.560
Chicago Hgts.	*.239	—	.084	.063	—	—	.060	.044	.019	.045	.162	.716

TABLE 21 (continued)

MUNICIPAL TAX RATES, 1960 LEVY YEAR, 41 ILLINOIS MUNICIPALITIES (in per cent)

	Corporate	Public Benefit	Library	Garbage Disposal	Fire Protection	Street and Bridge	Bonds and Interest	Police Pension	Fire Pension	Illinois Mun. Retirement Fund	All Other Funds	Total Municipal
Cicero	*.683	—	*.045	—	—	—	.071	—	—	.029	.014	.842
Des Plaines	.222	.014	*.074	—	*.065	—	.051	.007	.003	.032	.020	.488
Elgin	*.182	*.050	—	*.050	*.050	.009	.033	.019	.009	.051	.093	.546
Elmhurst	*.102	—	.063	*.031	*.031	*.044	.021	.015	.011	.031	.002	.351
Evanston	.376	—	.079	.057	—	.057	.150	.047	—	.060	.116	.942
Harvey	*.330	—	.044	*.065	—	—	.225	.045	.017	.028	.002	.756
Highland Park	*.136	.022	.114	.020	—	*.038	.117	.031	.038	.032	.055	.603
Joliet	*.296	*.040	.082	*.043	—	—	.010	.010	.015	.058	.117	.671
Maywood	*.239	*.040	.065	—	*.111	*.061	—	.041	.033	.063	.047	.700
Oak Lawn	*.217	—	.062	*.065	.091	—	.036	.014	—	.019	.010	.514
Oak Park	*.339	—	*.080	*.065	—	.074	—	.031	.031	.054	.046	.720
Park Forest	*.333	—	*.100	—	*.116	—	.098	.004	—	.029	.146	.826
Park Ridge	*.338	.013	.068	*.077	—	—	.075	.019	.005	.029	.002	.626
Skokie	*.239	.008	*.067	*.065	—	—	.077	.009	—	.034	.001	.500
Waukegan	*.284	.013	.079	*.060	*.038	*.018	.010	.033	.017	.025	.063	.640
Wilmette	.240	—	.095	.069	—	—	.059	.018	.005	.051	.053	.590
Average	.267	.011	.069	.043	.026	.019	.065	.024	.012	.039	.057	.631
Chicago	.834	—	.072	—	—	—	.315	.085	.071	.124	.225	1.726

[a] An asterisk before rate indicates it equals or exceeds reported rate limits.

SOURCE *Illinois Municipal Review* (June, 1962), and data gathered from Illinois county clerks and private files.

provisions of the General Revenue Law.[5] The rate may be increased to .20 by referendum. An additional tax not to exceed .0833 per cent may be levied for purchase or repair of sites, buildings, or equipment. No referendum is required, even if bonds are issued.[6]

The garbage disposal tax of .10 per cent which may be levied without referendum is subject to formula scaling and is in addition to the corporate fund. The statutes regulating the garbage disposal levy allow municipalities to jointly operate garbage disposal facilities. A 1965 amendment allowed municipalities with a garbage tax limit of less than .10 per cent to increase their limit by .04 per cent by action of the corporate authorities taken before December 31, 1965.[7]

The fire protection tax is another addition to the corporate fund and is subject to referendum. The formula provisions of the General Revenue Law apply. The statutory limits had been .20 per cent, subject to the General Revenue Law, but a 1963 amendment allows any municipality that in 1960 levied at least .20 per cent to extend their levy to .30 per cent without referendum, and from .30 per cent to .40 per cent on the basis of a referendum.[8] These conditions are met in few municipalities. Property in a fire protection district which is annexed to the city is subject to a special district levy and not to the municipal fire protection tax.

The street and bridge tax is used for street and bridge purposes within the municipality. Municipalities which contain an entire township or road district within their boundaries may levy a tax up to .06 per cent. An additional .04166 per cent may be levied upon a favorable vote of three-fourths of the corporate authorities. The formula provisions of the General Revenue Law apply. If the municipality does not contain an entire township or road district within its boundaries, it may levy a similar amount; however, the municipality receives one-half of the tax levied by the township or road district upon property within the corporate limits and the county clerk abates an equivalent amount of the municipal tax.[9] Several additional levies can be made if approved by referendum.

The bond and interest fund receives the proceeds of tax levies which are used to pay principal and interest upon bonds issued by the municipality. There is no limit upon the levies for this purpose but bond

---

[5] *Ibid.*, ch. 81, sec. 3-1-4; Opinion of the Attorney General, F 1520, *Libraries, Referendum Required for Increased Tax.*

[6] *Ill. Rev. Stat.*, ch. 81, secs. 5-2, 5-3 (1965).

[7] *Ibid.*, ch. 24, sec. 11-19-4 (1965).

[8] *Ibid.*, ch. 24, secs. 11-7-1–11-7-3 (1965).

[9] *Ibid.*, ch. 24, secs. 11-81-1, 11-81-2; ch. 121, sec. 6-507 (1965).

issues must be approved by referendum. Taxes to pay the principal and interest due during the years the bond will be outstanding are levied when the bonds are issued and the county clerk extends the necessary taxes each year until the obligation is retired, but these levies may be abated if other funds are used to pay the bond service obligations.

Current law and practices in the financing of police and fire pension funds were discussed in Chapter 2. Tax levies to pay the municipal portion of contributions to these funds are limited to the amount needed to meet the annual requirements of the funds.[10]

The Illinois Municipal Retirement Fund covers municipal employees other than policemen and firemen in municipalities other than Chicago which have a population of 10,000 or more. Smaller municipalities may elect coverage by referendum or ordinance. This fund is administered by a board of trustees which determines the municipal contribution from a formula provided in the statutes. The municipal tax levy is limited to the amount required to produce the necessary contribution.[11]

Many of the funds for which property taxes can be levied have not been discussed or listed separately in Table 21. Most of those funds grouped under "all other funds" in Table 21 are enumerated in Table 17. Few of these funds can be levied without prior approval by referendum and in a number of cases, a particular fund may have its own limit but still be included in the corporate fund and its limit for levy purposes.

THE PROPERTY TAX CALENDAR

Another parameter in the property tax system that concerns the municipal official is the property tax calendar. Before a municipality may levy a property tax, it must first enact and publish a detailed appropriation ordinance for those sums of money necessary to meet anticipated expenditures for the fiscal year.[12] The appropriation ordinance must contain a detailed, item-by-item classification of expenditure, and, generally, no expenditures may be made during the year which have not been anticipated in the appropriation ordinance.[13] After the appropriation ordinance is enacted and published, a property tax levy ordinance is enacted. The levy ordinance is certified to the county clerk by a specified date, and he extends the tax over the taxable property in the municipality.

Much confusion arises from the fact that the property tax adminis-

---

[10] *Ibid.*, ch. 108½, secs. 3-125, 4-118 (1965).
[11] *Ibid.*, ch. 108½, sec. 7-171 (1965).
[12] *Ibid.*, ch. 24, sec. 8-2-9 (1965).
[13] Matthews, *op. cit.*, p. 4.

trative cycle is long and not well coordinated with the budgeting and expenditure process of a municipality. There is often question as to which year's taxes are related to the expenditure of a given fiscal year. This problem is illustrated in Table 22 which relates a simplified tax calendar to the fiscal year of a municipality, using the very common May 1 to April 30 fiscal year. Assessment for 1966 taxes takes place as of January 1 for real estate and April 1 for personal property. The fiscal year of the municipality begins on May 1. By usual custom and the practices of the U.S. Census Bureau, a fiscal year is identified by the year in which it ends. Thus, the year used as an example in the table is fiscal year 1967. The appropriation ordinance for the 1966 tax year must be passed during the first three months of the fiscal year. The levy ordinance must be passed at least ten days after the appropriation ordinance is adopted and published but before the second Tuesday in September. Thus the appropriation and levy ordinances may be passed several months after the beginning of the fiscal year. The tax bills are sent out by the county clerk around April 1 and the fiscal year ends before there has been any substantial collection of property taxes for that year. Most of the 1966 taxes are collected in the 1968 fiscal year.

This situation creates confusion in the mind of the citizen who tries to understand the municipal financial process and also creates problems for municipal officials who must finance the operation of municipal government pending the collection of taxes. Probably the most com-

TABLE 22

PROPERTY TAX CALENDAR FOR A MUNICIPALITY WITH FISCAL YEAR BEGINNING ON MAY 1

1966 real property assessment day	January 1, 1966
1966 personal property assessment day	April 1, 1966
1967 fiscal year begins	May 1, 1966
Appropriation ordinance	May 1, 1966 to July 31, 1966
Levy ordinance	10 days after appropriation ordinance is published until 2nd Tuesday in September, 1966
1966 tax bills sent out by county clerk	April 1, 1967
1967 fiscal year ends	April 30, 1967
1968 fiscal year begins	May 1, 1967
1966 personal property taxes and first installment real estate taxes become delinquent	June 1, 1967[a]
Second installment 1966 real estate taxes become delinquent	September 1, 1967

[a] May 1 in Cook County.

mon method of doing this is through the sale of tax anticipation warrants. The statutes permit the sale of tax anticipation warrants in amounts up to 75 per cent of the amount of taxes levied although bond attorneys and investment houses sometimes insist upon a smaller percentage. The interest rate is limited to 6 per cent.

The statutes also provide that municipalities may establish a revolving fund known as a working cash fund. Money is transferred on a loan basis from this fund to the general and special funds of the municipality to meet expenses pending property tax collections.

In order to establish a working cash fund, the statutes provide for the issue of bonds in an amount not to exceed $400,000.[14] These bonds may be authorized, and the taxes necessary to repay them may be levied by the corporate authorities, without referendum.[15] Municipalities which have not issued the maximum amount of bonds to establish a working cash fund may also levy an annual tax for the purpose of providing money for the working cash fund. There is a statutory limit of .05 per cent and the limit is subject to the formula provisions of the General Revenue Law. The working cash fund levy need not be included in the appropriation ordinance, and no tax anticipation warrants may be issued against it.

THE TAX BASE

Although the financial procedures which are imposed by the property tax system play important roles in the financial decision-making process, the size of the property tax base is of even more importance. This, in turn, is determined by the amount of taxable property within the municipality and the level at which it is assessed and equalized.

The Quality of Assessment The quality of property tax assessment not only influences the total assessed value which can be taxed by a municipality, but also has important indirect influences upon the tax process. High quality assessment not only insures that tax burdens will be distributed uniformly among property owners but increases taxpayer respect for local government.

Unfortunately, assessment in Illinois is not generally of high quality. As indicated in Chapter 3, assessment organization in many counties is not well suited to the complex technical job of assessing modern property.

Professor Leo Cohen's analysis of tax uniformity within Madison and

[14] Eight million dollars for Chicago.

[15] *Ill. Rev. Stat.,* ch. 24, secs. 8-7-2, 8-7-3 (1965).

St. Clair counties probably illustrates the type of inequities that exist in most of the counties and taxing districts in the state. He found that:

1. Assessment inequality increased as the level of local assessment decreased.
2. Improved properties, whether rural or urban, are generally assessed at higher levels.
3. The parcel of property within a municipality will tend to be assessed higher than a similar parcel in an unincorporated area.
4. Regressive assessment is common. That is, as the value of the property increases, it is assessed at a lower percentage of its market value.
5. Incentives for competitive underassessment among taxing districts is built into the formulas for state subventions, particularly to school districts.[16]

Other indications of poor assessment are found in the results of the 1962 Census of Governments. Table 23 shows the coefficients of dispersion, a measure of the equality of assessment within the county. The figures are the average percentage by which assessments differ from

TABLE 23

U.S. BUREAU OF THE CENSUS COEFFICIENTS OF DISPERSION FOR NONFARM, SINGLE FAMILY HOUSES IN SELECTED COUNTIES, 1961

County	Coefficient of Dispersion
McLean	13.7
La Salle	15.1
Lake	16.2
Du Page	16.9
Kane	19.2
Winnebago	21.6
Champaign	21.8
Madison	22.4
Rock Island	24.1
Sangamon	24.5
Cook (entire county)	26.1
Will	26.7
Knox	28.0
Tazewell	28.8
McHenry	30.1
Peoria	31.6
Macon	32.3
Chicago (city only)	32.4
St. Clair	33.5
Whiteside	36.3

SOURCE U.S. Bureau of the Census, *Census of Governments: 1962,* Vol. II, Table 22.

[16] Leo Cohen, *Intra-County Tax Uniformity in Madison and St. Clair Counties, Illinois* (Edwardsville: Public Administration and Metropolitan Affairs Program, Southern Illinois University, 1965), pp. 6, 22, 30, 37, 41-42.

the median ratio. Students of property tax assessment often state that a coefficient of 15 or 20 per cent represents a "good" assessment but even this figure represents a considerable amount of inequality in assessment. Larger coefficients, such as the 36.2 per cent in Whiteside County, represent extremely inequitable assessments.

If the data in Table 23 seem shocking, a greater shock is in store when it is recalled that they are based upon nonfarm, single family houses, probably the easiest type of property to assess. Specialized real properties and properties of a type which seldom sell are much more difficult to assess than a single family house. The quality of personal property assessment is, of course, even worse. The values assigned to personal property often bear no relationship to true values.

The Size and Composition of the Tax Base For the most part, the municipal official has no control over the assessment process and must accept the property tax base as given, at least in the short run. Table 24 provides a general picture of the composition of the property tax base in the state and within SMSA's. From these data it would seem that about one-half of the tax base in a typical municipality consists of

TABLE 24

THE ILLINOIS PROPERTY TAX BASE, 1961

	Amount (in millions)		Per Cent of Total	
	State	SMSA's Only	State	SMSA's Only
Residential Real Estate	$15,086	$12,853	43.3	50.2
Acreages and Farms	4,487	1,106	12.9	4.3
Vacant Lots	684	619	2.0	2.4
Commercial Real Estate	3,197	2,757	9.2	10.8
Industrial Real Estate	3,245	2,952	9.3	11.5
Other Locally Assessed Real Estate[a]	351	16	1.0	.1
Total Real Estate	27,050	20,305	77.6	79.3
State Assessed Property	1,602	914	4.6	3.6
Personal Property	6,206	4,393	17.8	17.2
Tangible Commercial and Industrial	3,793	NA[b]	10.9	
Agricultural	291	NA	.8	
Household	403	NA	1.2	
Motor Vehicle	938	NA	2.7	
Other Tangible Personalty	299	NA	.9	
Intangible Property	483	NA	1.4	
Grand Total	$34,858	$25,612	100.0	100.0

[a] Largely separately assessed mineral rights.

[b] NA indicates data are not available.

SOURCE U.S. Bureau of the Census, *Census of Governments: 1962,* II, 30, 32, 154.

residential real property. The other half is divided among several classes of property including vacant lots, commercial and industrial real estate, and business and nonbusiness personal property. The complete breakdown of the assessment of intangible personal property is indicated by the very small amount of such property that is assessed.[17]

Statewide data give only a hint as to the nature of the tax base of a given city since it is clear that there is much variation in the composition and size of the tax base. Column 4 of Table 25 indicates the variation in the size of the tax base that occurs among the 41 larger cities.

TABLE 25

PER CAPITA EQUALIZED ASSESSED VALUE, 41 ILLINOIS MUNICIPALITIES, 1960 TAX YEAR

	Real Estate	Personalty	Railroads	Total
Municipalities Outside Chicago SMSA				
Alton	$2,148	$ 693	$ 41	$2,882
Belleville	2,243	718	27	2,988
Bloomington	2,562	735	53	3,350
Champaign	2,183	553	8	2,744
Danville	1,818	481	55	2,353
Decatur	2,470	615	57	3,142
East St. Louis	1,485	581	233	2,271
Freeport	2,184	753	16	2,953
Galesburg	2,020	598	115	2,733
Granite City	2,079	1,421	45	3,545
Kankakee	2,374	642	33	3,049
Moline	2,621	1,036	49	3,706
Pekin	1,893	866	66	2,825
Peoria	3,098	1,197	50	4,346
Quincy	1,993	1,643	21	3,657
Rockford	2,924	1,066	32	4,023
Rock Island	2,257	823	44	3,124
Springfield	2,471	516	56	3,043
Urbana	1,743	419	20	2,182
Average	2,239	808	54	3,101
Municipalities in Chicago SMSA				
Arlington Hgts.	2,610	359	13	2,982
Aurora	2,522	948	42	3,512
Berwyn	2,312	229	31	2,574
Calumet City	1,805	160	65	2,030
Chicago Hgts.	2,273	649	107	3,028
Cicero	2,829	825	135	3,789
Des Plaines	2,532	324	22	2,878
Elgin	2,297	633	17	2,947

[17] For a detailed study of the assessment of personal property see: H. K. Allen, "General Property Tax," Chapter XII, *Report of the Commission on Revenue* (Springfield: 1963).

TABLE 25 (continued)

PER CAPITA EQUALIZED ASSESSED VALUE, 41 ILLINOIS MUNICIPALITIES, 1960 TAX YEAR

	Real Estate	Personalty	Railroads	Total
Elmhurst	$3,581	$316	$ 20	$3,917
Evanston	3,218	388	16	3,622
Harvey	2,050	472	23	2,545
Highland Park	4,908	466	51	5,426
Joliet	2,089	430	117	2,636
Maywood	2,209	675	21	2,905
Oak Lawn	2,313	199	9	2,521
Oak Park	2,988	435	12	3,435
Park Forest	1,993	226	15	2,234
Park Ridge	3,234	314	10	3,558
Skokie	3,946	485	10	4,441
Waukegan	2,914	947	38	3,899
Wilmette	3,719	489	13	4,221
Average	2,778	475	37	3,290
Chicago	2,259	615	69	2,943

SOURCE *Illinois Municipal Review* (June, 1962).

Per capita assessed value varies from a high of $5,426 in Highland Park to a low of $2,030 in Calumet City. Even greater variation occurs in smaller cities. Data from a recent study of Madison and St. Clair counties indicate the tremendous variations which occur in these counties.[18] The greatest extremes occur in St. Clair County, where the per capita assessed value ranged from $1,002 in Centreville to $180,522 in nearby Monsanto. These differences in the size of the base are closely related to differences in the composition of the tax base. Monsanto is the location of a large industrial plant but contains few people, while Centreville is a low income residential city. Unfortunately, data which would permit systematic study of the relationship between composition of tax base and its size are not available. The breakdown of the tax base into real estate, personalty, and railroad property of Table 25 only hints at the substantial variations in composition which exist.

OTHER CLAIMS ON THE TAX BASE

Municipalities are only one of several kinds of local government which utilize the property tax. Table 26 indicates that in the average

[18] Leo Cohen, *Comparative Fiscal Capacity and Tax Effort of Units of Government in Madison and St. Clair Counties, Illinois, 1950-1960* (Edwardsville: Public Administration and Metropolitan Affairs Program, Southern Illinois University, 1963), pp. 85, 87, 89, 91.

large municipality outside the Chicago SMSA municipal levies make up 23 per cent of the total tax levy. In the suburban areas of northeastern Illinois the average is only 14.5 per cent. The city of Chicago, on the other hand, receives 37 per cent of the property taxes paid by its taxpayers.

It is difficult to determine just how much effect the levies of over-

TABLE 26

TAX RATES, 41 ILLINOIS MUNICIPALITIES, 1960 TAX YEAR

	Municipal (per cent)	School (per cent)	All Other (per cent)	Total (per cent)	Municipal as Per Cent of Total
Municipalities Outside Chicago SMSA					
Alton	.769	2.019	.416	3.204	24.0
Belleville	.733	2.337	.417	3.487	21.0
Bloomington	.798	1.877	.452	3.127	25.5
Champaign	.715	2.178	.674	3.567	20.0
Danville	1.060	2.080	.646	3.786	28.0
Decatur	.472	2.550	.728	3.750	12.6
East St. Louis	.931	2.210	1.152	4.293	21.7
Freeport	.783	2.043	.610	3.436	22.8
Galesburg	.919	1.805	.464	3.188	28.8
Granite City	.670	2.220	.776	3.666	18.3
Kankakee	.522	2.095	.598	3.215	16.2
Moline	.859	2.299	.421	3.579	24.0
Pekin	.867	2.173	.392	3.432	25.3
Peoria	.805	1.590	.520	2.915	27.6
Quincy	.897	1.677	.434	3.008	29.8
Rockford	.601	1.768	.637	3.006	20.0
Rock Island	.808	1.818	.472	3.098	26.1
Springfield	.876	1.891	.679	3.446	25.4
Urbana	.895	2.417	.749	4.061	22.0
Average	.788	2.055	.591	3.435	23.1
Municipalities in Chicago SMSA					
Arlington Hgts.	.418	3.326	1.016	4.760	8.8
Aurora	.654	2.216	.491	3.360	19.4
Berwyn	.598	2.255	.902	3.755	15.9
Calumet City	.560	3.151	.929	4.640	12.1
Chicago Hgts.	.716	3.002	.884	4.602	15.6
Cicero	.842	2.060	.914	3.816	22.1
Des Plaines	.488	3.202	.982	4.672	10.4
Elgin	.546	2.489	.647	3.682	14.8
Elmhurst	.311	2.773	.486	3.570	8.7
Evanston	.942	2.788	.790	4.520	20.8
Harvey	.756	3.430	.844	5.030	15.0
Highland Park	.603	3.430	.668	4.701	12.8
Joliet	.671	2.463	.441	3.575	18.8
Maywood	.700	3.156	.773	4.629	15.1
Oak Lawn	.514	3.775	.922	5.211	9.9

TABLE 26 (continued)

TAX RATES, 41 ILLINOIS MUNICIPALITIES, 1960 TAX YEAR

	Municipal (per cent)	School (per cent)	All Other (per cent)	Total (per cent)	Municipal as Per Cent of Total
Oak Park	.720	2.720	.910	4.350	16.6
Park Forest	.826	4.162	.657	5.645	14.6
Park Ridge	.626	3.200	.967	4.793	13.1
Skokie	.500	2.490	1.149	4.139	12.1
Waukegan	.640	2.827	.643	4.110	15.6
Wilmette	.590	3.018	.890	4.498	13.1
Average	.630	2.949	.805	4.384	14.5
Chicago	1.726	1.850	1.092	4.668	37.0

SOURCE See Appendix B.

lapping units have upon the revenue capacity of a municipality, but it seems likely that municipalities find it more difficult to raise rates when the overlapping levies are high. Most city officials feel that the possibility of a successful tax rate or bond issue referendum is greatly reduced for several months following a referendum by an overlapping unit of government. There is also a strong feeling that referenda for school purposes are much more apt to be successful than are municipal referenda.

Several municipalities have found it advantageous to follow the policy of cooperating with other units, especially schools, in the scheduling of referenda. In a few cases, municipalities have even agreed to forgo increases in municipal property tax rates in an effort to aid school districts which have no source of nonproperty tax revenue.

THE ROLE OF MUNICIPAL OFFICIALS

The Illinois property tax system, as it has been described in this and the two preceding chapters, is very complex. The constitutional, statutory, and judicial laws which define the procedures which must be followed by tax-levying bodies are numerous and sometimes conflicting.

These "rules of the game" are the result of many past decisions which have become crystallized into the law and custom of property taxation. They require or permit many persons to have a role in the levy and collection of current taxes.

The typical municipal official does not find it possible or necessary to understand fully the entire system. Upon election or appointment to a position of responsibility in the municipal finance process, he is likely to perceive a rather limited number of alternative responses to the particular situation which the municipality faces.

Typically, a municipal official will find that the municipality is levying property taxes for several different funds. There is a better than even chance that several of the more important special funds are being levied at the maximum legal rate. Current levies for the bond and interest fund and for the pension funds are largely or entirely out of the control of municipal officials. While it is likely that the heads of many municipal departments are able to make convincing cases that more money is needed, if the official inquires of the corporation counsel, he will be told that the legal limits on tax funds can be increased by means of a referendum and that there are a number of other special funds which the city could levy after a referendum. Older hands around city hall will probably tell him that the chances of a successful referendum to increase the corporate fund limit are small, but that it might be possible to get an increase in one of the special funds or authority to levy for a fund not now being levied, if the service to be financed is a popular one. Even this, however, requires an all-out effort to sell the voters on the idea. The accuracy of this advice is indicated by Table 27. In the 169 cities from which data concerning rate limit referenda were received, only 48 referenda were held in a five-year period and only 14 of these were successful. In the same years, there were 115 bond issues submitted to the voters of which 84 were passed. Several of the bond issues, however, were revenue bonds or street improvement bonds which are repaid from the revenues of the facility to be built or from motor vehicle tax funds and thus involved no increase in property tax rates.

The new official will also discover that the municipality has little control over the assessment and collection process and that little can be done if either of these jobs is poorly performed.

Under these circumstances it is not surprising that in many municipalities the role of the corporate authorities in the property tax process is rather passive. Taxes are levied for existing funds and levies are calculated so as to produce the maximum legal rate or a rate equal to or slightly higher than the rate of the prior year. A considerable amount of care is taken to insure that the appropriation and tax levy ordinances are in correct legal form. Given the uncertainties of the law in this area, this usually is best accomplished by making as few changes from the prior year as possible.

There are, on the other hand, cases in which municipal officials are well informed about the property tax system and take a positive and active role. If a municipal official is well informed about the property tax system, he can, in some instances, have an effect upon matters which are often assumed to be outside his control. For example, an

TABLE 27

TAX RATE REFERENDA, ILLINOIS MUNICIPALITIES, 1959-64

Municipality	Year	Fund	Carried	Lost
Bartonville	1962	Police protection		X
Bensenville	1964	Library		X
Cairo	1960	Police protection		X
Calumet City	1963	Police protection		X
	1963	Fire protection		X
Champaign	1963	Police protection		X
	1963	Fire protection		X
Clarendon Hills	1960	Corporate		X
	1961	Fire protection	X	
Creve Coeur	1960	Corporate		X
	1962	Corporate		X
	1962	Corporate		X
	1962	Corporate	X	
Deerfield	1963	Police protection		X
Elgin	1960	Forestry		X
Elmhurst	1961	Police protection	X	
Elmwood Park	1963	Fire protection	X	
Hinsdale	1959	Community building		X
	1959	Fire protection		X
	1959	Forestry		X
	1959	Parks		X
	1959	Police protection		X
	1961	Street lighting		X
	1961	Fire protection		X
	1961	Police protection		X
	1961	Corporate		X
	1964	Corporate	X	
Kewanee	1963	Fire protection		X
	1963	Airport authority	X	
Macomb	1963	Fire protection		X
	1963	Police protection		X
	1963	Forestry		X
Moline	1962	Park and recreation		X
	1963	Park, playground, & recreation		X
Naperville	1961	Fire protection		X
Ottawa	1961	Forestry		X
River Forest	1964	Corporate	X	
Rockford	1960	Forestry		X
	1962	Forestry	X	
Rock Island	1963	Fire protection		X
	1963	Police protection		X
	1964	Fire protection	X	
	1964	Police protection	X	
Villa Park	1961	Recreation	X	
Western Springs	1964	Corporate	X	
Westmont	1963	Police protection		X
Wilmette	1961	Corporate	X	
Worth	1963	Library	X	

SOURCE Questionnaires sent to city clerks and managers of 201 cities over 5,000 population. Tabulation based on 169 replies.

official who is knowledgeable about the rate limit situation may be able to extend taxes at a rate higher than the accepted limit. This is sometimes accomplished by proving the accepted limit was incorrect. In other cases higher limits have been achieved by negotiating and compromising disputed points of law with the county clerk, attorneys for protesting taxpayers, and bond attorneys.[19]

In some municipalities, officials also attempt to influence the size and composition of the tax base. This may be accomplished by such short-run tactics as persuading or pressuring the local assessor to follow a particular policy with regard to the assessment of certain classes of property. It may also include a campaign to sell owners of property eligible for annexation upon the advantages of being within the corporate limits. This policy has been followed with considerable success in several of the cities included in the 41-city group. In fact, two of these cities, Peoria and Decatur, have carried out large annexation programs which have greatly increased their area, population, and tax base. In other cities there have been many smaller and less spectacular annexation programs — sometimes involving annexation of single lots. It is true, of course, that annexation increases municipal costs as well as revenue. Whether it represents a net financial gain to the municipality depends upon the nature of the area annexed, the amount of new facilities and services which must be provided to the newly annexed areas, and other factors.

Longer range aspects of a campaign to increase the tax base may include industrial development programs, which may or may not include negotiations over assessment levels. In a number of cities housing code enforcement, urban renewal programs, and zoning laws have the maintenance or building up of the tax base as one of their goals. Many municipal governments carry out continuing or special programs intended to inform taxpayers as to the financial affairs of the municipality and to build support for tax limits or bond issue referenda.

Although the need for revenue often means that active municipal policies in the property tax field are directed toward increasing property tax collections, it is also possible that a municipality may have a policy of decreasing property taxes. One sizable downstate city is pursuing a policy of de-emphasizing property taxes and at least some of the officials of that city envision complete elimination of property taxes as a method of municipal finance.

---

[19] In the article, "The Politics of Property Taxation," *Administrative Science Quarterly,* Vol. 12, No. 1 (June, 1967), pp. 48-71, the authors describe such negotiation in more detail. It is noted in that article that opening the issue as to the proper rate limit involves danger that the final result could be a lower rate.

6 NONPROPERTY TAX REVENUE

Although the property tax is still an important source of revenue for municipalities, they receive a smaller percentage of total revenue from property taxes than does any other level of government in Illinois. Furthermore, municipalities are the only type of local government which receives substantial sums from nonproperty taxes. As indicated in Table 28, counties, townships, and school districts receive a higher proportion of general revenue in the form of intergovernmental grants but receive very little from nonproperty taxes. Charges and miscellaneous general revenues are most important as sources of revenue for special districts and municipalities.

MUNICIPAL REVENUE PATTERNS

Table 29 shows the 1962 revenue receipts for the 41 largest cities by major source in per capita terms. These data are noncommercial general revenues only and do not include current charges from those operations which are designated as semi-commercial in Chapter 2 nor from those operations classified as utility expenditure by the U.S. Census Bureau. Examination of these data reveals that property tax collections ranged from a low of $12.85 per capita in Elmhurst to $43.97 per capita in Chicago. The average for the 41 cities was $22.54 per capita. Some idea of the importance of the tax in financial decisions can be gained by viewing the data on a percentage basis. Property taxes made up as much as 62.9 per cent of total general revenue in Quincy and as little as 21.1 per cent in Oak Lawn, with an average of 43.0 per cent.

Nonproperty taxes provide a low of $7.11 in Granite City and a high of $28.46 in Chicago. In the average city, nonproperty taxes provided 25.8 per cent of total revenues.

TABLE 28

LOCAL GOVERNMENT GENERAL REVENUE BY MAJOR SOURCE, ILLINOIS, 1962[a]

Source	Municipalities	Counties	Townships	School Districts	Special Districts	All Local Units
			(in millions)			
Property Taxes	$248	$122	$48	$ 767	$130	$1,314
Other Taxes	159	8	1	—	—	167
Charges and Miscellaneous Revenue	120	30	2	68	59	279
Intergovernmental Revenue	93	118	14	213	15	453
Total	$621	$277	$65	$1,048	$204	$2,214
			(per cent)			
Property Taxes	40.0	43.9	73.7	73.2	63.7	59.4
Other Taxes	25.6	2.8	1.0	—	—	7.5
Charges and Miscellaneous Revenue	19.4	10.8	3.1	6.5	28.9	12.6
Intergovernmental Revenue	15.0	42.5	22.3	20.3	7.4	20.5
Total	100.0	100.0	100.0	100.0	100.0	100.0

[a] These data are based on the U.S. Census Bureau definition of general expenditure. They do not include utility revenue but do include gross revenue from sources classified as semi-commercial elsewhere in this volume.

SOURCE U.S. Bureau of the Census, *Census of Governments: 1962*, Vol. VII, No. 13, p. 26.

TABLE 29

PER CAPITA GENERAL REVENUE COLLECTIONS BY MAJOR SOURCES, 41 ILLINOIS MUNICIPALITIES, 1962 FISCAL YEAR

	Total	Property Taxes	Nonproperty Taxes: General Sales Tax	Nonproperty Taxes: Motor Vehicle Licenses	Nonproperty Taxes: Liquor Licenses	Nonproperty Taxes: All Other	All Other Revenue
Municipalities Outside Chicago SMSA							
Alton	$54.25	$16.98	$7.51	$1.70	$ .86	$3.62	$23.58
Belleville	42.85	16.93	7.69	1.73	1.26	1.19	14.05
Bloomington	63.66	24.60	9.70	2.87	1.21	2.61	22.67
Champaign	46.17	18.71	8.07	—	.58	.82	17.99
Danville	40.68	24.07	8.79	—	1.25	1.28	5.29
Decatur	43.33	15.25	8.35	—	1.26	1.51	16.96
East St. Louis	64.19	18.00	6.39	1.18	1.80	7.48	29.34
Freeport	44.83	23.10	7.81	—	1.54	.71	11.67
Galesburg	48.81	28.16	6.92	1.76	1.05	.40	10.52
Granite City	42.50	24.96	5.10	1.00	.45	.56	10.43
Kankakee	57.11	16.31	11.38	.22	1.70	1.37	26.13
Moline	73.78	31.09	7.86	1.71	1.77	1.50	29.85
Pekin	47.87	23.68	6.53	—	.75	.30	16.61
Peoria	58.56	33.83	10.82	—	1.22	2.02	10.67
Quincy	50.05	31.47	7.23	—	1.27	.54	9.54
Rockford	51.68	25.29	9.65	4.19	1.44	2.73	8.38
Rock Island	65.49	24.21	5.57	1.58	1.99	1.71	30.43
Springfield	67.91	25.22	9.32	—	1.45	2.33	29.59
Urbana	33.19	18.30	4.49	1.47	.62	.81	7.50
Average	52.47	23.17	7.85	1.02	1.24	1.76	17.43
Municipalities in Chicago SMSA							
Arlington Hgts.	44.92	12.68	6.61	2.75	.64	4.90	17.34
Aurora	49.99	23.28	8.90	1.21	1.09	1.16	14.35
Berwyn	31.62	15.50	7.22	—	1.25[a]	2.16	5.49
Calumet City	41.56	14.48	3.73	3.63	6.17	3.42	10.13
Chicago Hgts.	46.06	20.99	9.03	2.57	1.70	4.68	7.13

TABLE 29 (continued)

PER CAPITA GENERAL REVENUE COLLECTIONS BY MAJOR SOURCES, 41 ILLINOIS MUNICIPALITIES, 1962 FISCAL YEAR

			Nonproperty Taxes				
	Total	Property Taxes	General Sales Tax	Motor Vehicle Licenses	Liquor Licenses	All Other	All Other Revenue
Cicero	$ 62.12	$36.23	$ 7.88	$1.80	$2.24	$ 1.59	$12.38
Des Plaines	47.81	14.33	8.47	3.44	.78	4.48	16.31
Elgin	40.40	17.13	8.80	.16	.71	1.06	12.54
Elmhurst	41.41	12.85	6.33	2.22	.46	1.22	18.33
Evanston	65.05	32.50	7.90	5.78	—	3.01	15.86
Harvey	53.32	18.39	7.83	2.70	—	3.63	20.77
Highland Park	71.76	30.84	7.46	6.56	—	2.35	24.55
Joliet	42.51	18.54	9.93	1.16	2.17	.67	10.04
Maywood	44.77	18.96	5.04	3.70	.04	3.28	13.75
Oak Lawn	63.66	13.45	8.66	2.77	.42	4.46	33.90
Oak Park	55.45	26.42	10.38	3.13	—	2.69	12.83
Park Forest	37.65	18.22	4.41	2.15	.43	1.06	11.38
Park Ridge	53.88	24.59	5.79	5.20	—	3.88	14.42
Skokie	51.44	20.71	10.58	4.70	.52	2.99	11.94
Waukegan	50.41	22.89	8.98	1.68	1.72	1.42	13.72
Wilmette	56.04	27.18	6.51	5.82	—	1.80	14.73
Average	50.08	20.96	7.64	3.01	.97	2.67	14.86
Chicago	101.01	43.97	6.45	6.27	2.40	13.34	28.58

[a] 1963 data.

SOURCE Columns 1, 2, 3, 4, 7: U.S. Bureau of the Census, unpublished worksheets for the 1962 Census of Governments; Column 5: Auditor of Public Accounts, *Statewide Summary of Municipal Finance, 1962,* Chicago data from comptroller's reports; Column 6: computed residual.

The large variation in municipal revenue structure which is revealed by Table 29 suggests the possibility that municipal officials have a considerable amount of freedom in raising revenue. Before this can be accepted as a conclusion, however, it is necessary to look in much more detail at the revenue sources, their history, and the statutory provisions governing their use.

NONPROPERTY TAXES

The principal taxes other than property taxes levied by Illinois municipalities are general sales taxes, motor vehicle (wheel) taxes, and liquor license taxes. Several municipalities receive substantial sums from utility sales taxes and the number of cities using this tax is increasing rapidly. Table 29 shows the per capita yield of each of these taxes in 41 Illinois municipalities.

Municipal Sales Taxes In 1947 the Illinois legislature passed a measure permitting municipalities to impose a municipal sales tax, as a supplement to the state sales tax, after approval in a public referendum. During the period from 1947 to 1955, six cities held such referenda and the tax was defeated in every case.

In 1955 the governor and the mayor of Chicago agreed to eliminate the referenda requirement and permit the imposition of the tax by action of the city council.[1] Legislation implementing this agreement became effective July 1, 1955, and within one month 114 municipalities had passed ordinances imposing the tax. Today the tax is imposed by virtually every municipality.

The tax is a privilege tax, imposed upon persons engaged in the business of selling tangible personal property at retail in municipalities at a rate not to exceed .5 per cent of the gross receipts from retail sales.[2] The tax is collected by the State Department of Revenue and the tax base is generally identical to the base of the state sales tax, although the service occupation tax imposed by the 1961 legislature and the leasing occupation tax imposed by the 1965 legislature do not apply unless specifically enacted by the city. Cities may not impose a use tax.[3]

---

[1] Jack F. Isakoff, Gilbert Y. Steiner, and June G. Cabe, *Illinois Municipal Revenue,* Second Edition (Urbana: The Institute of Government and Public Affairs, University of Illinois, 1958), p. 51.

[2] *Ill. Rev. Stat.,* ch. 24, sec. 8-11-1 (1965).

[3] For constitutional reasons, the "sales tax" in Illinois is not legally a tax upon the sale, but upon the privilege of engaging in retail selling or upon the privilege of using (use tax) the property within the state. For detailed discussions of this situation and the effect which it has had upon Illinois tax policy and administration see: John Due, "The Unique Illinois Use Tax," *National Tax Journal* (September, 1959), pp. 260-64; A. James Heins, "Sales and Use Taxes," *Report*

Although the municipal sales tax is imposed by the municipality, it is administered by the Illinois Department of Revenue as an integral part of state sales tax administration. Additional lines are added to the state sales tax forms upon which the retailer enters the amount of municipal tax due. These amounts are allocated to municipal accounts as the returns are processed and are paid to the municipality monthly. The state retains a 4 per cent administration fee as reimbursement for the added cost of collecting the municipal tax. There are important advantages of this system to both taxpayers and municipalities. The taxpayer is not required to make returns to each municipality and face the possibility of separate audits by each municipality. Cities avoid the necessity of setting up the specialized administrative machinery needed for proper administration of the tax and avoid the ill-will which would result from the unavoidable frictions between taxpayers and tax collectors. The fee paid the state is less than cities would spend to obtain equally good administration and probably returns a "profit" to the state. Another advantage of state administration is that disputes concerning which municipality is entitled to jurisdiction over a particular sale are eliminated by having the decision made by the State Department of Revenue, which has no vested interest in the matter and can make decisions on a uniform basis.[4]

Retail sales taxation is familiar to Illinois taxpayers since the state has imposed a retail sales tax since 1932 and depends more heavily upon general and specific sales taxes than do most states. The imposition of the .5 per cent city tax has aroused relatively mild opposition in most cities, although retail merchants in a city are often concerned with the effect which a new or increased sales tax will have upon their competitive position vis-à-vis untaxed merchants outside the municipality. During the first years of the Illinois municipal sales tax, there was concern in some cities about the construction of shopping centers just outside the corporate limits. In 1959 the state legislature passed legislation permitting counties to levy a .5 per cent sales tax supplement to be effective only in unincorporated areas. When this tax is imposed by the county, it removes any sales tax incentive to shop or to locate shopping

---

of the Commission on Revenue (Springfield, Illinois: 1963), pp. 652-701; and Glenn W. Fisher, *Financing Illinois Government* (Urbana: University of Illinois Press, 1960), pp. 58-73.

[4] The other side of the coin is that the Revenue Department's decisions are not subject to check or review by municipal officials and errors can go undetected for a long period of time. Legislation approved by the governor on April 23, 1965, requires the Department of Revenue to submit to municipalities, upon request, a list of the taxpayers who have paid municipal sales tax to the city. *Laws of Illinois* (1965), pp. 398-400.

facilities outside of the municipality. Although the county tax has not spread as rapidly as did the municipal tax, it is imposed by about 80 counties including the metropolitan counties where the problem had been most acute. At present, concern about the effect of the municipal sales tax upon the location of retail trade occurs in cities which are close to states which tax retail sales at a lower rate than Illinois. Officials of a few such cities express the opinion that their city would not levy a higher sales tax rate should the legislature authorize it.

Under present law, responsibility for imposing a city sales tax rests squarely upon the city council. It is clear from the history of the tax that city councils have been willing to assume this responsibility and that the political disturbances which have resulted from the decision have been relatively mild. Once the tax has been in effect for some time and taxpayers become accustomed to the higher combined city-state rate, many taxpayers probably do not distinguish sharply between the state and the municipal portion of the tax.

Among 188 cities with a population of more than 5,000, the average per capita municipal sales tax collection in 1962 was $6.85. Among the 41 largest cities shown in Table 29, the per capita collection was $7.71 and ranged from a high of $11.38 in Kankakee to a low of $3.73 in Calumet City. For the average city with a population in excess of 25,000 the general sales tax provided 57 per cent of the revenue produced by nonproperty taxes and amounted to 16.4 per cent of total nonenterprise general revenue.

During the 1965 session of the General Assembly, a bill to permit the municipal sales tax to be raised to 1 per cent was part of a package designed to give municipalities a wider choice of nonproperty taxes. These bills, with strong backing from the Illinois Municipal League, the mayor of Chicago, officials of a large number of downstate cities, union leaders, and leaders of police and fire organizations, passed the House early in the session. The sales tax increase was strongly opposed by retailers' groups who suggested that additional municipal revenue might be obtained by broadening the sales tax to include services or by the imposition of a payroll tax upon those who work in the city. In the Senate the bills apparently became a key element in the bargaining over reapportionment and were lost when no agreement was reached.[5]

Municipal Utility Taxes and Franchise Fees Taxation of utilities by

[5] Although supported by downstate municipal officials of both political parties, the municipal tax package was considered to be of particular importance to Chicago. Leaders of the Republican-controlled Senate attempted to use it in bargaining over the number of Senate seats to be allocated to Chicago.

Illinois municipalities takes two forms, in addition to ad valorem property taxation discussed previously. Franchise fees may be paid to the municipality by privately owned utilities in exchange for the right to use public streets and alleys. Utility sales taxes (legally occupational privilege taxes) may be levied at rates of as much as 5 per cent of gross receipts.

Franchise fees are usually established in long-term agreements, called franchises, between the city and the utility company. In this agreement the municipality grants the company the exclusive right to sell certain utility services within the municipality, and the utility may agree to pay fees to the municipality or to provide the city with free services.

Utility franchise fees are collected by relatively few Illinois cities, although they have been a source of substantial revenue in Chicago and a few other cities. In 1945 a study committee of the Illinois Municipal League reported that there was no uniformity in the matter of franchise fees.[6] The committee found that telephone companies often granted a limited amount of free telephone service in exchange for its franchise but that there was a great variance among cities of similar size. In some cities the only concession granted was to permit the use of poles for municipal fire and police alarm boxes. In the great majority of cases, companies furnishing gas and electricity contributed nothing for the use of city streets, alleys, and other public places.

A survey of municipal revenue sources completed ten years later suggests that franchise fees grew little in importance in the interim. Data for 45 cities for 1956 indicated that only 16 of them were obtaining any revenue from franchise fees and that in only two of these did revenue exceed $1.00 per capita.[7] One of these, Chicago, received a fee of 4 per cent of gross revenue from Commonwealth Edison and 3 per cent from Illinois Bell, but received no fee from Peoples Gas Light and Coke Company.

In 1955, as the result of an agreement between the governor and the mayor of Chicago, the General Assembly passed legislation which permits municipalities to levy a tax upon the occupations or privileges of persons engaged in the business of transmitting messages by means of electricity or distributing or selling gas, water, and electricity. The tax may not exceed 5 per cent of gross receipts and applies only to receipts

[6] "Report of the Committee of the Legal Section of the Illinois Municipal League Appointed to Consider the Subject of Compensation or Rental to Be Paid to Municipalities by Public Utilities Operating Within a Municipality for Use of Its Streets, Alleys and Other Public Places," *Illinois Municipal Review* (January, 1946), pp. 12-21.

[7] Isakoff, Steiner, and Cabe, *op. cit.*, pp. 60-61.

from messages originating within the city limits or from the consumption or use of gas, electricity, and water within the city limits.[8] The statutes make clear that the tax may be in addition to payments received as compensation for the use of streets and alleys for the installation and maintenance of equipment. Thus, a municipality may levy both a franchise tax and a gross receipts tax upon the same company.

Chicago adopted the tax to become effective on January 1, 1956. Electric companies are taxed at a 5 per cent rate with a credit for the amounts paid as a franchise fee, message companies are taxed at 2 per cent, and gas companies are taxed at 5 per cent. These rates coupled with the previously existing franchise fees mean that gas, electric, and telephone companies pay a total of 5 per cent of gross receipts. Since there is no franchise fee for Western Union, the tax on telegraph messages is 5 per cent.[9] This rate structure was challenged in a suit brought by Peoples Gas Light and Coke Company on the grounds that (1) the tax was not uniform as to class since the gas company was assessed a 5 per cent tax while the rate for Commonwealth Edison was only 1 per cent and (2) the tax was really a "street use" tax and thus a violation of the contract between the company and the city which was established when the charter was granted. The State Supreme Court held that the city had express authority from the legislature to enact the tax and that the classification was a reasonable one.[10]

Considerable confusion has resulted from the fact that the operation of the statute results in an increase in the consumer's utility bill which is noticeably higher than the rate of tax imposed. The statutes provide[11] that the amount of the municipal utility tax plus an accounting charge of 3 per cent of the amount of the tax may be added to its charge to customers. The effect which the imposition of the tax has upon the utility bill is further complicated by the fact that the tax is imposed upon gross receipts which is defined to include the city tax, the state utility tax, and the accounting charge as well as the basic charge for services. The result is that the imposition of the tax at a given rate results in a larger percentage rise in the utility bill.

In 1964, 48 municipalities were levying a utility sales tax. Information concerning the coverage of the tax and its yield in the 11 cities of more than 5,000 population which levied the tax at that time is pro-

---

[8] *Ill. Rev. Stat.*, ch. 24, sec. 8-11-2 (1965).

[9] Dale H. Weeks, "Taxation of Public Utilities," *Report of the Commission on Revenue* (Springfield, Illinois: 1963), p. 804.

[10] *Peoples Gas Light and Coke Company* v. *City of Chicago*, 9 Ill. 2d 348 (1956).

[11] *Ill. Rev. Stat.*, ch. 111 2/3, sec. 36 (1965).

TABLE 30

RATES AND PER CAPITA YIELDS, MUNICIPAL UTILITY TAXES, CITIES OVER 5,000 POPULATION

City	Year Adopted	Applicable To[a]	Rate[b] (per cent)	Per Capita Yield 1962[c]
Cairo	1957	egmw	5	$6.55
Carmi	1957	egmw	5	7.80
Champaign	1962	egmw	2¾	—
Chicago	1955	egm	5	9.71[d]
East Moline	1955	egm	5	8.62
East St. Louis	1960	egmw	5	6.26
Freeport	1963	egm	3	—
North Chicago	1962	egm	5	—
Robbins	1960	egm	5	4.09
Urbana	1962	egmw	2	—
Zion	1955	egmw	5	6.16

[a] Type of utility indicated as follows: e — electricity; g — gas; m — telephone and telegraph messages; w — water.

[b] Rates as stated in ordinances; this does not include extra charges resulting from imposition of tax. See text.

[c] Per capita yield computed from 1962 Census of Governments. Cities for which no data are given did not impose the tax during all or part of the fiscal year.

[d] Chicago data include receipts from franchise tax. See text.

SOURCE Illinois Municipal League, *Municipal Utility Tax* (mimeographed report dated May 12, 1964); U.S. Bureau of the Census, unpublished worksheets for the 1962 Census of Governments; letter from Professor Dale H. Weeks, Northern Illinois University, October 27, 1964.

vided in Table 30. Information from questionnaires and interviews with municipal officials in 1964 indicated that a number of Illinois cities had considered the imposition of the utility tax but that the idea often met with considerable opposition. Arguments raised against the tax are that it discourages location of industry in the city, that it places an undue burden on low income residents, and that it discriminates against certain fuels (gas and electricity as compared with oil).[12] Since these interviews were completed, however, the tax has spread rapidly and has been adopted by a number of the cities in the over-25,000 population group which were not using it in 1964.

Information concerning utility franchise fees is difficult to obtain, but it appears that the situation has changed little since the 1945 and 1956 surveys. A few cities are known to receive cash franchise fees and a substantial number receive free services which range in value from nominal to as much as $2.00 per capita. Since franchise fees are contractual, municipalities cannot increase them during the life of a valid franchise without the consent of the utility company and legal difficul-

[12] For an appraisal of the administrative and equity aspects of Illinois municipal utility taxes see: Weeks, *op. cit.*, pp. 802-12.

ties are sometimes encountered even after franchises expire.[13] Nevertheless, officials of some cities report that they have successfully negotiated increases in cash or services granted as franchise fees.

Motor Vehicle Licenses Municipalities are also empowered to license motor vehicles owned by residents. This tax, popularly known as the wheel tax, is levied by a majority of the larger municipalities and by many smaller ones.[14]

Fees upon not-for-hire passenger vehicles are limited to $15.00 and $30.00 in Chicago and $10.00 and $20.00 in other municipalities. The lower fee, in each case, applies to vehicles of 35 taxable horsepower or less and the higher fee to more powerful vehicles.

Funds collected from motor vehicle licensing must be utilized for improving, paving, repairing, or maintaining streets and other public roadways except that municipalities of more than 3,000 population may use up to 35 per cent of the gross receipts for the salaries of traffic policemen. Municipalities of more than 40,000 may also use these funds for the construction, maintenance, and operation of testing stations.[15]

As shown in Table 29, the amounts collected from motor vehicle licenses in the 41 larger cities go as high as $6.27 per capita in Chicago. The average in the 32 larger cities which reported revenue from this source in 1962 is $2.77 per capita.

Wheel taxes are administered locally and evidence of payment is a numbered decal affixed to the windshield of the vehicle. Municipal authorities have used roadblocks at which vehicles are checked for current stickers and the cross-checking of municipal license records against state license records to secure compliance. Unfortunately, the first method creates traffic congestion and generates a certain amount of ill-will, while the effectiveness of the second method is reduced by the fact that the post office address does not necessarily indicate whether or not the licensee lives within the corporate limits of a municipality. At least one municipality in the Chicago area issues free courtesy decals to

---

[13] *Village of Lombard* v. *Illinois Bell Telephone Co.,* 405 Ill. 209 (1950); *City of Chicago Heights* v. *Public Service Co.,* 408 Ill. 310 (1951); *City of Peoria* v. *Peoria Transit Lines, Inc.,* 11 Ill. 2d 520 (1957).

[14] Thirty-two of the 41 cities of more than 25,000 population are reported as receiving revenue from motor vehicle licenses in the 1962 Census of Governments; however, two of these report revenues amounting to less than 25 cents per capita (see Table 29).

In a 1963 survey, the Illinois Municipal League collected rate and collection data from 338 municipalities of all sizes. Illinois Municipal League, *Illinois Municipal Review* (May, 1963), pp. 10-20.

[15] *Ill. Rev. Stat.,* ch. 24, sec. 8-11-4 (1965).

their residents to prevent their being detained by police in neighboring communities which impose the tax.

The wheel tax has the advantage of raising revenue for street purposes from those who use the streets. Since it is imposed only on residents, however, commuters into or through a municipality contribute nothing to defray the costs which they occasion. In some cases, use of a municipality's streets by nonresidents may be balanced by residents' use of streets in other municipalities. In other cases no such balance exists.

Foreign Fire Insurance Tax Since 1895 municipalities have had the power to tax premiums of fire insurance policies written by insurance companies not incorporated in Illinois. For many years few municipalities took advantage of this tax because the cost of collection and enforcement was apt to exceed the revenue from the tax. In the late 1920's, however, an accountant engaged in municipal audit work began to enter into contracts with municipalities to collect the tax at commission rates of 33⅓ to 50 per cent of collections. As other individuals began to enter the field, a rather chaotic situation developed which created much ill-will between municipalities and the local insurance agents and produced little revenue.

In 1935 the Illinois Municipal League established a collection system under which the league collects the tax from the home or district office of the insurance company and remits the tax to the municipality. Since the tax paid to municipalities or fire protection districts can be taken as credit against the state tax, insurance companies have no incentive to cheat on the amount reported to each municipality. Originally each company wrote a check to each municipality and it was common for a municipality to receive a large bundle of checks, many for only a few cents. Since 1952, the process of allocating the amount due each city has been computerized so that each city receives a single check from the Municipal League.[16]

The statutes provide that the fire department of each municipality of less than 50,000 population is to be organized and that municipal treasurers are to pay all sums collected from the foreign fire insurance tax to the fire department treasurer who is to pay it out as directed by the fire department for the maintenance, use, and benefit of the department. If a firemen's pension fund exists, the proceeds may be paid into the fund.

---

[16] Historical information concerning the foreign fire insurance tax reported above is based upon an Illinois Municipal League newsletter to clerks and finance officers dated January 6, 1964.

It is difficult to determine what use has been made of these funds. Reports that they are used primarily for social events are widespread, but it is also known that a number of departments have used the funds to purchase additional firefighting and rescue equipment. In 1965 a bill to limit departmental control of funds to cities of less than 5,000 population[17] passed the Senate but died in House committee after representatives of a firemen's organization appeared in opposition.

The *Statewide Summary of Municipal Finance in Illinois,* published by the Auditor of Public Accounts, shows that four cities of over 25,000 population did not receive funds from the foreign fire insurance tax in at least one of the two years 1962 and 1963. Since, in the past, some city treasurers have not entered collections from this source as municipal revenue but have merely endorsed the check over to the treasurer of the fire department, it is possible that these cities may have received these funds. The largest amount collected among the cities of more than 25,000 population was 34 cents per capita in Joliet. The average was 22 cents per capita.

Business License Fees Municipalities have the power to license a wide variety of businesses and license fees are a substantial source of revenue for some municipalities. Municipalities, of course, have no inherent power to license or regulate business and the specific authority to license a particular business must be found in the statutes. Furthermore, such statutes are subject to strict interpretation.[18]

Legally, it is necessary to distinguish between regulatory and taxing powers delegated to municipalities. If only regulatory powers are delegated, there is implied a power to charge a fee on the theory that the fee goes to pay the expense involved in regulation. Illinois courts have held that for a license fee to be valid under these circumstances there must be some regulation involved and that the fee must bear some reasonable relationship to the cost of regulation. On the other hand, a license fee is not invalid merely because the fee is large enough to cover the cost of regulation and leave something over for the general treasury.[19]

Although lists of the businesses which may be regulated have been compiled,[20] no such list can be considered definitive since the power to license may involve more than one statute and vary with circumstances. Furthermore, it is difficult to compile a meaningful summary of all the

---

[19] *Ibid.*

[17] S.B. 681, 74th General Assembly.

[18] Thomas A. Matthews, "Municipal Powers to License Business," *Illinois Municipal Review* (February, 1962).

[20] *Ibid.*, p. 9; Isakoff, Steiner, and Cabe, *op. cit.*, pp. 49-50.

businesses which are actually licensed and the revenue produced by each kind of license. It is clear, however, that liquor licenses are by far the largest revenue producers.

The city council may determine the number, kind, and classification of retail liquor licenses to be issued and set the fee to be charged.[21] The fee is not limited to the cost of regulations,[22] and the method of classification varies considerably. Some municipalities have only one class of license while others have several classes. License fees commonly run as high as $1,000 per year for "Class A" licenses and sometimes drop to less than $100 for a "beer only" license. Several of the cities shown in Table 29 are "dry" and thus report no collections.

Table 31 shows business license fees charged and annual collections for the City of Rock Island and gives an indication of the variety of

TABLE 31

BUSINESS AND MOTOR VEHICLE LICENSES, CITY OF ROCK ISLAND

Business	Annual Rate	Annual Collections
LIQUOR, BEER, WINE		
Tavern	$ 750	
Restaurant	750	
Night Club	1,250	
Fraternal	1,000	$103,250
OTHER BUSINESS		
Auctioneer ($10 per day)	100	230
Automatic Musical Instrument	25	2,700
Billiard and Pool Tables	15	470
Bill Poster and Distributors	50	250
Bowling Alleys	15	825
Dairy Trucks ($15 for first truck)	10	525
Electrical Contractors	25	300
Express Trucks	15	75
Ferry Boat	150	150
Filling Station (per pump)	10	2,974
Food Establishment		
Less than 2,000 sq. ft.	25	
2,000-3,000 sq. ft.	50	
Over 3,000 sq. ft.	100	5,775
Gun or Electric Ray (amusement)	25	75
House Movers	25	50
Junkyard	200	800
Kennel (5-20 dogs)	10	10

[21] *Ill. Rev. Stat.,* ch. 43, sec. 110 (1965).

[22] *Sager et al.* v. *City of Silvis,* 402 Ill. 262 (1949).

TABLE 31 (continued)

BUSINESS AND MOTOR VEHICLE LICENSES, CITY OF ROCK ISLAND

Business	Annual Rate	Annual Collections
Loud-Speaker Advertising (per day)	5	5
Pawnbrokers	150	150
Peddlers	varies	330
Public Bench	5	275
Refuse Removal Truck	25	700
Sales (going out of business)	25	225
Taxicab	30	750
Taxicab Drivers	2.50	542.50
Theater		
500 seats or less	10	
500-1,000 seats	15	
Over 1,000 seats	25	50
Trailer Court (annual rate plus $3.00 per space)	50	349
Tree Trimmer	15	450
WHEEL TAX		
Pleasure Car	$ 4	
Truck		
Less than 8,000 lbs.	6	
8,000-14,000 lbs.	10	
Over 14,000 lbs.	20	
Commercial Semitrailer	30	
Trailer		
2,000 lbs. or less	4	
Over 2,000 lbs.	10	
Motor Bus — over 10 people	20	
Motor Bike	2	
Motor Tricycles	3	
Dealer Plates (first plate $10)	1	
Parochial School or Municipal Vehicle	1	$165,835

SOURCE City clerk of Rock Island, *Annual Report for Year Ending March 31, 1964;* letter from City Manager Raymond P. Botch, May 27, 1966.

such licenses and the magnitude of fees charged by Illinois cities, although as stated above, there is so much variation from city to city that it would probably be a mistake to consider Rock Island or any other city as "typical."

Several of the licenses listed as business licenses are levied upon a per vehicle basis and thus might be described as vehicle taxes. They are legally business license taxes which rest upon the use of the vehicle for a particular business purpose. Listed at the end of the table are rates of the "wheel tax" upon vehicles owned by residents of the city.

INTERGOVERNMENTAL REVENUE

Table 32 details the intergovernmental revenue of Illinois municipalities by the level of government from which it was received.

Clearly the major portion of intergovernmental revenue of municipalities comes from the state government in the form of a share of the motor fuel tax. Municipalities receive 32 per cent of the collections of this tax after administrative cost and the statutory allocation to the grade-crossing protection fund. This 32 per cent is allocated to particular municipalities on a population basis.

The purposes for which motor fuel tax funds may be spent and the conditions surrounding their expenditure were analyzed in some detail in Chapter 2. It should be noted that per capita allocations in a given year are identical for every city in the state since allocations are on a population basis. These funds are released to the municipality to pay for completed projects and to meet debt service requirements of street improvement bonds which are being retired from motor fuel tax funds.

Motor fuel tax receipts and expenditures need not be included in the appropriation ordinance since such funds are not municipal funds but are state funds administered in part by local officials.[23]

Intergovernmental revenues as reported by the U.S. Census Bureau also include small amounts paid to municipalities by other units of government for services rendered or as payment for property purchased. For example, some municipalities maintain and clean state highways under a contract with the Division of Highways.

In view of the great amount of publicity which has been given to new federal programs directed to the solution of urban problems, the rather small amount of federal funds paid directly to cities is somewhat surprising. Most cities receive nothing in the way of a direct grant from the federal government. A few cities do receive funds under federal programs set up to aid urban renewal, airport construction, or the elimination of water pollution.

In some cases, due to apathy or lack of information, there has been little serious consideration of the possibilities of obtaining federal funds for projects such as housing, urban renewal, or airport construction. In other cases, as in Rockford, such programs have been rejected after public discussion.

In some cases funds for such projects have come into the community, but have been administered by agencies other than the municipal government. For example, the importance of housing and urban renewal authorities in Illinois means that most of the federal grants for these

[23] Matthews, *op. cit.*

TABLE 32

PER CAPITA INTERGOVERNMENTAL REVENUE, 41 ILLINOIS MUNICIPALITIES, FISCAL YEAR 1962

	STATE	LOCAL	FEDERAL	TOTAL
Municipalities Outside Chicago SMSA				
Alton	$8.12	$ —	$ —	$ 8.12
Belleville	1.40	—	—	1.40
Bloomington	3.31	—	1.40	4.71
Champaign	5.31	—	—	5.31
Danville	4.28	.17	—	4.45
Decatur	10.53	.10	—	10.63
East St. Louis	5.58	—	—	5.58
Freeport	5.55	—	—	5.55
Galesburg	5.63	.07	—	5.70
Granite City	5.07	.09	—	5.16
Kankakee	6.37	—	4.44	10.81
Moline	10.65	.02	2.51	13.18
Pekin	5.29	—	—	5.29
Peoria	6.36	.15	—	6.51
Quincy	5.69	.21	—	5.90
Rockford	3.19	—	—	3.19
Rock Island	5.70	.10	—	5.80
Springfield	12.31	2.73	—	15.04
Urbana	4.99	.13	—	5.12
Average	6.07	.20	.44	6.71
Municipalities in Chicago SMSA				
Arlington Hgts.	3.89	—	—	3.89
Aurora	10.46	.20	—	10.66
Berwyn	3.79	—	—	3.79
Calumet City	6.60	.40	—	7.01
Chicago Hgts.	5.07	—	—	5.07
Cicero	5.44	—	—	5.44
Des Plaines	9.74	.85	—	10.59
Elgin	5.87	—	.54	6.41
Elmhurst	5.45	—	—	5.45
Evanston	7.75	—	—	7.75
Harvey	5.42	—	—	5.42
Highland Park	5.59	—	—	5.59
Joliet	6.90	.15	—	7.04
Maywood	4.42	—	—	4.42
Oak Lawn	6.32	—	—	6.32
Oak Park	6.04	.12	—	6.16
Park Forest	5.21	.51	—	5.73
Park Ridge	5.43	—	—	5.43
Skokie	3.57	—	—	3.57
Waukegan	5.53	—	.05	5.58
Wilmette	6.10	—	—	6.10
Average	5.93	.11	.03	6.07
Chicago	14.54	.84	3.45	18.83

SOURCE U.S. Bureau of the Census, unpublished worksheets for the 1962 Census of Governments.

purposes have gone to special district government rather than to municipal government. In 1962 Illinois local governments received $30.5 million directly from the federal government.[24] Municipal governments received less than 17 million of this.[25] By 1965, the latest year for which data are available as this is written, the total amount received by all levels of local government in Illinois was $39 million.[26]

It is possible that the rather small amount of funds which comes directly to local governments will increase substantially as a result of the recently enacted "Great Society" programs. For example, the Urban Mass Transportation Act of 1964 initiated a new system of grants and loans to provide for improvements in mass transportation facilities in urban areas. The Economic Opportunity Act of 1964 provides federal grants for community action programs developed by public or private nonprofit agencies or a combination of these. The Manpower Development and Training Act of 1962 was broadened in 1963 to provide a wider variety of training and education programs. Municipalities must submit proposals for projects through appropriate state agencies. The Land and Water Conservation Fund Act of 1964 set up a 25-year program to provide federal matching grants to public agencies for planning, developing, and acquiring outdoor recreational facilities which are in accord with a comprehensive statewide recreational plan.

These, and a number of other federal programs, are all possible sources of revenue for municipal governments. None of them are designed specifically to aid municipal governments and, in many cases, grants can be made to private nonprofit agencies, to governmental units, or to bodies composed of both public and private groups. Often, grants will be approved only if the proposed program is part of a community or statewide plan. It is difficult to predict what the eventual impact of these programs on municipal finance will be, but it is clear that several of them open up new sources of revenue. It is also clear that the number and complexity of the programs and the requirement for planning and cooperation with other agencies will require municipal officials to devote more attention to federal programs and to the municipal government's role in the community if any substantial amount of financial aid is to be received.

NONENTERPRISE CURRENT CHARGES

Current charges are collected by the municipality in exchange for the

[24] U.S. Bureau of the Census, *Census of Governments: 1962,* Vol. VII, No. 13, p. 26.

[25] *Ibid.,* Vol. IV, No. 3, p. 15.

[26] U.S. Bureau of the Census, *Governmental Finance in 1964-65,* p. 31.

provision of a particular service. In many cases they are more like "prices" than taxes.

In Chapter 2, a distinction was made between enterprise and nonenterprise functions. Although classifying functions on this basis required certain rather arbitrary judgments, such classification is necessary in order to arrive at a core of "general government" expenditures which can logically be compared from city to city. The same classification is preserved in this section so that the revenue classification will conform with the expenditure classification.

The provision of sewers and sewerage disposal is traditionally a general rather than an enterprise function but there is a growing tendency for Illinois municipalities to apply service charges to sewer use. In several cases revenue bonds secured by a pledge of sewer service charges have been sold to finance new collection or treatment facilities. The service charge to residential users may be a flat monthly fee or it may be related to the amount of water used. Charges for commercial and industrial users may be related to water use or determined on the basis of a formula embodying measures of use or cost.

Table 33 shows per capita receipts for cities of over 25,000 population. Twenty of the 41 cities report collections from this source. Per capita collections among these 20 cities averaged $4.03, but run as high

TABLE 33

PER CAPITA NONENTERPRISE CURRENT CHARGES, 41 ILLINOIS MUNICIPALITIES, FISCAL YEAR 1962

	Sewers	Refuse Collection	Recreation	Other Current Charges	Total
Municipalities Outside Chicago SMSA					
Alton	$9.10	$ —	$ —	$ .60	$ 9.70
Belleville	8.78	.57	1.59	1.12	12.06
Bloomington	6.38	—	1.74	1.86	9.98
Champaign	—	.08	.01	.28	.37
Danville	.01	.02	—	.24	.27
Decatur	—	—	—	—	—
East St. Louis	1.35	—	—	21.08[a]	22.43
Freeport	3.14	—	—	.84	3.98
Galesburg	.01	—	.77	.36	1.15
Granite City	3.52	—	—	.70	4.22
Kankakee	7.53	2.03	—	1.32	10.88
Moline	5.05	.10	.87	—	6.02
Pekin	.02	1.84	—	.77	2.63
Peoria	—	—	.16	.65	.81
Quincy	—	—	—	.17	.17

TABLE 33 (continued)

PER CAPITA NONENTERPRISE CURRENT CHARGES, 41 ILLINOIS MUNICIPALITIES, FISCAL YEAR 1962

	Sewers	Refuse Collection	Recreation	Other Current Charges	Total
Rockford	$ .14	$ .89	$ —	$1.18	$ 2.21
Rock Island	6.25	—	1.16	9.71[a]	17.12
Springfield	6.21	.88	.57	1.10	8.75
Urbana	—	—	.10	.11	.21
Average	3.03	.34	.37	2.22	5.95
Municipalities in Chicago SMSA					
Arlington Hgts.	—	—	—	1.15	1.15
Aurora	—	—	.76	.20	.96
Berwyn	—	—	—	.11	.11
Calumet City	—	—	—	1.00	1.00
Chicago Hgts.	—	—	—	.17	.17
Cicero	3.66	—	—	—	3.66
Des Plaines	—	3.35	—	.66	4.01
Elgin	—	.26	.64	1.86	2.76
Elmhurst	6.52	3.08	—	.03	9.62
Evanston	—	.52	.71	.98	2.21
Harvey	6.07	—	—	—	6.07
Highland Park	.63	2.19	1.51	1.68	6.01
Joliet	—	—	—	.15	.15
Maywood	—	3.18	.05	.77	4.00
Oak Lawn	—	2.80	—	.72	3.52
Oak Park	2.14	—	.35	1.00	3.48
Park Forest	—	—	.55	2.12	2.67
Park Ridge	—	—	—	.40	.40
Skokie	—	—	—	1.08	1.08
Waukegan	4.06	—	.11	.37	4.54
Wilmette	—	3.32	2.45	.67	6.44
Average	1.10	.89	.34	.72	3.05
Chicago	—	—	—	2.22	2.22

[a] Includes receipts from toll bridges.

SOURCE U.S. Bureau of the Census, unpublished worksheets for the 1962 Census of Governments.

as $9.10 in Alton where these charges produce more revenue than the retail sales tax.

A far less lucrative source of revenue than sewerage charges is charges for refuse collection. Only 16 of the 41 cities collect such fees and the average collection amounts to $1.57. In some cases, charges are made only for collections from industrial and commercial establishments. In others, fees are charged for each residence. As indicated in Chapter 2, some cities depend upon private scavengers to collect garbage and refuse and thus spend nothing for this function except for cleaning streets and other public places.

Most park and recreation facilities are provided free to all who care to use them. Some, such as organized recreational programs, involve an enrollment procedure which makes it possible to limit the program to residents of the municipality or park district. For other facilities, such as golf courses and swimming pools, it is common to charge an admission fee which may be higher for nonresidents. In a few cases such facilities are entirely self-supporting and might logically be classified as enterprise operations but separate financial statistics are not available. As indicated in column 3 of Table 33, the sums collected are relatively small, averaging 78 cents per capita in the 18 cities which report collection from this source.

The category "other general charges" is a residual classification to which all general charges not otherwise classified are assigned. Relatively small sums are involved except for the cities of East St. Louis and Rock Island, where charges include receipts from toll bridges owned by the municipality. These charges clearly should be classified as enterprise charges but the statistical information necessary to permit this to be done in a uniform way for both expenditures and revenue was not available.

MISCELLANEOUS REVENUE

Special assessments are levied against property owners to finance the cost of permanent improvements such as streets, sidewalks, and sewers which benefit property owners in a particular area rather than the municipality as a whole.

The cost of the project is prorated among the property owners of the area in proportion to the benefits received. Part of the cost may be assessed against the city as a public benefit. Bonds payable from the proceeds are usually issued and the property owner is permitted to pay his assessments in annual installments which are used to retire the bonds. A board of local improvements is responsible for administering special assessment programs. In Chicago, this board consists of the superintendent of special assessments and five members nominated by the mayor and confirmed by the council. In cities and villages with a population from 50,000 to 500,000, the board consists of five municipal officials who are ex officio members of the board. In smaller municipalities the board is composed of three members serving ex officio. Special provisions apply to municipalities with a commission form of government where the board may consist of the mayor and two commissioners and in council-manager cities where the board is appointed by the manager.

The board of local improvements can initiate local improvements on its own although in many cities it is the practice to order projects only when a majority of the property owners affected petition for the improvement.

In 1947 a new special assessment act was passed with the intention of simplifying procedures and improving the security of the bond holders by improving and simplifying foreclosure procedures. This act has never been used, apparently because bond houses are reluctant to handle bonds issued under these procedures since the law has never been tested in court and no case law interpreting the act is available.[27]

Special assessments are not used as widely in Illinois as in some other states, due, undoubtedly, to the lingering memory of the widespread defaults that occurred in the depression of the 1930's.[28] These defaults were a direct result of overexpansion of municipal facilities in the 1920's.

Although the statutes spell out special assessment procedures in detail and prohibit municipalities from pledging the general credit of the city, special assessment financing can be rather flexible. Some municipalities have encouraged advance payment, reducing the interest cost to the property owner and sometimes reducing the construction cost since the contractor is assured of prompt payment. In some cities other available municipal funds are used as a revolving fund to expedite prompt payment of the contractor. In other cities, where it is believed to be difficult to sell special assessment bonds at par, the call for bids specifies that the contractor will be paid in special assessment bonds. This results in a higher cost for the project since contractors compute their bids to allow for selling the bonds at a discount.[29]

Table 34 shows the 1962 per capita revenue from special assessments and from other miscellaneous sources. Sale of property occasionally provides substantial amounts of revenue. In a recent year, for example, the city of Urbana financed the construction of a new city hall complex partly from the sale of streets to the University of Illinois and to the developer of a downtown shopping center. Obviously, sales of streets or other property cannot be considered basic or continuous revenue sources.

---

[27] Donald D. Herrman, *The Special Assessment in Oak Lawn* (Carbondale: Public Affairs Research Bureau, Southern Illinois University, 1962), pp. 6-7.

[28] William O. Winter and Robert W. Richey, *The Special Assessment in Illinois* (Carbondale: Public Affairs Research Bureau, Southern Illinois University, 1959).

[29] *Ibid.;* Herrman, *op. cit.,* pp. 18-20.

TABLE 34

PER CAPITA MISCELLANEOUS REVENUE, 41 ILLINOIS MUNICIPALITIES, 1962 FISCAL YEAR

	Special Assessment	Sale of Property	Earnings on Investments	Other	Total
Municipalities Outside Chicago SMSA					
Alton	$ —	$ .20	$2.38	$3.18	$ 5.76
Belleville	—	.08	—	.51	.59
Bloomington	1.38	2.66	1.20	2.74	7.98
Champaign	9.41	—	.09	2.81	12.31
Danville	.02	—	—	.55	.57
Decatur	2.52	1.24	1.26	1.30	6.33
East St. Louis	—	—	—	1.33	1.33
Freeport	—	—	.20	1.94	2.14
Galesburg	2.31	.01	.17	1.17	3.67
Granite City	.01	—	.22	.83	1.05
Kankakee	1.70	—	.22	2.52	4.44
Moline	7.71	1.50	.43	1.01	10.65
Pekin	8.16	—	.10	.43	8.69
Peoria	1.63	.04	.02	1.66	3.35
Quincy	—	.13	1.19	2.16	3.47
Rockford	—	.09	.86	2.03	2.98
Rock Island	3.15	.32	2.05	2.00	7.51
Springfield	.55	.12	2.18	2.95	5.80
Urbana	.16	—	.06	1.95	2.17
Average	2.04	.34	.66	1.74	4.78
Municipalities in Chicago SMSA					
Arlington Hgts.	5.34	4.44	.77	1.75	12.30
Aurora	.68	—	.14	1.90	2.73
Berwyn	.59	—	—	1.00	1.59
Calumet City	.85	—	—	1.28	2.12
Chicago Hgts.	.22	.12	.38	1.17	1.89
Cicero	—	—	.10	3.18	3.28
Des Plaines	.11	—	.13	1.47	1.71
Elgin	.99	—	.98	1.40	3.37
Elmhurst	.08	—	.74	2.44	3.26
Evanston	1.38	.14	.34	4.04	5.90
Harvey	6.13	2.51	.08	.57	9.28
Highland Park	7.38	3.11	.87	1.59	12.95
Joliet	—	.78	.50	1.57	2.85
Maywood	1.32	1.30	.15	2.56	5.33
Oak Lawn	22.19	—	.19	1.68	24.06
Oak Park	—	.54	.17	2.48	3.19
Park Forest	—	.27	1.01	1.70	2.98
Park Ridge	4.60	1.66	.66	1.67	8.59
Skokie	5.06	—	.58	1.65	7.29
Waukegan	—	—	.40	3.20	3.60
Wilmette	.61	—	.84	.65	2.09
Average	2.74	.71	.43	1.85	5.73
Chicago	1.83	1.92	.65	3.13	7.53

SOURCE U.S. Bureau of the Census, unpublished worksheets for the 1962 Census of Governments.

Earnings on investment may result from investment of city operating funds or the investment of the receipts from bond sales prior to expenditure for designated purposes.

ENTERPRISE AND UTILITY RECEIPTS

As indicated in Chapter 2, the majority of Illinois municipalities operate a water utility. Operation of electrical utilities and transportation systems is less common. In order to improve the comparability of data for the various cities, revenue from these utilities and certain other "enterprise-type" operations have also been excluded from the data presented. The exclusion should not be taken to imply, however, that such operations do not affect municipal finances. In a number of municipalities, revenue is transferred from utility or enterprise operations to finance general functions. In other cities, there is no direct transfer of funds, but a portion of the general overhead and management expenses is paid directly from the enterprise operation. In other cases, the enterprises provide certain services which might otherwise be provided from general revenue. Unfortunately, the data which would permit an accurate calculation of the net contribution or net cost of these operations are not generally available.

GENERAL SUMMARY

Table 35 indicates the relative importance of the major revenue sources for the 41 largest cities. Illinois municipalities have available a

TABLE 35

GENERAL REVENUE COLLECTIONS BY MAJOR SOURCES, AS PER CENT OF TOTAL, 41 ILLINOIS MUNICIPALITIES, 1962 FISCAL YEAR

	Property Taxes	Nonproperty Taxes	Intergovernmental Revenue	Nonenterprise Current Charges	Miscellaneous Revenue	Total
Municipalities Outside Chicago SMSA						
Alton	31.3	25.2	15.0	17.9	10.6	100.0
Belleville	39.5	27.7	3.3	28.1	1.4	100.0
Bloomington	38.6	25.7	7.4	15.7	12.5	100.0
Champaign	40.5	20.5	11.5	.8	26.7	100.0
Danville	59.2	27.8	10.9	.7	1.4	100.0
Decatur	35.2	25.7	24.5	—	14.6	100.0
East St. Louis	28.0	26.2	8.7	34.9	2.1	100.0
Freeport	51.5	22.4	12.4	8.9	4.8	100.0
Galesburg	57.7	20.8	11.7	2.4	7.5	100.0
Granite City	58.7	16.7	12.1	9.9	2.5	100.0

TABLE 35 (continued)

GENERAL REVENUE COLLECTIONS BY MAJOR SOURCES, AS PER CENT OF TOTAL, 41 ILLINOIS MUNICIPALITIES, 1962 FISCAL YEAR

	Property Taxes	Nonproperty Taxes	Intergovernmental Revenue	Nonenterprise Current Charges	Miscellaneous Revenue	Total
Kankakee	28.6	25.7	18.9	19.1	7.8	100.0
Moline	42.1	17.4	17.9	8.2	14.4	100.0
Pekin	49.5	15.8	11.1	5.5	18.2	100.0
Peoria	57.8	24.0	11.1	1.4	5.7	100.0
Quincy	62.9	18.1	11.8	.3	6.9	100.0
Rockford	48.9	34.8	6.2	4.3	5.8	100.0
Rock Island	37.0	16.6	8.9	26.1	11.5	100.0
Springfield	37.1	19.3	22.1	12.9	8.5	100.0
Urbana	55.1	22.3	15.4	.6	6.5	100.0
Average	45.2	22.8	12.7	10.4	8.9	
Municipalities in Chicago SMSA						
Arlington Hgts.	28.2	33.2	8.7	2.6	27.4	100.0
Aurora	46.6	24.7	21.3	1.9	5.5	100.0
Berwyn	49.0	33.6	12.0	.3	5.0	100.0
Calumet City	34.8	40.8	16.9	2.4	5.1	100.0
Chicago Hgts.	45.6	38.9	11.0	.4	4.1	100.0
Cicero	58.3	21.7	8.8	5.9	5.3	100.0
Des Plaines	30.0	35.9	22.2	8.4	3.6	100.0
Elgin	42.4	26.6	15.9	6.8	8.3	100.0
Elmhurst	31.0	24.7	13.2	23.2	7.9	100.0
Evanston	50.0	25.7	11.9	3.4	9.1	100.0
Harvey	34.5	26.6	10.2	11.4	17.4	100.0
Highland Park	43.0	22.8	7.8	8.4	18.0	100.0
Joliet	43.6	32.8	16.6	.4	6.7	100.0
Maywood	42.4	26.9	9.9	8.9	11.9	100.0
Oak Lawn	21.1	25.6	9.9	5.5	37.8	100.0
Oak Park	47.6	29.2	11.1	6.3	5.8	100.0
Park Forest	48.4	21.4	15.2	7.1	7.9	100.0
Park Ridge	45.6	27.6	10.1	.7	15.9	100.0
Skokie	40.3	36.5	6.9	2.1	14.2	100.0
Waukegan	45.4	27.4	11.1	9.0	7.1	100.0
Wilmette	48.5	25.2	10.9	11.5	3.7	100.0
Average	41.7	28.9	12.5	6.0	10.8	
Chicago	43.5	28.2	18.6	2.0	7.5	100.0

SOURCE Computed from Tables 29, 32, 33, and 34.

wider range of revenue sources than does any other type of local government. The property tax remains basic to the revenue structure, not only because it yields 43 per cent of the revenue of the average city but because budgeting, appropriation, and borrowing procedures are closely tied to the property tax process.

Nonproperty taxes available include the municipal sales tax, which is levied by virtually all municipalities in the state, and the motor vehicle (wheel) tax which is levied by a substantial number of municipalities, especially in the Chicago metropolitan area. The utility tax is confined to a relatively few cities but shows signs of spreading at an accelerated rate.

Intergovernmental revenue is largely in the form of state motor fuel tax grants and is allocated on a per capita basis, although in any one year there may be a great variation in per capita receipts since the funds are paid to the city upon completion of an approved project.

The great differences in the extent to which sources such as special assessments, business licenses, and charges for service are utilized appear to represent both differences in the municipal environment and the energy which municipal officials devote to the task of raising money from these sources. In a few cases, there is a definite policy of relating revenue collections and services rendered whenever possible. In other cases there appears to be little awareness of this possibility.

7 MUNICIPAL INDEBTEDNESS

The authority to contract debt obligations is an important local government prerogative and most states have accorded sundry borrowing powers to their local units. For historical as well as political and economic reasons, numerous restrictions have been placed on borrowing powers. But most local officials find market constraints and referendum requirements a more effective curb on indebtedness than state debt limitations. The task of the local government official in entering the money markets becomes one of salesmanship, perseverance, and political gamesmanship.

Ample evidence exists indicating that local government officials have acquired some of these traits. As indicated in Table 36, the outstanding gross indebtedness of all U.S. local governments increased $45.6 billion from 1946 to 1962 as opposed to a $28.8 billion increase for the federal government. Of course, by 1946 the federal government had already contracted a record debt through the financing of World War II and its immediate financial needs had ebbed as the U.S. returned to a quasi-peacetime economy. Local governments, however, found themselves subject to the pressures of urbanization, the general state of prosperity, and the backlog of demands for capital improvements. Local capital expenditures had been curtailed during both the war and the depression of the 1930's, and municipal officials found themselves facing expanding service levels with deteriorated equipment.

One recent California study claims that for each new family moving into a particular area, demand is created for approximately $13,000 in public improvements.[1] Increasing urban population and the resulting

[1] John O'Donnell, "Some Postwar Trends in Municipal Bond Financing," *The Journal of Finance* (May, 1962), p. 259.

TABLE 36

GROSS DEBT OUTSTANDING, SELECTED GOVERNMENTS AND FISCAL YEARS, 1902-62

Fiscal Year	Gross Debt Outstanding (billions): Federal Government	All U.S. Local Governments	Illinois Local Governments	All Local Debt as a Percentage of Federal Debt	Illinois Local Debt as a Percentage of Federal Debt
1962	$298.2	$59.2	$3.8	19.8	1.3
1957	270.5	39.3	2.5	14.5	0.9
1952	259.1	23.2	NA[a]	9.0	NA
1946	269.4	13.6	NA	5.0	NA
1942	72.4	16.1	0.8	22.2	1.1
1932	19.5	16.4	NA	84.1	NA
1902	1.2	1.9	NA	158.3	NA
Per Cent Increase, 1946-62	10.7	335.3	375.0[b]		

[a] NA indicates data are not available.

[b] Increase for 1942-62.

SOURCE Compiled from U.S. Bureau of the Census, *Census of Governments: 1962,* Vol. VI, No. 4, Tables 3, 6, 17.

increase in the need for local services undoubtedly explain much of the increase in local government debt shown in Table 36. Local government indebtedness increased over 300 per cent in two decades and continues to grow. The purpose of this chapter is to review the major forms of debt contracted by Illinois municipalities and to analyze the problems encountered by municipal officials in deficit financing.

CLASSIFICATION OF DEBT INSTRUMENTS

Municipal debt may be classified in terms of the purposes for which it is issued, the length of time for which money is borrowed, or the type of security or the repayment guarantee offered to the lender. Table 37 is based upon the U.S. Census Bureau's classification of the debt instruments which make up the gross debt of U.S. and Illinois municipalities.

Borrowing for Capital Purposes Full faith and credit issues, or general obligation bonds, pledge the lender or investor that the full credit of the borrowing municipality guarantees the payment of principal and interest. That is, for any particular full faith and credit bond issue the city promises to use its taxing power to levy sufficient taxes to service the debt. In fact, the Illinois Constitution requires that municipalities

TABLE 37

MUNICIPAL INDEBTEDNESS IN THE UNITED STATES, BY TYPE OF DEBT, 1957 AND 1962

	U.S. Municipalities (in millions)		Illinois Municipalities (in millions)		Per Cent Increase 1957-62	
Type of Debt	1957[a]	1962	1957	1962	U.S.	Illinois
Gross Debt	$19,199	$26,857	$876	$1,446	39.9	65.1
Gross Long-Term	18,306	25,099	802	1,284	37.1	60.1
Full Faith and Credit	12,481	16,739	324	512	34.1	58.0
Nonguaranteed	5,825	8,360	478	772	43.5	61.5
Net Long-Term Debt	16,580	23,309	749	1,220	40.6	62.9
Full Faith and Credit as a Per Cent of Gross Long-Term	68.2	66.7	40.4	39.9		

[a] Hawaii and Alaska data added to conform with 1962 data.

SOURCE Compiled from U.S. Bureau of the Census, *Census of Governments: 1962,* Vol. IV, No. 3, and *Census of Governments: 1957,* Vol. III, No. 3.

levy a direct annual tax sufficient to retire bond issues within 20 years.[2] The bond and interest extension is determined in any year by the amount that needs to be collected to pay principal and interest on outstanding general obligation debt with allowances for tax delinquency and the cost of collecting the tax.

General obligation issues are primarily used to finance nonrecurrent capital expenditure projects such as street lighting, street improvements, or the construction of municipal buildings. The fact that this type of improvement will benefit residents of the community over a period of years justifies spreading the cost of the facilities through time. However, most general obligation issues require voter approval of the improvement project before the bonds can be issued and it is sometimes difficult to secure approval. Tax-conscious voters are aware that general obligation issues will raise their tax bills and are reluctant to approve general obligation issues for nonschool purposes. In fact, school districts have been so successful in securing approval for their bond issues that many municipal officials feel that the schools have practically forced other competing taxing bodies to finance capital projects with revenue bonds.

Municipalities have had much success in selling the voters on general obligation issues for street improvements. While such issues still call

[2] *Illinois Constitution* (1870), Article IX, Sec. 12.

for an annual property tax levy, the voters are informed that the levy will be abated by the use of motor fuel taxes distributed to the municipality by the state.[3] Thus, the bond and interest rate is still certified to the county clerk but he abates it once motor fuel tax funds become available. If the taxpayer is convinced the approval of a general obligation issue will not raise his taxes, he is far more likely to vote yes.[4]

Where the chances of financing capital improvements through general obligation bonds appear futile, municipal officials often seek to keep the project alive by turning to revenue bonds or nonguaranteed issues. These issues are not backed by the full faith and credit of the municipality but rather by the income or revenue-producing capacity of the improvement project; hence, they seldom require an election. The income from the facility is used to service the debt, and if it proves inadequate, the investors can seek redress through the courts. The courts may establish a service charge that will be sufficient to liquidate the debt, or they may appoint a receiver to do this. As the taxing power of the municipality is not pledged to secure the loan, revenue bonds generally mean higher interest costs to the borrower.

Despite the risk premium of revenue bonds, many officials believe they are actually a safe investment. Engineering estimates of cost and potential revenues are carefully prepared. Often city councils will not approve a revenue issue unless the revenues anticipated will equal one and one-half times the cost of servicing and retiring the debt obligation. The closer scrutiny of proposed revenue issues by municipal officials and investors indicates that, by comparison, general obligation issues are probably handled somewhat haphazardly. In fact, the risk premium might well be lower on revenue issues if investors realized the differences experienced by municipal officials in administering the two types of issues.[5] The fact that the full taxing power of the issuing body backs the general obligation issues appears more important to the investor than the relative care with which projects financed with either type of issue are approached by the municipalities themselves.

As Table 37 indicates, revenue issues have been extremely popular in Illinois. Sixty per cent of the outstanding debt of Illinois municipalities

---

[3] For authority to abate the bond and interest tax rate with motor fuel fund receipts, see: *Ill. Rev. Stat.,* ch. 24, sec. 8-3-4 (1965).

[4] From questionnaire material compiled by the Institute of Government and Public Affairs, University of Illinois, 1965.

[5] O'Donnell observes that the disparity between general obligation and revenue bond yields is surprising, given the shrinkage in yield differentials that have occurred since World War II between grades of corporate securities. This amounts to an overestimation of risk on municipal revenue bond issues. *Op. cit.,* p. 264.

is in the nonguaranteed category. The state first authorized its municipalities to issue nonguaranteed debt in 1899, and the state itself has issued the largest single nonguaranteed issue of any state or local government in the U.S.[6]

The popularity of the revenue bond issue is easily explained. First, since the bonds do not pledge the taxing power of the issuing unit, they are not subject to constitutional and statutory debt limitations. Second, a more direct relationship is provided between the consumer of the service and the price he pays for it. Municipal utilities, highways, and housing projects are often financed with revenue bonds on the basis that those who use the facility pay for it in the form of fees, tolls, rents, or other earmarked payments. This is, in effect, a private market type of transaction or a proprietary service in the public sector. Third, some argue it leads to much sounder governmental use of resources since the revenue bond issue must stand on the economic feasibility of the project undertaken.[7] Finally, revenue bonds have longer lives as repayment can be extended for as long as 40 years.

A somewhat different, and far more controversial, use of revenue bonds was made possible by the Illinois Industrial Building Revenue Bond Act of 1951. Municipalities were given the authority to issue revenue bonds, after approval by referendum, to purchase, construct, or improve industrial properties for lease to private industry.[8] The stated purpose of the act was to encourage the industrial development of the state and to reduce unemployment.[9] The bond holders are to have a lien on the rentals from the industrial buildings for which the bonds were issued. The main restrictions or limitations to such an issue are provided by the required referendum, a stipulation that interest on the bonds not exceed 6 per cent per annum and that the buildings be within ten miles of the boundaries of the issuing government.

Section 20, Article IV, and separate section 2 of the Illinois Constitution specifically prohibit cities from lending their credit to aid private corporations. This constitutional provision resulted from the overexpansion and default on municipal bonds issued in the nineteenth century to aid railroad expansion.[10] Whether or not the Industrial Building

---

[6] A $415 million issue for the Northern Illinois Toll Road. "Municipal Bonds," *The New York Times,* April 17, 1966, sec. 11, p. 7.

[7] Bankers Trust Company, *Financing Public Needs (Manual for State and Municipal Fiscal Officers)* (New York: undated), p. 9.

[8] *Ill. Rev. Stat.,* ch. 24, secs. 11-74-1–11-74-13 (1965).

[9] *Ibid.,* ch. 24, sec. 11-74-3 (1965).

[10] Irving Howards, *Selected Aspects of State Supervision over Local Government in Illinois* (Carbondale: Public Affairs Research Bureau, Southern Illinois University, 1964), p. 52.

Revenue Bond Act violates the Constitution is not clear since the Illinois Supreme Court sidestepped the constitutional issue in a recent case.[11] In view of the fact that the security of such a bond issue depends largely upon the credit and permanence of the leasing corporation, many such arrangements are attractive primarily for the lower interest rates that the municipality can obtain because income from municipal bond interest is exempt from federal income tax. In a sense, municipalities are loaning their tax exemption, rather than their credit, to the private corporation.[12]

Another type of bond falling into the nonguaranteed category is the special assessment bond. As pointed out in the last chapter, special assessments spread the cost of public improvements such as streets, sidewalks, or street lighting among the property owners in the area to be benefited. Special assessments bonds sold to finance the property owner's portion of the cost are backed by liens on the property against which the assessments are made. If part of the cost of the improvement is assessed against the city as a public benefit, the city must pay its share of the cost in the same fashion as owners of specifically benefited properties. The public benefit tax rate levied by the municipality to offset its share of the cost of the improvement need not be used solely to service special assessment issues. Frequently cities use the public benefit fund to finance projects such as alley repaving or sidewalk replacement on a current basis. Some cities pay for 50 per cent of alley or sidewalk repairs if the property owner agrees to pay the remaining 50 per cent.

A special category of revenue bond issues should be mentioned since they can create an indirect debt obligation for a municipality. The Public Building Commission Act of 1955 makes it possible to establish local building commissions empowered to issue revenue bonds to raise construction funds for public buildings. Once constructed, the commission can enter into lease agreements with local governments. According to Ch. 24, secs. 11-76.1-1 to 11-76.1-4 *Ill. Rev. Stat.*, the governing board of a municipality may lease either real or personal property from the commission for a period of not more than 20 years, and may by ordinance provide for the levy and collection of a direct annual tax sufficient to offset rental or annual installments connected with such leases. Once the city has passed such an ordinance, it has indirectly assumed responsibility for repayment of the revenue bonds issued by the building commission. The authority of the municipal governing

---

[11] *Slack* v. *City of Salem*, 31 Ill. 2d 174 (1964).

[12] For a detailed analysis of this type of finance see: Advisory Commission on Intergovernmental Relations, *Industrial Development Bond Financing*, Commission Report A-18 (Washington, D.C.: June, 1963).

board to enter into such lease agreements may be challenged by 1 per cent of the registered voters of the municipality, thereby forcing a referendum be held on the issue.

As the result of legislation passed in 1965, municipalities are also empowered to lease or purchase property on the installment basis.[13] Purchase of particular pieces of real estate or expensive personal property has previously been difficult. It is not feasible to vote a bond issue every time the municipality wishes to purchase property (e.g., a single lot to be used for parking facilities), yet it may not be possible to purchase the property on a current basis. This latest addition to the long-term borrowing powers of municipalities should facilitate additions to the capital plant of the city that previously have been difficult to acquire, even if they were high priority needs.

Borrowing for Noncapital Purposes Most commonly, indebtedness for noncapital purposes is contracted to pay for working cash, refunding bonds, tax anticipation warrants, and judgments entered in a court of record against the municipality.

Municipalities of under 500,000 population are authorized to establish working cash funds to enable the city to pay its bills during the long period between the levy and collection of property taxes. The city may, by ordinance and without referendum, issue general obligation bonds of no more than $400,000 at an interest rate of not more than 5.5 per cent to establish this fund. The indebtedness is to be repaid within 20 years. If the municipality prefers not to debt finance the fund, it can adopt a direct annual tax of not more than 5 cents for working cash that is independent of the general corporate rate, but subject to the General Revenue Law.[14]

Any transfer of money from the working cash to the general corporate or any other fund is to be reimbursed in full upon collection of the tax levy. If tax anticipation warrants have been issued against the tax levy for a particular fund, any transfer of working cash to that fund is supposed to be in anticipation of the taxes to be collected for the fund. That is, as tax funds are collected, tax anticipation warrants are to be redeemed before the working cash fund is reimbused. If the anticipated taxes are not sufficient to reimbuse the working cash fund, the deficiencies are to be made up in the next appropriation ordinance.[15]

Another way that corporate authorities meet current expenses is

---

[13] *Laws of Illinois* (1965), pp. 992-93, 2173-76. See: Louis Ancel and Edward M. Levin, Jr., "The Right to Lease or to Purchase Property on the Installment Basis," *Illinois Municipal Review* (December, 1965).

[14] *Ill. Rev. Stat.*, ch. 24, secs. 8-7-1–8-7-3 (1965).

[15] *Ibid.*, ch. 24, sec. 8-7-4 (1965).

through the issue and sale of tax anticipation warrants. These warrants are issued in anticipation of a particular tax levy in process of collection and are redeemed from the tax revenues forthcoming from the particular levy. Warrants may be issued for up to 75 per cent of a particular tax extension. Where working cash funds have been transferred to a fund in anticipation of those same tax revenues, the aggregate amount of all warrants issued and working cash funds transferred must not exceed 90 per cent of the expected tax collection.[16] As a matter of practice, bond attorneys will seldom approve any issue within 10 percentage points of the statutory limitation.[17] The amounts of outstanding warrants of this type are not to be included as liabilities falling within constitutional or statutory debt limits as long as the warrants have been issued against a specific tax extension.

The law provides for a maximum 6 per cent interest rate on tax anticipation warrants and requires repayment of warrants in the order they were issued. Some municipalities have made a practice of purchasing their own tax anticipation warrants using city treasury funds set aside for particular purposes. The interest on such warrants must not exceed 4 per cent per annum,[18] and warrants so purchased cannot be repaid until taxes have been accrued to pay all other warrants outstanding on a particular fund, regardless of the order issued. That is, all of the warrants not held in the treasury of the issuing municipality must be repaid first, or the money must be accrued and set aside to discharge these obligations. If the special purpose funds are needed before all of the warrants purchased and held by the municipality have been repaid, the warrants may be resold or reissued.[19]

Tax anticipation warrants partially fulfill short-term or temporary borrowing needs. In fact, municipalities sometimes borrow with tax anticipation warrants when the legislature increases tax rate limits. Budgets are based on the higher limits, but tax anticipation warrants are used to finance the budget until collection of taxes levied at the higher rate begins.

The fact that tax anticipation warrants usually have a life of less than 15 months renders them impractical for intermediate term financing. If, for example, a city wished to purchase a piece of firefighting equipment that it could pay for in three years, tax anticipation warrants would be of little help in raising sufficient funds for the purchase

[16] *Ibid.*, ch. 24, sec. 8-1-11 (1965).

[17] This is especially true if there are railroads in the taxing district since questions of valuation arise so frequently.

[18] *Ill. Rev. Stat.*, ch. 24, sec. 8-1-13 (1965).

[19] *Ibid.*, ch. 24, sec. 8-1-14 (1965).

and bond financing would be impractical. Installment purchasing of the equipment might be possible, but if it were not, the city might find its hands tied. Early in the 1900's, several local government units tried to issue warrants in anticipation of taxes for five- or ten-year periods. The State Supreme Court ruled such attempts at avoiding debt limits invalid.[20]

Several states have enhanced short-term municipal borrowing powers by authorizing municipalities to borrow for periods of from three to five years from local banks. Such legislation fills a gap in borrowing power that exists between bond issues and tax anticipation warrants.

The corporate authorities of a municipality may also by ordinance, and without referral to the voters, issue refunding bonds at any time regardless of debt limits. That is, debt obligtaions must be serviced even if assessments decline so rapidly that the ratio of indebtedness to equalized property values comes to exceed statutory or constitutional limits. Refunding bonds can be used to pay for matured coupons evidencing interest due on unpaid bonds, to pay off matured or callable bonds, or to refund bonds prior to their maturity.[21]

While refunding bonds, like general obligation bonds, are subject to a 20-year maximum life and an interest rate of not more than 6 per cent,[22] they are more likely to be made callable. Actually, these bonds act as an extension of time in liquidating the outstanding debt. Making the bonds callable raises the premium or interest rate on the bonds but could mean substantial interest savings in the future. If the circumstances which made repayment on the original schedule impossible are expected to be temporary, the callable feature is of special importance. The refunding operation preserves the municipality's credit rating and the callable feature permits rapid liquidation of the obligation when the financial crisis is past.

Revenue bonds for municipal utilities, swimming pools, and airports may also be refunded provided the refunding bonds are guaranteed as payable solely from the income of these facilities.[23]

Still another type of bond issued by municipalities is the judgment funding bond. These bonds may be issued by a municipality after a creditor obtains a court judgment that the city is obligated to pay its bills. After the judgment has been obtained, the city, without referendum, issues judgment funding bonds to pay its creditor and levies a

---

[20] Illinois Tax Commission, *Bonded Indebtedness of Local Governments, 1927-1940* (Springfield: 1940), p. 132.

[21] *Ill. Rev. Stat.*, ch. 24, sec. 8-4-3 (1965).

[22] *Ibid.*, ch. 24, secs. 8-4-4–8-4-7 (1965).

[23] *Ibid.*, ch. 24, sec. 8-4-14 (1965).

direct annual tax to retire these bonds. In 1960, five municipalities levied for judgment funds,[24] but the most extensive use is in East St. Louis. This city is financially unable to provide adequate city services due to high tax delinquency rates and an inadequate property tax base. Yet, some of these services have been provided from monies borrowed from local creditors — usually banks.[25] The creditor obtains a judgment against the city so that judgment funding bonds may be issued and a judgment fund rate extended against the property tax base of the community. Judgment fund tax rates are not subject to tax limits and warrants may be issued in anticipation of these taxes. Chicago has a special judgment fund tax, or an additional tax to the corporate fund. In the other municipalities the court may set the rate or determine how much of the judgment is to be repaid annually.

Municipalities establish sinking funds in which they accumulate monies to meet principal and interest payments on their indebtedness as it falls due. Excess tax collections or revenues that result from the sale of bonds at a premium accrue in the sinking fund. Investments are made in federal or state securities or in the municipalities own debt issues.

Illinois statutes provide that in every municipality there shall be a sinking fund commission made up of the mayor or president, the chairman of the finance committee, and the comptroller or municipal clerk The commission manages the sinking fund assets, and it has the authority to invest accumulations in the fund not currently needed to repay principal or interest on a given issue.[26] Refunding bonds have special sinking fund accounts and accumulations in these accounts may be invested by the corporate authorities if refunding issues cannot be called or purchased before maturity.[27]

Numerous authors have questioned accumulations in sinking funds as a temptation to dishonesty and have asked if they might not be diverted into corporate uses other than repaying indebtedness. Also, especially for smaller municipalities, sinking funds cause administrative management problems. It takes skilled personnel and constant attention to the market to manage a large sinking fund in such a fashion that debt obligations can be retired as they fall due. Admittedly, proper management of sinking funds can yield substantial savings on the cost of retiring any debt issue. However, most municipal obligations are

---

[24] See Table 17.

[25] David A. Meeker, "East St. Louis Expects Deficit of $900,000; Tax Hike Likely," *St. Louis Post-Dispatch,* May 8, 1966.

[26] *Ill. Rev. Stat.,* ch. 24, secs. 8-4-11, 8-4-12 (1965).

[27] *Ibid.,* ch. 24, sec. 8-4-8 (1965).

issued in the form of serial bonds, maturing in various years during the period of indebtedness. Repaying portions of the principal on the indebtedness each year not only makes the bonds more marketable[28] but also reduces the administrative responsibility for maintaining large sinking funds over long time periods.

Several court actions have questioned the proper use of sinking funds. In one instance, the objector sought to have the loss and cost portion of the bond and interest tax rate abated on the basis that earnings from interest-bearing sinking fund securities and other nontax earnings would offset the loss and cost of collection. The court ruled that the Constitution requires not only the levy, but also the collection, of sufficient taxes to repay indebtedness within 20 years.[29] The legislature has not indicated that tax levies are to be abated even if unexpected tax collections provide a surplus in the sinking fund. In a similar case, the court ruled a sanitary district did not have to abate its tax levy for principal simply because it had larger accumulations in the sinking fund than in other years. In cases other than the purchase and cancellation of bonds, questions of abatement of tax levies are to be left solely to the discretion of the taxing authorities.[30]

DEBT LIMITATIONS

A partial list of specific powers granted to municipalities by the state legislature has been provided above. However, this authority is subject to several kinds of limitations, including constitutional limitations. At the time the Illinois Constitution was adopted in 1870, municipalities had not been granted the authority to issue nonguaranteed debt. Municipal debt issues were all backed by their taxing powers, and since the property tax was the main tax, debt limits related the amount of outstanding debt to the assessed value of the taxing unit.[31]

The Constitution prohibits municipal indebtedness in excess of 5 per cent of the assessed valuation of the taxing unit.[32] A statutory limitation of 2.5 per cent was imposed in 1927 when the basis for state equalization of local assessment was increased from 50 to 100 per cent.[33]

---

[28] Short-, medium-, and long-term investors can be attracted because of the varying maturities making up the serial issue.

[29] *People ex rel. Korzen* v. *Englemann,* 32 Ill. 2d 196 (1964).

[30] *People ex rel. Brenza* v. *Gebbie,* 5 Ill. 2d 565 (1955).

[31] For a history of the development of debt limitations see: Illinois Tax Commission, *op. cit.,* pp. 93-112; and Howards, *op. cit.,* ch. 4.

[32] *Illinois Constitution* (1870), Article IX, sec. 12.

[33] Illinois Tax Commission, *op. cit.,* p. 95; and *Ill. Rev. Stat.,* ch. 24, sec. 8-5-1 (1965).

The legislature has made several exceptions to the statutory debt limit,[34] granted municipalities authority to issue nonguaranteed debt, and permitted the formation of numerous kinds of special districts. Each of these actions has eased the restrictiveness of percentage limitations based on assessed value of property. Special districts are subject to the 5 per cent constitutional debt limit, but to the extent one or more special districts overlap a municipality, the debt limit becomes additive. Instead of 5 per cent of assessed value providing the maximum amount of indebtedness for a particular area, the maximum becomes 10, 15, 20, or even a greater per cent of assessed value if enough special districts overlap the same area.

Aside from strict percentage limitations based on property values, the legislature has also sought to restrict debt issues by restricting the terms of issue. Most of the statutes authorizing debt issues require voter approval, although there are exceptions here also.[35] Other statutes specify maximum dollar amounts of bond issues, maximum interest rates, or restrictions regarding sale prices and selling procedures. The lack of regularity in these restrictions[36] is confusing. It is not clear whether the legislature simply lacks enthusiasm for debt restrictions or attempts to tailor the restrictions for each type of issue. It is clear, however, that the legislature is not prepared to accept market limitations as sufficient to protect the taxpayer and to maintain the solvency of municipalities.

Regardless of legal limitations, the amount of debt that a municipality can sell and its cost depend upon the municipality's credit rating. Among the factors which determine this rating, other than population and location, are the following:

1. Continuous responsible financial management over a period of years.
2. Past record of debt service.
3. The general economy of the area.
4. The amount of industry in the area, its diversification and susceptibility to recessions.
5. Average income of the population and trend in population changes.
6. Per capita debt, size and trend in debt, and taxable resources.
7. Prospective borrowing needs.
8. Assessed value of property, the rate at which it is increasing, and the ratio of debt to such valuation.

---

[34] *Ibid.*, ch. 24, secs. 8-5-2–8-5-15 (1965).

[35] *Ibid.*, ch. 24, sec. 8-4-1 (1965). The exceptions noted earlier in this chapter and those falling under the Illinois Highway, Election and School codes are included.

[36] See Howards, *op. cit.*, pp. 56-60.

9. Past record of tax collections and delinquencies. Whether there are restrictions on assessment ratios.[37]

Changes in credit ratings can provide substantial savings or losses, depending upon the direction of the change. But a municipality with an Aa rating that is suddenly changed to A will find that interest costs of borrowing have risen as much as .375 to .5 per cent, depending on the time at which the market is entered. Many municipal officials simply accept their rating when they actually might have a good chance to alter it. One Chicago area city manager flew to New York recently to talk with officials of a leading rating service. His feeling was that he received an extremely fair hearing. He was able to present them with enough information on the assessed value and trends in ownership in the community that the earlier, higher credit rating was restored. The savings in interest costs from a small bond issue would more than offset the expenses involved in checking how the ratings were established. Often the ratings do not reflect the most recent information, and a municipality's rating may be influenced by the fact it is "in the Chicago area" or some other generality.

Aside from the characteristics listed above, the rating services are interested in the stability of the community and the trend in apartment building. Although it is not mentioned, racial mix of property owners or a changing population balance most assuredly affects credit ratings. One rule of thumb in judging municipal credit ratings involves the proportion of the city's budget that goes into debt servicing. If it is over 25 per cent, it indicates the city may not be in the best financial shape and its credit rating could suffer.[38] Another factor affecting credit ratings is the number and size of recent and contemplated debt issues. Two things are of interest to the rating services here: (1) does the city have a long-range financial plan, and (2) has it used debt issues to build a strong financial position. The city without any debt may not be in the best financial shape, especially if it has let its physical assets deteriorate. Such deterioration can mount up rapidly. Also, if a municipality has issued only general obligation bonds, it may indicate that they have not carefully considered the debt program or that voters in the area are extremely "easy."

GOING TO MARKET

When a local government decides to debt finance a particular project,

---

[37] Based upon a list of factors in Bankers Trust Company, *op. cit.*, pp. 13-14.

[38] Column 4 of Table 38 presents a similar index for the largest 41 municipalities in Illinois.

it means a trip to the capital or money market. Evidence cited earlier in this chapter indicated municipalities have been taking an increasing number of such trips in the postwar period. Interest costs on local government indebtedness increased from 2.4 per cent of total general revenue in 1952 to 3.6 per cent in 1963.[39] Nor is this the only cost that has to be paid. Debt issues must be sold and there is generally an expense to marketing bond issues. The amount of the marketing expense will depend largely on the community's credit rating and how frequently the municipality borrows, since the regular borrower may have learned some of the complexities of the capital and money markets.

To the uninitiated, the first venture to the financial markets must indeed seem complex. Bond attorneys are needed to check the legality of the issue before a syndicate will purchase it. Someone must prepare a prospectus for the issue, notify underwriters of the proposed issue, and circulate invitations for bids. A bank note company must be engaged to print the bonds, agents have to be selected to service the bonds for customers, and an accounting procedure must be established for assuring that interest will be paid and principal retired promptly. Fortunately, private firms provide all of these services. As noted by the Advisory Commission on Intergovernmental Relations: ". . . professional legal and financial services are made available to governmental borrowers by the investment market itself. . . . While these services are useful to the localities, it is the financial community's aim to put together a marketable bond package — *one that will attract investors.*"[40]

Although those who provide these professional services are interested primarily in protecting the investor, they must be given credit for increasing the marketability of municipal debt. In the growing postwar economy, the rating on local general obligation bonds has been high. A 1957 to 1961 Investment Bankers Association study found that over 45 per cent of the dollar volume of local guaranteed debt was rated either Aaa or Aa, the highest ratings.[41] Again, high credit ratings mean a reduced interest cost to the issuer.

The market for general obligation bonds has consisted primarily of commercial banks, fire and casualty insurance companies, and individual wealthy purchasers. All are concerned with the tax-exempt

---

[39] Advisory Commission on Intergovernmental Relations, *State Technical Assistance to Local Debt Management,* Information Report M-26 (Washington, D.C.: January, 1965), p. 6.

[40] *Ibid.*, p. 11. Italics added.

[41] Roland I. Robinson, *Money and Capital Markets* (New York: McGraw-Hill Book Co., 1964), p. 211.

earnings and will sell or buy these securities depending upon what they judge their taxable income will be for the immediate future.

Investors in revenue bonds are more apt to represent the general investing public and especially the life insurance companies. Yields are greater on revenue issues and usually they are term bonds so that they attract long-term investors. Unlike general obligation bonds, which are usually sold to a syndicate or investment banking house on the basis of sealed bids, revenue bond sales are often negotiated with an underwriter.

For both types of debt issue many technicalities such as the timing or the form of a bond issue plague the municipal fiscal officer. The advice of the professionals who serve the investment community is necessary in these matters, although an experienced finance officer often knows enough about the market to dispense with some of these services. In fact, good finance officers generally handle general obligation issues largely on their own. The market for revenue bonds is an entirely different one from the general obligation market and the municipal official finds professional advice indispensable.

Many municipalities make a practice of preparing for debt issues by keeping the banking community apprised of the city's financial position. Officials may send budgets and other financial data to banks in the large financial centers. Part of successfully marketing a debt issue is being known in the investment community. Finance officers often keep track of who purchased their last bond issue, who is likely to purchase the next one, and what banks and bankers can be cultivated and made responsive to future borrowing needs. When a prospectus on a bond issue is sent to the investment community, its reception is enhanced if the investors are already aware of the financial position of the municipality.

For short-term borrowing, especially for tax anticipation warrants, it is important that the municipality be aware of its tax rate limits. In some instances the city may find bond attorneys have a different limit listed than the city has been levying. If the limit determined by the bond attorneys is lower than the rate being extended, tax anticipation warrants might not bring in nearly as much as the city hoped to raise. Some municipalities operate at the limits on all or most of the tax rates they levy. Differences of opinion about tax rate limits are not infrequent. One Cook County municipality once found itself in the rare position where the bond attorneys allowed a substantially higher rate limit on a fund than the county clerk did. In fact, it was possible to borrow *more* in tax anticipation warrants than could be raised in taxes. This situation is nearly always the reverse.

DEBT PROFILE

A debt profile for Illinois' 41 largest municipalities is presented in Table 38. Net long-term debt per capita in 1962 ranged from $6.76 in Peoria to $255.34 in Highland Park.[42] These figures do not indicate the financial soundness of a given community, however. A city with a relatively low per capita debt is not necessarily any better off than a city with a higher per capita debt, since it may not have the capital facilities needed to provide municipal services, or it may be allowing its physical plant to deteriorate. In private accounting it is customary to present balance sheets on which outstanding debt is set against the total asset of the firm. In governmental accounting, no attempt is made to determine the value of fixed assets so it is impossible to know whether a large per capita debt results from recent construction of long-lived assets or whether it is an indication of serious financial difficulties. A related problem of interpretation results from the fact that the individual debt issues that make up the total indebtedness of a given city may not be comparable. In some cities a high proportion of the debt may be revenue bonds issued in connection with bridges, hospitals, utilities, or other income-producing enterprises. Since these bonds will not be repaid from tax revenue, they have a significantly different impact upon municipal finance than do bonds which are to be retired from tax revenue.

The debt profile presents a very general picture of the indebtedness of municipalities. It becomes more meaningful as more details are considered. For example, columns 3 and 4 of Table 38 provide some further indication of the burden which debt retirement is placing upon the taxpayers in the municipality, a factor often affecting the community's credit rating. A full appraisal of the debt conditions of the municipalities shown in the table would require more detail than it has been possible to provide.

SUMMARY

Most Illinois municipalities make considerable use of their power to borrow money. Many long-lived capital projects are financed by the sale of general obligation bonds which are repaid from property taxes

[42] Net long-term debt figures were arrived at by subtracting sinking fund cash and deposits from gross long-term debt outstanding at the end of fiscal year 1962. This does not yield an entirely accurate net indebtedness figure since some municipalities purchase securities with sinking fund monies but it was not possible to classify which securities were offsets to long-term debt issues. Many municipalities hold securities for employee retirement programs, but these were not separately classified either.

TABLE 38

DEBT PROFILE OF ILLINOIS MUNICIPALITIES OF OVER 25,000 POPULATION, 1962

	Per Capita, Net Long-Term Debt, 1962	Guaranteed Long-Term Debt as a Percentage of: Gross Long-Term Debt, 1962	Guaranteed Long-Term Debt as a Percentage of: Equalized Assessed Value, 1962	Bond and Interest Tax Rate as a Percentage of Total Municipal Rate, 1962	Per Cent Increase in Per Capita, Net Long-Term Indebtedness, 1957-62
Municipalities Outside Chicago SMSA					
Alton	$152.70	24.7	1.3	15.1	2081.4
Belleville	68.32	39.5	1.9	11.8	−8.0
Bloomington	154.35	30.1	1.3	7.2	26.5
Champaign	43.68	6.6	0.1	1.5	19.6
Danville	30.47	100.0	1.3	10.7	−28.7
Decatur	102.65	41.9	1.4	—	9.3
East St. Louis	192.53	22.1	2.1	36.4	337.9
Freeport	64.74	25.5	0.6	13.5	−8.9
Galesburg	160.74	40.9	2.4	23.7	602.8
Granite City	33.72	100.0	1.1	—	−29.0
Kankakee	93.24	8.6	0.3	11.0	96.3
Moline	130.85	8.2	0.3	2.6	89.5
Pekin	28.35	66.0	0.7	3.7	−40.0
Peoria	6.76	100.0	0.2	1.1	−64.3
Quincy	233.42	63.5	4.0	38.0	133.0
Rockford	91.40	59.6	1.3	14.0	185.8
Rock Island	166.90	1.8	0.1	1.6	109.8
Springfield	247.44	2.6	0.2	0.9	94.2
Urbana	85.15	88.7	3.3	33.1	1114.7
Average	112.68	30.2	1.1	11.9	91.4
Municipalities in Chicago SMSA					
Arlington Hgts.	60.09	30.6	0.6	31.1	−6.9
Aurora	22.15	47.9	0.4	7.8	62.6
Berwyn	64.44	30.0	0.8	9.6	35.3
Calumet City	23.36	51.4	0.6	15.2	−38.2
Chicago Hgts.	70.55	28.7	0.6	8.3	63.2

TABLE 38 (continued)

DEBT PROFILE OF ILLINOIS MUNICIPALITIES OF OVER 25,000 POPULATION, 1962

	Per Capita, Net Long-Term Debt, 1962	Guaranteed Long-Term Debt as a Percentage of:		Bond and Interest Tax Rate as a Percentage of Total Municipal Rate, 1962	Per Cent Increase in Per Capita, Net Long-Term Indebtedness, 1957-62
		Gross Long-Term Debt, 1962	Equalized Assessed Value, 1962		
Cicero	$ 90.17	61.9	1.6	7.8	17.0
Des Plaines	32.81	31.3	0.3	8.3	−40.8
Elgin	23.90	19.2	0.2	5.7	−13.5
Elmhurst	23.23	4.1	0.02	3.0	−57.0
Evanston	89.52	51.2	1.4	5.1	−3.7
Harvey	70.33	41.5	1.5	27.5	−32.0
Highland Park	255.34	53.5	2.4	27.8	543.8
Joliet	98.09	1.6	0.1	1.3	−25.1
Maywood	9.74	—	—	0.8	−38.8
Oak Lawn	41.59	11.9	0.2	5.7	−43.6
Oak Park	47.92	54.4	0.8	3.9	491.6
Park Forest	171.09	33.9	2.6	11.0	1592.3
Park Ridge	93.26	95.0	2.2	13.1	−20.6
Skokie	54.37	46.0	0.7	10.0	−25.0
Waukegan	69.23	5.3	0.1	1.7	−20.4
Wilmette	131.42	19.0	0.6	1.3	−20.8
Average	70.14	37.5	0.8	9.8	15.3
Chicago	205.95	39.6	2.9	17.9	63.9

SOURCE Compiled from data of U.S. Bureau of the Census, *Census of Governments: 1957* and *Census of Governments: 1962*, and data from the Illinois Department of Revenue, Property Tax Division.

or motor fuel tax funds. On the other hand, income-earning assets such as parking lots, hospitals, and utility facilities are often financed by the sale of revenue bonds. Special assessment bonds are commonly used to fund projects whose costs are to be assessed against benefited property owners, and tax anticipation warrants are sold to finance municipal operations during the long period between tax levy and tax collection. Although floating a municipal bond issue involves the financial officers of a municipality in a maze of complicated and unfamiliar procedures, there exists a well-coordinated group of specialists who will guide him through the process. Although the specialist's primary loyalty is not to the municipality, he does provide a valuable service by providing a smoothly functioning market for municipal securities.

Unfortunately, data which would permit a complete appraisal of the debt position of Illinois municipalities are not available. It is clear, however, that Illinois municipalities have been doing an increasing amount of borrowing in the postwar period and that there is great variation in the amount and composition of debt outstanding among the various cities.

8 FINANCIAL DECISIONS AND COMMUNITY CHARACTERISTICS

The preceding chapters include a great many details concerning the expenditure and revenue patterns of Illinois municipalities. They describe the financial powers and responsibilities which are delegated to municipalities and provide information about some factors external to the political system which influence financial decisions. This chapter is concerned with two related questions. The first of these involves the impact which municipal financial decisions have upon the community and its residents. Briefly stated, the question is: "Does it make any difference what expenditure and revenue policies are followed?"

If financial policies do make a significant difference, then it is important to inquire into the way decisions are made and the factors which influence the process. The second question is an inquiry into the factors which determine the financial policies pursued in a particular city.

THE IMPORTANCE OF FINANCIAL POLICY

As indicated in Chapter 1, Illinois cities differ greatly in character and function. Perhaps the greatest differences occur within the Chicago metropolitan area where cities tend to be highly specialized. Some suburbs are high income residential areas, some are low income residential areas, some are industrial, and some are balanced. Some suburbs are new cities in the sense that a high proportion of buildings, streets, and other improvements is of recent construction. Other suburbs are mature with a high proportion of old construction and little vacant land on which further construction could occur.

Downstate there is less specialization. Almost all municipalities serve as regional shopping and marketing centers, but there are other differences. Several downstate cities are highly industrialized. Some, like Springfield, depend heavily upon governmental activities and tourism. Others, like Champaign and Urbana, exist almost solely because of a single state institution. A few, like Bloomington, are characterized as "white collar" cities due to the existence of firms and industries employing large numbers of clerical workers.

Regardless of the existing characteristics of the city, every municipality is in the process of transformation. As new structures are built, new residents and new types of activities are brought into the city. Also, existing structures become obsolete for existing purposes and are converted to satisfy new demands. The result is a change in the intensity of use of land and structures, in population mix, in income or age distribution, or in other socio-economic characteristics. Unlike other units of general government, municipalities may also change in size as the result of annexation.

The speed and direction of municipal change are determined in part by the existing characteristics of the municipality and its surroundings. It is probably inevitable that new residential suburbs will age and that deterioration of housing will bring about an influx of lower income residents. It is clear that some industrial areas are likely to become the sites of high income housing or major office buildings, and it is probable that downstate municipalities economically dependent upon a declining industry will lose both population and tax base.

The fact that future developments are shaped and constrained by the existing situation does not mean that this is an immutable process. Transformations frequently occur which are the result of decisions made by governments and by private individuals within the constraints imposed by existing situations.

Municipal governments may influence these developments through control measures, leadership, or financial policy. Control involves direct regulation of land use and activities within the municipality by zoning, housing regulation, business regulation, and ordinances controlling air and water pollution. Leadership involves municipal officials in leading and coordinating private and public activities which affect the nature and development of the community. City government can play an important role in developing and promoting plans for industrial development, improvements in race relations, or other broad-gauged programs aimed at conservation and development of a particular community asset, although the results may not always be as intended because of the complex interactions which occur.

Both control and leadership measures may require the expenditure of funds, but the limitations on these functions are seldom solely financial. Consequently, these activities are given little attention in this study. It is important to note, however, that the presence or absence of governmental activity in these areas can often be the variable needed to explain the character of financial decisions within a community.

Financial policy in turn affects both the character and development of a municipality, directly and indirectly. The direct effects are the immediate consequences of taxes and expenditures upon the community. Indirect effects are those which result from private actions which were induced by tax or expenditure policy.

The effectiveness of police protection in reducing crime rates, and the adequacy of street and sewerage systems, are matters that relate to the health and safety of residents and visitors alike. In a broader, but less tangible sense, municipal services, or the lack of them, can be said to affect the "life-style" of the community. The quantity and quality of municipal services have a direct effect upon the day-to-day activities of residents and visitors.

On the other side of the ledger, the tax payments that finance municipal services are drawn from income that might otherwise be spent for private purposes. The existence of high taxes may contribute to the slow growth of the city or to its actual decline. Considerable residential development on the fringes of municipalities is due to the desire of owners and developers to avoid municipal taxes. In Champaign, for example, an area of expensive residences extends as an unincorporated peninsula into the corporate limits.

The existence of fringe area developments often leads to disgruntled citizens and creates immediate financial problems for the city. A good many of the benefits of municipal services are enjoyed by residents of these fringe areas. Residents frequently drive to work on city streets and utilize city parks and playgrounds. In many cases municipal officials hesitate to refuse emergency police and fire protection services to the fringe resident. Occasionally, when city limits are irregularly shaped, services are even provided inadvertently.

The exact way that the indirect effects of financial policies come about varies from place to place, but where these policies affect private activities, they must be taken into account because of their effects on the character and development of a given community. Downstate, for example, population growth is closely related to employment opportunities and the effect which municipal financial policies have upon employment is given a good deal of attention. Low taxes are an attraction to the potential employer, but, at the same time, adequate roads, sewerage facilities, and police and fire protection for the plant are also important. A firm considering an investment in a downstate municipality may also be concerned with the quality of governmental services available to the plant personnel who will live in the community. Too often municipalities think more in terms of attracting new industry than in promoting the industry they already have. Certainly, attention must be paid to both alternatives if sound financial policy is to prevail. Low taxes may thwart the service desires of domestic industries while failing to provide inducements to the new industry sought.

It is difficult to state with precision just how important municipal taxes are as a factor in the process of municipal change and development. Popular opinion commonly holds that taxes are a major factor in the choice of industrial location but popular opinion can be misleading. Almost all the reputable studies have concluded that taxes are usually minor factors in industrial location.[1] Apparently, the minor role of taxes in industrial location decisions results from the fact that differences in state and local taxes are relatively small as compared with differences in other costs associated with different location. Variations in taxes are usually paralleled by differences in the level of governmental services that the business firm and its employees will enjoy. It is important to note here that most of the studies of the developmental effects of taxation have involved interstate comparisons. Industrial location decisions involving municipalities within a state differ somewhat from decisions involving choices among states. The smaller geographic area involved means that the "spillover" of governmental benefits is greater and this increases the possibility of finding a low tax location for an industrial plant situated so that the plant and its personnel reap the benefits of services provided by other municipalities. On the other hand, *municipal* taxes make up such a minor portion of total taxes that the savings resulting from municipal tax differences are usually relatively minor and may be easily offset by other considerations.

Residential location choices may be another matter. One writer has pointed out that a person is free to move from one community to another and thus to seek out the community that has the combination of public services and taxes that suits him best.[2] Clearly, a choice of residence is possible in a metropolitan area, and taxes and municipal services are among those factors which should be considered. On the other hand, the cost of moving from municipality to municipality and

[1] For a summary of the major studies of this subject see: John F. Due, "Studies of State-Local Tax Influences on Location of Industry," *National Tax Journal* (June, 1961), pp. 163-73.

[2] Charles M. Tiebout, "A Pure Theory of Local Expenditure," *The Journal of Political Economy* (October, 1956), pp. 416-24.

other barriers to free movement are so great that it seems unlikely that many persons move principally for this reason. Those most free to move, the wealthy, often choose to live in suburbs where control and regulation of land use virtually insures that many municipal services will be inefficient and per capita taxes high.[3]

THE DETERMINATION OF FINANCIAL POLICY

To answer the second question, "What determines municipal expenditure and tax policy?" attention must be directed to the way financial decisions are made.

Local decisions about municipal expenditure and tax policy are political decisions made within the framework established by state law. They are incremental decisions — not in the sense envisioned by economic theorists, but in a temporal sense — since all decisions are made as changes from an existing situation. Essentially, the process is one of reconciling demands for more government expenditures with demands that taxes not be increased. The decisions which are reached are affected by a number of factors external to the political process as well as by the attitudes and political skills of those involved in the process. Insights into the process and the factors which influence it can be gained by examining the demands and pressures which come to bear upon municipal officials and by analyzing the more common responses which they make.

Demand for increased municipal expenditures reaches municipal officials from several sources, both internal and external to the financial process, and varies in urgency depending upon the particular situation. A prime source of such a demand is the general citizenry of the municipality. Occasionally, pressure from this source takes the form of a well-organized, articulate demand for more expenditure in a broad programmatic or functional area. More commonly, such a demand is in the form of a complaint or request involving a very specific item. Thus, citizens may demand repair of a particular hole in the street or cleaning of a particular catch basin. The city official who expects to be retained

---

[3] Minimum lot sizes and other land use requirements are often set to insure wide spacing of houses and a minimum of commercial and industrial developments. The wide spacing means high costs for many governmental services such as streets and sewers and insures that total population will be small and overhead costs per person high. The exclusion of commercial and industrial property eliminates the possibility that industry will share governmental costs with the homeowner. The higher taxes in such a municipality are the price of obtaining a given community characteristic, not the cause of the characteristic. See: Wilbur R. Thompson, *A Preface to Urban Economics* (Baltimore: Johns Hopkins Press, 1965), pp. 259-63.

in office must realize that such requests are of great importance to the person involved and that his performance in office is apt to be judged by the way in which they are handled.

Department heads are another major source of pressure for additional expenditure. Sometimes this results from the fact that in a prosperous economic period it takes more money merely to do the same job. Rising costs of materials and labor require that departments receive periodic increases in their budgets in order to avoid the painful necessity of reducing the level of services and perhaps discharging employees. In many cases, however, department heads are not content with maintaining operations at the same level. It is almost inevitable that a department head is aware of needs which seem to justify increasing the level of services which his department provides, and he often carries these concerns to higher officials. The department head may be the first to appreciate the extent to which spillovers from similar programs of other governmental units affect his own service levels, positively or negatively. If higher officials appear unresponsive, he may even develop a constituency of his own which reinforces his request for a higher budget.

Employees often bring requests for wage and salary increases directly to higher municipal officials. Pressure for such increases is especially strong in the case of policemen and firemen who are well organized and make their demands at both local and state levels, but even unorganized workers make a strong case in a period of rising general wage levels. It is difficult to resist such wage demands, particularly where employees in neighboring governmental units and private industry have been receiving increases.

As noted, pressure or requirements that municipal government increase expenditure often arise outside the municipality itself. State legislative acts may require minimum pay scales for employees or set compulsory standards for retirement plans and other employee benefits. State and federal governments may also affect the level of municipal expenditure in such fields as public health, air pollution, and water pollution. Illinois cities have spent many millions of dollars in the last few years as a result of federal orders that they discontinue discharge of untreated sewage. Developments in overlapping or neighboring local governmental units can pressure a municipal official into financial decisions he might not have otherwise made. The official may find himself providing fire protection to property adjacent to the municipality or he may withhold the service in an effort to force annexation of these properties. In either case, the policies set by another governmental unit create pressures on the official which he cannot totally ignore.

Still another source of demand for increased municipal expenditure arises from the official's own ambitions for himself and his city. He is often aware that many of the needs of the city are not supported by organized interest groups and that demands for municipal services are not stimulated by the constant advertising which creates demand in the private sector of our economy. Thus, more than one person elected to municipal office as a "conservative" or an "economy advocate" have later found themselves promoting higher levels of municipal expenditure.

Against the impressive list of sources of demand for additional expenditure is an equally impressive list of constraints which prevent the meeting of all requests.

One of these constraints is the knowledge that increased taxes will encounter opposition. The city official who attempts to "sell" a new or expanded service is in a much different position than is a businessman who would sell a product or service. The businessman can offer immediate delivery of the product in exchange for a given sum of money. Sales are made one at a time so that there is no need to sell all prospective customers at once. The city official who offers increased city services in exchange for increased taxes is not in such a favorable position. The service is prospective and there is often no direct and immediate connection between the service and the payment of the tax. If taxes are imposed by public referendum it is necessary to have at least a majority of voters in favor on the date of the election; a poorly timed election has often spelled the difference between success and failure. Also, even the voter who favors the increased expenditure may vote against a given tax increase in the hope that another method of financing more favorable to him will be used

Legal limitations upon the revenue power of municipalities provide a potent constraint. No tax or revenue source may be utilized without the specific consent of the legislature. Property tax rate limits and the procedural requirements involving the tax levy and appropriation ordinance often circumscribe the action of municipal officials. Fragmented and highly decentralized administration of the property tax imposes rigidities in the tax system that have been noted in Chapters 3-5. The correlation analysis which is reported in Appendix A indicates that tax rate limits are an important factor in explaining variations in the level of expenditure of Illinois municipalities.

Still another set of constraints is economic. Although it is questionable that the notion of an economic limit to the level of taxation has much validity or usefulness, it is clear that it is much more difficult to raise funds in a municipality in which the tax base is small. Correlation analysis indicates that assessed value of taxable property is the variable most closely associated with variations in municipal expenditure.

The demands for more expenditure and the constraints which make it impossible to satisfy all of the demands create a conflict situation which must ultimately be settled through political processes. Many of the factors which enter these processes and affect the outcome are beyond the control of municipal officials, yet they are inevitably heavily involved and have a considerable amount of freedom in choosing the role which they can play. The responses described below represent two extremes among the many which municipal officials might make. A majority respond in ways which fall between these extremes or vary strategies depending upon the issues involved, the facts of the case, and the gains or losses anticipated to result from given actions.

One possible response can be described as passive. It amounts almost to a withdrawal from the decision-making process, except for performing clerical or ministerial functions. Such a role is possible, even for the principal officials of a municipality, because of the nature of the constraints on municipal action and because of the complex political system which tends to obscure responsibility. Related to the fact that new or increased taxes always cause complaint is the fact that old, familiar taxes usually cause little active complaint. Thus, while the municipal official is at a disadvantage in selling new services that require new taxes, he usually has no problem in maintaining existing levels of taxation. Further, some of the legal constraints upon expansion of tax revenue have the effect of making it easy to maintain existing levels. In some municipalities it is a long-established custom to levy certain property taxes at the maximum legal rate and few question the implication that the rates are "set" by the state.

Much the same clerical approach can be taken to the allocation of available funds among the various departments and activities. The city official who follows the passive strategy begins his budgeting process with the previous year's budget, makes necessary adjustments to allow for the automatic or unavoidable increases, and makes whatever additional changes are necessary to reconcile the total with the receipts expected from existing taxes at existing rates. Departments with earnings of their own or with earmarked property tax levies may regard any increases from these sources as "theirs," and often no effort is made to reallocate such sums.[4] In the case of those municipal functions such as

[4] Most departments for which there are special tax levies also receive funds from the general corporate fund or other sources so that it would be possible to offset increases in earmarked levies by reducing appropriations from other sources.

parks and libraries, which involve special boards within the structure of city government, it is especially easy for all parties to assume a clerical approach with the result that no real responsibility is assumed by anyone involved in the process.

In a municipality where the clerical or ministerial approach is followed, emphasis is put upon procedural details, and much responsibility is apt to fall upon the individual who has a detailed knowledge of these matters. Often this is a long-time member of the city council, the corporation counsel, or the city clerk. Occasionally, the expert on these matters is a person who has no official position in the city government.

Situations sometimes develop which disturb the "inactive" strategy and result in a period of change and crisis. This may occur because city services are shown to be inadequate in an emergency situation or because of the development of an obvious hazard to health and safety. An adverse court decision can reduce the permissible property tax levy and force a drastic curtailment of city services or the utilization of a new revenue source. Political opponents of incumbent officials are sometimes able to dramatize poor services or high taxes with such success that positive action must be taken. And, during the period of change, the political process becomes intensified, drawing into active participation many persons who ordinarily take little part in the decision-making process. The crisis period may end when new or surviving municipal officials are able to resume an inactive policy — perhaps at a different level of expenditure or with a slightly different revenue structure. In other cases, the end of the crisis finds a new set of officials committed to a more active role in the local fiscal process.

Many city managers and some elected officials are not content to assume the passive role. Although aware of the constraints upon their freedom to make decisions, some officials are determined to utilize the opportunities available to influence municipal policies. There are several positive actions which they can take in an effort to reconcile the demand for better services with revenue constraints.

One type of action is to attempt to secure better use of the available funds through a more satisfactory allocation of funds among the various purposes for which expenditures are made. This is essentially a problem of budgeting, since the legal requirements for appropriation and tax levy ordinances in Illinois tend to focus attention upon the funds from which expenditures are made and the objects for which money is spent rather than upon the services which are provided by a given expenditure. The detailed itemization of the appropriation ordinance and the fact that nothing may be spent for which an appropriation has not been made tend to encourage appropriations in excess of expected expenditure and render the appropriation ordinance largely meaningless as a budget document.

The municipal official who wants a budget document that focuses upon the kinds of services provided and that can be reconciled with the legally required appropriation ordinance must add classifications which focus upon the function or activity to be performed and then recombine items in the desired fashion. For example, the 1964 budget of the city of East St. Louis contained the following appropriations for fire protection:

	Personal Services	Contractual Services	Commodities	Other Charges	Capital Outlay	Total
General Fund						
Fire Department	$494,213	$96,130	$15,850	$1,600	$57,600	$665,393
Fire Commissioner	14,730	425	100	—	2,250	17,505
Fire Protection Fund	126,824	—	—	—	—	126,824
Total	$635,767	$96,555	$15,950	$1,600	$59,850	$809,722

In order to meet appropriation ordinance requirements, each of these major object classes has to be broken down in detail. Thus, personal services for the fire commissioner's office were itemized as:

Regular Salaries	$14,430
Temporary Salaries	300
Total	$14,730

and contractual services were broken down into the following items:

Services to Maintain Office Equipment	$ 50
Telephone	25
Maintenance of Automotive Equipment	300
Postage	50
Total	$425

Altogether, appropriations for fire protection were broken down into 52 separate appropriation items ranging in amount from $25.00 for the fire commissioner's telephone to $426,476 for regular salaries of firefighters.

In the city budget these items were regrouped and summed to provide the following functional or programmatic summary of fire protection expenditures:

General Fund	
Operating Expenses	
Fire Commissioner's Office	$ 15,255
Fire Department:	
Administration	17,210
Training	4,564
Communication	13,340
Fire Prevention	22,100
Firefighting	535,206
Building Maintenance	15,373
General Fund Operating Expenses	$623,048

Capital Outlay	
Fire Department	$ 57,600
Fire Commissioner's Office	2,250
Total Capital Outlay	$ 59,850
FIRE PROTECTION FUND	
Fire Department:	
Firefighting	$126,824
Total Fire Protection Expenditure	$809,722

It is clear that the latter classification focuses attention upon the kinds of services rendered rather than upon the object of expenditure and that decisions about the use of available funds may well differ when attention is focused in this way.[5] City officials who intend to take the role described as positive and creative ordinarily prefer the functional classification while those who prefer the passive role are content with the object-fund classification required for the appropriation ordinance. To those who prefer a functional classification the appropriation ordinance requirements are an unnecessary hindrance but by no means an unsurmountable obstacle.

Another aspect of improved utilization of existing funds involves seeing that the services which are being rendered are performed more cheaply and efficiently. Such an approach might include personnel policies designed to insure that well-qualified personnel are working at maximum efficiency and cost and accounting control techniques which enable city officials to know and control costs of doing a particular job.

Efforts to control costs have, in some instances, resulted in incorporating unit cost data in the budget document. In Decatur, the budget document includes a great deal of data concerning costs of performing particular tasks. Past and expected costs per unit of performance are included for such items as vehicle operation (per mile for each vehicle), traffic lines painted (per foot), sign posts installed, truck loads of tree limbs hauled and burned, catch basins pumped, police patrol (miles), and deaths recorded. Some activities, of course, are not subject to this kind of cost comparison. For example, the only unit cost estimates provided for the executive department are operating and maintenance cost data for a single vehicle. Unit cost data for the legal and engineering departments include instances where the unit is an hour of work and thus tells little about the cost of output.[6]

A determined effort to inform the public about the services per-

---

[5] For an excellent analysis of the role which the informational system has upon budget decisions see: Thomas J. Anton, *The Politics of State Expenditure in Illinois* (Urbana and London: University of Illinois Press, 1966).

[6] City of Decatur, *1964-65 Annual Budget.*

formed by the municipality and about the financial affairs of the city has been found by some officials to be the key to building support for expenditure programs. A number of cities publish budget documents and some also publish separate annual financial reports. Usually copies of these documents are sent to newspapers, civic organizations, banks, and bond houses and are made available upon request to other interested persons. A few cities publish periodicals which contain items of interest to residents. For example, the April, 1965, issue of *Around the Village,* published by the president and board of trustees of Skokie, was a four-page publication of which three pages were devoted to explaining the tax bills received by residents of the village. The fourth page was devoted to a review of the first year of operation of the "Skokie Swift," a demonstration rapid transit line connecting Skokie and the elevated line to downtown Chicago.

Other cities emphasize the use of leaflets and pamphlets on particular subjects. For example, Elgin publishes a 16-page pamphlet which includes a brief description of Elgin's finances, a table of organization of the city government, a short summary of the responsibilities of the boards and commissions, and a description of major city services. The publication concludes with a two-page directory of city services complete with appropriate telephone numbers. The city of Elgin also publishes a number of small leaflets dealing with particular subjects such as dog control, sidewalk repair and replacement, tax levies, and various aspects of the park and recreation program.

Other cities publish annual reports as supplements to local newspapers and almost all city officials accept invitations to speak on city government and to participate in sundry civic functions.

In some municipalities a good deal of attention has been devoted to increasing revenue by developing fees and charges which are related to the cost of the services rendered. In cases where such charges can be appropriately levied, they serve much the same function as do prices in the private sector — that is, they finance the production of the service and also limit the amount of service demanded.

City officials who follow the positive strategy usually think in terms well beyond the services rendered by the municipality within its boundaries. Some have taken the initiative to develop cooperative relations with overlapping or neighboring units of government in planning for development of the community or in working out cooperative agreements for the provision of services. Others play an active role in planning and guiding the development of the community itself. Thus some officials have been deeply involved in efforts to encourage annexation and industrial development as a way of enlarging the tax base.

The form which such efforts may logically take varies greatly from municipality to municipality. It can by no means be assumed that either annexation or industrial development will automatically improve the financial situation of a municipality.[7] Actions which Illinois city officials take to encourage annexation or economic development range from intense involvement in efforts to attract industry to relatively minor efforts to encourage and support the activity of private groups. In one large downstate city effort has been directed toward securing the annexation of industrial plants which surround the municipality. In another, there has been a large annexation which includes a considerable amount of low income and thinly developed residential property. In some other cities municipal officials have been active in selling the developers of small subdivisions and owners of existing houses upon the advantages of being within the city. In at least one downstate community, there was serious talk of merging two adjoining municipalities.

In all, it is clear that there are many possible ways in which a municipal official may move in an effort to meet the problems imposed by the demands for public services and the constraints which prevent the fulfillment of all the demands. He may attempt to use existing funds more effectively, either by reallocation of the funds to the different functions or purposes or by greater efficiency in accomplishing existing purposes. He may attempt to sell citizens upon the value of municipal services in order to improve acceptance of additional taxes that may become necessary. Another approach sometimes used is to attempt to increase revenue by imposing service charges or fees for specific services or by trying to enlarge the tax base through annexation and industrial development. All of these methods have been successfully used in Illinois but not all of them are useful in every situation. On the other hand, the methods may be complementary. For example, improving efficiency with which funds are used may be an important part of selling taxpayers on the value of the services being rendered.

Throughout this section reference has been made to "a municipal official" as if each city were governed by a single official responsible only to the voters. This is an oversimplification of the situation, result-

---

[7] Studies directed toward the effect which industrial development has upon the financial position of local government are commonly called cost-revenue studies. Examination of several such studies reveals that the impact depends upon the type of industry and the specific location involved. Even with regard to a specific location and a specific industry, it is not always easy to be sure what the net effect will be. For a selected list of such studies, see: Ruth L. Mace, *Costing Urban Development and Redevelopment* (Chapel Hill: Institute of Government, University of North Carolina, 1963).

ing from the fact that this study does not contain a detailed analysis of the political process. Actually, of course, there are several officials such as the mayor, councilman, manager, and others who potentially have the power to undertake the positive creative roles discussed. If only one of these persons attempts to do so or if several work to carry out a common policy, the oversimplified account given here is reasonably adequate. If several attempt to carry out active strategies which conflict at some point, intense political interaction will occur and only a more detailed study of the political process can present an accurate picture of what happens. It is also possible that different kinds of policies will be carried out at the same time. This is particularly likely to happen under the commission form of government since each commissioner heads his own department, but it can also occur under other forms of government. In one city a mayor who is of a different political party than the majority of the council has been able to pursue a generally positive policy, but one department head has succeeded in maintaining an independent position and follows a passive or status quo policy.

Municipal officials, then, and less directly, those who choose and influence them, have a choice of roles. They may choose a relatively inactive role and respond to pressure for change only when absolutely necessary or they may choose to play a positive, creative role, attempting to guide and shape the kind and quality of municipal services rendered and perhaps to project municipal government into an active role in the development of the community. Often the official who plays a positive role is a city manager who conceives of himself as a professional manager and who has at his disposal a great deal of information and a wide variety of techniques to improve efficiency and to shape budgets and reports so that citizens and elected officials are aware of the significance of the financial decisions which must be made. Often the city manager has a better idea of the level of service considered adequate by professionals and presents this information to the city council in a way that brings about a different decision than would result from the purely clerical or ministerial approach to financial decisions.

Officials of nonmanager cities are often part-time and are much more apt to follow a passive role but there are significant exceptions. A number of mayors take an active and effective interest in exploring the policy alternatives open to them and effectively employ the services of well-qualified finance officers, city planners, and other professionally trained assistants. Often this means the replacement of patronage employees the mayor may no longer feel are necessary for political support. The complexion of local politics itself changes once the active role is adopted.

Regardless of how active municipal officials may be, however, it is important to note that all decisions are made in the light of an existing situation. The level and pattern of expenditures and revenues are never determined *de novo* at any time but result from incremental decisions made in the context of an existing situation so that abrupt changes rarely occur.

9 AN APPRAISAL OF THE FINANCIAL PROBLEMS OF ILLINOIS MUNICIPALITIES

Few Illinois municipalities face financial crises, in the sense that there is serious question as to whether they will be able to maintain even a minimum level of city services from existing revenue sources. East St. Louis, with its low income population, low tax base, and high level of needs for police protection, urban renewal, and other "central city" services, does face such a crisis. Despite some encouraging signs of economic revival, it appears doubtful that the city will be able to finance the services needed to sustain such a revival. Only a reorganization of local government which would permit the city to obtain revenue from some of the industrial concerns which lie outside its limits or large infusions of state or federal funds are likely to solve a financial problem of this type.

In most Illinois municipalities financial problems are of a different sort. There is no doubt that the city is able to pay for services at existing expenditure levels. In fact, the present revenue structure will support moderate increases in expenditure in the coming years. At the same time municipal officials are aware that strong and conflicting pressures for better services prevail side by side with demands for lower taxes. It is doubtful that this type of financial problem can or should be "solved." As long as the political mechanism operates to transmit normal expenditure demands to municipal officials, they will remain in a position of having to mediate and compromise among conflicting positions. The important problem is whether or not the process results in decisions which produce "proper" levels of service and reasonable distributions of cost.

Naturally there is a lack of agreement as to what constitutes "proper" levels. One possible approach to an analysis of the situation is to focus upon the system or "machinery" used to reach decisions rather than upon the decisions themselves. This method is somewhat analogous to that of the economist who assumes that correct economic decisions will be reached if the system corresponds to or is at least an approximation of the competitive model. Another approach is to compare the results achieved with a separately determined list of desirable results. Either method involves a considerable amount of subjectivity and is certain to reflect personal preferences. Those who disagree with the appraisal in this chapter will undoubtedly find material in the first eight chapters which can be used to support alternative appraisals.

AN APPRAISAL OF THE SYSTEM

There are a number of reasons why a state government creates a local government and gives it power to make financial decisions.

First of all, it is essential to subdivide the process of decision-making. The number of decisions which must be made in providing a simple service such as garbage collection to the several million urban households in Illinois could not possibly be made by a single individual. There must be a division or delegation of responsibility for making these decisions. The creation of local government units with power to provide garbage collection services is a convenient and logical method of breaking the management problem into reasonable sizes.

The delegation of certain kinds of decisions to local government automatically means that they will be made by people with a knowledge of local conditions. To carry the garbage collection example one step further, it is entirely possible that technicians in Springfield could set up the routes and schedules for every garbage truck in the state, but there are many advantages of having this task done locally.

Still another reason for establishing local governments is to facilitate local variations in response to local conditions or local preferences. Residents of one municipality may prefer to have less frequent garbage collection and more parks while residents of another municipality may have the opposite preference.

There are, however, definite constraints or limits upon the amount of local variation which is desirable. There are a number of functions in which there is such a wide interest that it seems desirable to require minimum levels of service in all areas. It is clear, for example, that a municipality with an inadequate police force can become a base for criminals operating in a wide area and that inadequate sewerage treatment can affect health far beyond the city limits. For these reasons, the federal and state governments perform certain functions directly and impose minimum requirements for other functions which are performed by local units. The interdependence of geographic areas in a modern economy is such that local units of government should not be permitted to become low tax havens whose industries and residents enjoy the governmental services provided by neighboring units without making a proportionate tax contribution. Conversely, local units of government should not be given powers which permit them to levy discriminatory taxes upon nonresidents who do not receive a reasonable return in governmental services.

Two other requirements which should be met by a system which delegates power to local units are extremely important. The first of these is that responsibility and power should be coordinated so that the person or unit of government which has the responsibility for a given task has the power to perform it and the resources to finance it. Services which are of purely local interest should be financed locally and those which are of wider interest should be a charge against the entire area. The other requirement is that the system insure that those who make decisions, whether they are state legislators, municipal officials, or local voters, have a maximum amount of information about a proposed policy and its consequences.

Inevitably, some of the criteria used in appraising a system of local government finance are in conflict with others. For example, the requirement that a minimum level of service be provided limits the amount of variation that can occur as a result of local needs or local preferences.

The "decision-making machinery" for municipal finance in Illinois fails to strike a proper balance at several points. For example, the constraints are not always strong enough. Tax havens exist in the most flagrant forms in the St. Louis Metropolitan Area. Many municipalities throughout the state are plagued by the problem of having to provide services to residents of incorporated or unincorporated areas which are not matched either by tax contributions or by the provision of reciprocal services to residents of the municipality. Conversely, there are cases in which nonresidents or corporate taxpayers are subject to unfair taxation.

Perhaps the greatest weaknesses of the system involve the making of decisions and the fixing of responsibility for them. Specifically, (1) power and responsibility are not well coordinated, and (2) the information at the disposal of decision-makers often is not adequate.

To a considerable extent the lack of coordination between power and responsibility results from the way that the local fiscal process focuses on the property tax. The high degree of interrelatedness that exists among municipal revenue, debt, and expenditure procedures is a survival from the time when the property tax was virtually the sole source of municipal income. Appropriation and levy ordinances, rate limits, debt limits, assessments, and equalization procedures are all tied together by laws governing the property tax — albeit not always neatly. The highly fragmented administration of the local property tax is partially the result of historical accident and the changing nature of the units of government assigned portions of the administrative task. The result of this fragmentation is a wide diffusion of responsibility for maintaining adequate standards of equity and fairness.

In attempting to alter tax policy the municipal official often finds it necessary to deal with officials from other governmental units and with private parties instrumental in policy decisions. The technical expert interpreting property tax law enjoys wide prerogatives, consciously or unconsciously. Note, for example, the bond attorney who in ruling on the legality of bond issues becomes an authority on property tax rate limits. Without the mandate of local residents or the legislature his decisions as to what rate limits are can affect revenue, expenditure, and borrowing decisions in the community.

It is very difficult if not impossible for all of the officials involved in assessing, levying, equalizing, extending, abating, and collecting taxes to comply with all the details prescribed in the statutes. Errors are almost certain to be made in some of these procedures and, legally, the taxpayer can protest any time the law is not followed. Expert legal advice which would help to prevent errors is costly. Thus, the whole property tax process invites outside interference, litigation, and apathy and makes it very difficult for an ordinary taxpayer to participate in decision-making or to fix responsibility for the decisions that are made.

The linking of appropriation and levy ordinances also combines with the lengthy property tax administrative cycle to deny municipal officials and taxpayers the information that they need for rational decision-making. It is difficult to budget efficiently when the expenditure side of the budget document is executed as much as a year in advance of the due date for property tax revenues. The result is a clouded expenditure-revenue relationship which makes it difficult to make enlightened decisions.

Detailed statutory and case law, which prescribes the form in which appropriations and expenditures must be itemized in the appropriation ordinance and the published treasurer's report, contributes further to the obscuring of important facts about municipal finance. The kind of detail demanded in these documents may have been of value in preventing fraud or favoritism in a small rural government in the past but is of little value in telling a taxpayer what kinds of services his tax dollars are buying.

The large number of overlapping units of local government which exist in Illinois also contribute to confusion and lack of accurate knowledge about the operations of local government. The existence of several overlapping units of government tends to fragment local government budgeting and decision-making and to remove certain service functions from the scrutiny of the voter. The result may well be that certain special districts tend to become separate entities responsible more to their own administration and a limited number of supporters or constituents than to the citizens as a whole. Municipal officials sometimes find their own freedom of action reduced because they are held responsible for actions and tax levies over which they have absolutely no control.

In summary, the system within which Illinois municipal government financial decisions are made seems to differ considerably from the one described as a model or ideal at the beginning of the section. In part, this stems from the large number of units of local government which fragment both the tax base and the administrative process. In part, it stems from substantive and procedural requirements which the state imposes upon municipal government and which, intentionally or unintentionally, tend to separate power from responsibility and to make it difficult for decision-makers (voters or officials) to obtain information in the form which would be most useful to them.

AN APPRAISAL OF THE RESULTS

If one looks at the results of the decisions which are made under the existing system, one finds an uneven picture.

In a great many instances, municipal governments are performing a minimum number of traditional municipal service functions. The exact number of functions and the quality of services are strongly affected by the past. Residents are accustomed to certain kinds of government services performed in a particular way and in some cases, performed by specific people. Municipal employees have acquired job rights which may or may not be formalized into law, and municipal suppliers are accustomed to doing business on a certain basis. There is little discussion of the need for new or expanded services and less discussion of the possibility of eliminating or reducing any existing service. In many of these cities the visitor sees many tangible signs of the low level of municipal services. Streets are in bad repair, sidewalks and curbs are broken or nonexistent, and street lighting is inadequate. Sometimes sidewalks are overgrown with bushes, and trees obstruct motorists' views. In a few cities dead elms line the boulevards. Discussions with officials at city hall will usually reveal that they are aware of these conditions although rarely are they as vivid to the city officials as to the visitor seeing them for the first time. In some cases municipal officials are utilizing all of the revenue which they can obtain without new referenda. In other instances referenda have been held and defeated, but in the majority of cases, the decision to tolerate existing conditions has been an unconscious one. No advertising agency sells civic beauty, safety, or public health and so, almost by default, the decision has been made to buy things other than municipal services with the income of the residents.

On the other hand, there are a number of Illinois cities which are obviously well kept and well governed. Municipal officials in these cities have often made systematic studies of needs and have established a priority list of needed improvements. Often citizens' advisory groups have been involved in surveying community needs. These municipalities are not able to do all the things that they would like to, but there has been a weighing of alternatives and citizens have been confronted with the possible choices. There is evidence that the residents of Illinois municipalities are willing to pay higher taxes for better services if the alternatives are clearly spelled out and if they have confidence in the honesty and efficiency of the government. One municipal official uses the concept of a "disappointment gap" to illustrate the fact that improved municipal services often create demand for even more improvement. "I make speeches about our improved street cleaning program and get more complaints than before the program started."

In too few Illinois cities, municipal government not only provides a high level of government services but also fills a role as innovator and planner. In these cities municipal government is active in developing plans for the future development of the community and is interested in playing a role in the life of the community that goes far beyond the provision of tangible municipal services. In these cities municipal government is active in developing long-range community plans for the physical and social development of the community. Often such plans are developed in cooperation with private groups and other governmental agencies, and they may go beyond physical planning to deal with such matters as race relations, employment, and education. Unfortunately, special private interests may thwart the best planning efforts when citizens are lulled into apathy and regard city hall as the enemy to be avoided if not fought.

THE CHALLENGE TO MUNICIPAL GOVERNMENT

Within the week that these words were written the mayor of the nation's largest city declared that it will take $50 billion to make New

York livable and two prominent U.S. Senators castigated the Secretary of Urban Affairs for inaction and lack of imagination in attacking urban problems. Civil rights marchers in Chicago were showered with rocks and other debris despite a massive display of police strength. The sheriff of Cook County, in words which could have been borrowed from a counterpart in rural Mississippi, warned that a march of civil rights demonstrators into Cicero would be "suicidal."

In the light of these dramatic, intensely human events it is appropriate to ask whether or not the mundane facts of municipal finance which have been presented in this volume are of any relevance to the more dramatic and pressing problems which face urban areas in America. Does it matter how many dollars are spent on street cleaning and police protection in 41 Illinois cities, and what is the significance of the procedural details of tax levy ordinances?

The answer, of course, is that there are many direct and immediate connections. Municipal government is clearly in a key position to deal with urban problems. Despite the large sums of money spent by school districts and other special purpose districts, only the leaders of municipal government are apt to have the political connections and prestige to deal with the many facets of the problem. To solve the problems, however, will require large amounts of money, large amounts of courage, and much imagination.

Unfortunately, the ability of Illinois municipalities to deal with the problems which face them is greatly reduced by restrictions on their ability to raise money and by procedural requirements which encourage inaction and divide responsibility. It is true that municipalities with an unusually alert citizenry, a group of capable and devoted civic leaders, or an unusually good city manager may overcome most of the handicaps. Nevertheless, it remains true that the system within which municipal financial decisions are made in Illinois imposes handicaps which most municipalities have not overcome.[1]

There are three general areas in which the state legislature might

[1] As indicated in the Introduction, the material in this volume focuses largely upon the cities of over 25,000 population other than Chicago. Although a considerable amount of the analysis is applicable to Chicago, it should be recognized that there are a number of modifications which need to be made. It is clear, for example, that because of the lack of a limit on the Chicago corporate fund, the fact that the mayor appoints the governing boards of several of the overlapping special districts, and the important role which a Democratic mayor plays in the Democratic party in Illinois, the government of the City of Chicago is in a better position to deal with many problems than is the mayor of a smaller Illinois city. Perhaps this is fortunate, given the magnitude of the problems facing very large cities.

take action to strengthen the ability of municipalities to deal with their financial problems.

The first of these involves financial procedures. Archaic, overlegalistic appropriation and tax levy procedures need to be eliminated. Municipalities should be encouraged to utilize modern budgeting techniques which place the emphasis upon the functions for which expenditures are made and which are useful as a means of measuring the efficiency with which funds are spent. The municipality should be required to make its financial decisions public and full and useful reports should be made to the citizens, but mandatory publication of the treasurer's report in its present detailed form should be eliminated.

Property tax procedures should be reformed in order to produce a more equitable distribution of the tax burden and also to eliminate the uncertainties which lead to tax protests and tax negotiations.

The second area which should be given attention by the legislature involves the whole question of local government organization. It is fashionable to belabor the confusion and lack of coordination among the many overlapping units of government. It is realistic to point out that there are political barriers which make wholesale reorganization or consolidation unlikely. Nevertheless, it is a problem which deserves constant attention. The great progress which has been achieved in reducing the number of school districts suggests that the task may not be an impossible one.

Finally, there is a strong case for liberalizing the taxing powers of municipal government. The complications and inequities brought about by the Hodge-Downing Amendments should be eliminated and the statutory rates should again become controlling unless raised by local referendum. The equalization level is now approximately the same as the statewide average before the enactment of the Butler legislation in 1945 which reduced statutory rates by one-half. Thus, a return to statutory rates would give municipalities, on the average, only about one-half the property taxing power which they had in 1945. It would, however, eliminate the present city-to-city variation in the tax limits and, for most cities, it would represent an increase over present limits. Serious attention should also be given to provide municipalities with increased authority to utilize nonproperty taxes. Nonproperty taxes are more suitable for use by municipalities than by most other units of local government and several municipalities have voluntarily chosen to restrict property tax levies in favor of school or other units of local governments. Wider authority to levy such taxes would give all municipalities more freedom to choose the revenue package most suitable for their particular situation.

As it is unlikely that reorganization of local government will ever completely solve the problems created by the fact that benefits for municipal services extend beyond municipal boundaries, attention should also be given to designing revenue sources which collect revenues from areas that correspond more closely to the areas of benefit. Properly designed federal and state aid programs can contribute much but it is also possible to design local taxes which contribute to this end.

It is quite possible that reforms in the areas indicated would result in increased municipal taxes. At the same time, however, responsibility would be more clearly established and local voters would have a simple remedy if they decided that they preferred fewer services and lower taxes. Local government should be designed to maximize local choice within the constraints which must be imposed due to the interdependent nature of modern society.

APPENDIX A
MULTIPLE CORRELATION ANALYSIS

Some of the results of multiple correlation analysis of differences in per capita municipal expenditures have been reported in the text. This appendix is devoted to a discussion of the nature of such an analysis and a more detailed report of the results.

THE NATURE AND PLACE OF MULTIPLE CORRELATION ANALYSIS

Attempts to use multiple correlation analysis to explain differences in the level of per capita government expenditure may arise from any one of three motives. The researcher may be interested in understanding the decision-making process, he may be interested in changing or controlling the results of the process, or he may want to predict the results.

Regardless of the motive, multiple correlation analysis is a powerful tool. It is obvious, for example, that differences in the level of expenditures may arise, in part, from differences which can be measured quantitatively. For example, one would expect variations in the percentage of population which is of school age to be positively correlated with per capita expenditures. This hypothesis can be checked in a rough way by drawing a scatter diagram or by grouping school districts by the percentage of school age children and computing the average expenditure for each group. Unfortunately, however, there may be other factors at work. It could be, for example, that wealthy communities spend more per child enrolled in school and also tend to be the communities with the lowest percentage of school age children. Simple ranking or diagrammatic methods take account of only one factor at a time, while multiple correlation permits several variables to be considered simultaneously.

The ready availability of electronic computers in the last few years and the development of increasingly sophisticated programs have greatly stimulated the use of multiple correlation analysis to solve problems in the field of public finance. Although these studies have made important contributions to understanding the importance of some of the factors which influence the level of government expenditure, it is becoming increasingly clear that multiple correlation analysis will not, in itself, provide all the answers that are needed. Before the first such study, one might have entertained the thought that certain variables largely independent of each other would be discovered which, collectively, are highly correlated with the level of expenditure. Such a result would be highly satisfactory to researchers primarily interested in predicting the level of expenditures and would have revealed much about the possibility of controlling the result, but would have left rather important questions unanswered for the researcher interested in understanding how decisions are made.

Actually, of course, no such results have been obtained. Even in those studies in which the percentage of variation explained has been the highest, there has been a considerable amount of unexplained variation. Perhaps even more frustrating is the fact that variables which work best in a study of a particular area or level of government do not necessarily work equally well for other areas or levels of government. Furthermore, it is not unusual to find that two different sets of variables do an almost equally good job of explaining the same variation. Some of the weaknesses of correlation analysis which explain the less than perfect results are as simple and prosaic as the fact that needed data are unavailable or inaccurate. Others involve complicated explanations of the mathematical assumptions upon which correlation formulas rest.

Seven weaknessses of multiple correlation analysis, as it has been utilized in an effort to explain variations in the level of expenditure of governmental units, are discussed below. The relative importance of each varies from analysis to analysis but all should be kept in mind in interpreting the analyses reported in this appendix.

1. Weaknesses in the data. Little more need be said about this problem since much attention has been devoted to it in this volume. Clearly any attempt to correlate financial data is hampered because the basic records from which such data are obtained are set up with primary emphasis upon meeting legal requirements which emphasize statutory funds rather than broad purposes or functions. There is also a certain amount of variation in accounting treatments of similar items. Transforming these data to a standardized classification for use in correlation analysis involves both conceptual problems and inevitable human error.

Another type of weakness in the data results from differences in the structure of local government and in the way that the performance of certain functions is allocated among the various governmental and non-governmental units and agencies in a particular community. These differences create problems of comparison among communities which must be solved in a somewhat arbitrary fashion.

2. Correlation not causation. Correlation analysis is a mathematical technique which measures the degree of association among two or more variables. It provides various measures of the extent to which one (dependent) variable changes as other (independent) variables change. It is important to note, however, that correlation analysis does not determine causation. The researcher must determine which variable is to be designated as the dependent variable on the basis of his own knowledge and judgment. In some cases, such a judgment can be made with confidence; in other cases, the direction of causation must be arbitrarily assumed. Often there exists a very real possibility that a third variable affects both.

3. Arbitrary models. The mathematical relationship between the variables being analyzed may take many forms. The dependent variable may vary in direct proportion to the independent variable. It may vary in proportion to the square or the log of the independent variable or in more complicated ways. There is rarely any a priori basis for choosing a particular model, except previous experience with similar data. When the researcher chooses a regression model to be fitted to the data, he may assume that changes are proportional and use a linear model when some other model would be more appropriate. Electronic computers do make trial and error fitting of several models relatively easy, but the number of possible models is very large and there is a strong tendency to utilize linear models on the basis of greater simplicity of computation and easier explanation of the results.

4. Proxy variables not identified. Still another problem with correlation analysis is that it does not indicate whether an independent variable which appears to be important is important in its own right or as a proxy for another unknown variable. The simple correlation between assessed value of owner-occupied houses and median family income in the 39 cities (2 cities are excluded as noted below) which make up the group of cities with a population of over 25,000 population is .96. If a researcher were to include only one of these variables in the analysis without being aware of the close relationship between the two, he might easily offer an erroneous explanation of the relationship involved.

5. Multicollinearity. A somewhat different problem arises if two

highly correlated variables are included in the analysis. In this case the usual measures of the relative importance of the variables become unreliable.

As an extreme example of the erratic results that may follow when closely correlated variables are utilized in a correlation analysis, consider the attempt to analyze per capita assessed value, using a stepwise correlation procedure and including both median value of owner-occupied houses and median income of families as independent variables. Median value of houses was the first variable to enter and by the usual tests of importance of an independent variable it continued to rank as the most important variable as other variables were added in steps 2 and 3. In step 4, however, median income of families entered and the value of houses dropped in importance so drastically that it was removed in step 5.

In this case the correlation between the two variables was so high that it was decided to drop one of them completely and, in effect, to consider them as the same variable. A more troublesome case arises when the level of correlation among the two variables is so low that dropping one of them represents a sacrifice of important information.[1]

6. Process not revealed. Multiple correlation itself provides no information about the mechanics of the decision-making processes. A high correlation between a measure of municipal expenditure and a set of independent variables suggests that the variable or variables, for which they are proxy, influence the level of expenditure but tell nothing as to how this comes about. For example, if it should be determined that a high per capita assessed value is closely related to high per capita expenditures, one is faced with at least two plausible explanations of the nature of that relationship. One is that a high assessed value means that moderate tax rates, perhaps well under the legal limit, will yield large per capita revenues and that municipal officials take advantage of this by spending freely. A second possible explanation is that high per capita assessed values are characteristic of well-to-do municipalities and that residents of such communities demand and get a high quality of public service. If it is desired to understand, predict, or control the results of governmental decision-making, it makes a great deal of differ-

---

[1] An alternative solution to the problem is to use factor analysis to combine variables so that a smaller number of principal components, independent of each other, are identified. The main problem with this procedure is the interpretation of the components. It is often difficult to say just what is being measured by a factor which is a combination of several variables. George Bernard Pidot, Jr., "The Public Finances of Local Government in the Metropolitan United States" (unpublished Ph.D. thesis, Harvard University, 1965), pp. 197-230.

ence which of the two explanations is correct. The first explanation implies that municipal officials make expenditure decisions largely in response to the availability of funds and that there is either little public concern with the level of spending or little response to the concern. The second explanation implies that municipal officials make expenditure decisions in response to public demands for governmental services and that these demands are positively related to the level of private affluence.

Since either explanation is consistent with an identical set of relationships among such measurable variables as levels of income, assessed value, and tax rates, multiple correlation analysis cannot determine which is correct. It is necessary to know something more about the mechanics of decision-making.

7. Nonquantifiable variables. Clearly, one important weakness of multiple correlation analysis is that many variables which should be included in the analysis cannot be quantified. In some cases this is due to a lack of conceptual techniques; in other cases, methods of quantifying the variable are available, but only at a cost which is beyond the research budget. In general, it is easier to quantify factors which describe the conditions external to the political system such as demographic and economic characteristics than it is to quantify factors describing the governmental system or the decision-making process itself. It is undoubtedly for this reason that correlation studies of the level of expenditure have concentrated on the effect of such conditions upon expenditures and have paid little attention to the political system and the process of decision-making. Conversely, many studies of the political aspects of the problem have not utilized multiple correlation analysis even in those situations where it can make an important contribution.

AN ANALYSIS OF ILLINOIS MUNICIPAL EXPENDITURE

In the text of this volume emphasis has been placed upon describing the environment in which municipal financial decisions are made. This has involved both numerical data which describe the economic and demographic features of the community and verbal descriptions of the political system within which the decisions are made. The former produced a great deal of data which are well suited to use in correlation and regression analysis. The remainder of this appendix is devoted to a report on the analysis of this data and the results obtained. The most important reason for presenting this material in the appendix is to avoid the impression of overemphasis on the importance of multiple correlation analysis. Because there may well be a kind of multicollinearity among some quantified and some nonquantified variables, emphasis upon the proportion of variation "explained" by correlation analysis may obscure equally important nonquantified variables.

The relationships between the dependent variable and the independent variables are analyzed with the aid of a stepwise multiple correlation program prepared by the Statistical Service Unit of the University of Illinois. This program fits the data to linear regression equations of the form $Y = a + b_1x_1 + b_2x_2 + \ldots$ in a stepwise fashion. At each step, the variable which provides the biggest improvement in the "goodness of fit" is added to the equation until all variables which give a specified degree of improvement have been added. Since the significance of a variable may change as other variables are added, provision is also made for the deletion of variables from the equation when its significance drops below a predetermined F level. In the analyses reported here, variables are entered at an F of 2.5 and removed at 1.5.

Emphasis is placed upon analysis of cities of more than 25,000 population, but since there is no limit on the Chicago corporate fund and some tax limit data for Oak Lawn were not obtained, these cities were omitted, leaving a group of 39 municipalities.

In several cases correlations have also been run for a group of 107 cities, largely outside of Cook County, with population between 5,000 and 25,000.[2]

Fifteen variables are utilized in the analysis of total expenditure. They are:

X_1 Population of the municipality.
X_2 Population per square mile.
X_3 Per cent of population under 18.
X_4 Per cent of population living in group quarters.
X_5 Per cent increase in population, 1950-60.
X_6 Per cent of population nonwhite.
X_7 Per cent of population foreign born.
X_8 Median years of schooling.
X_9 Per capita assessed value.
X_{10} Per capita sales tax collections.
X_{11} Tax limits, six municipal funds.
X_{12} Per cent of families with incomes under $3,000.
X_{13} Median value of owner-occupied houses.
X_{14} Per capita nonenterprise general expenditure and park and sanitary district levies.
X_{15} Per capita current general expenditure and park and sanitary district levies.

[2] As indicated in Chapter 4, tax limit data for many Cook County municipalities could not be obtained from the Cook County clerk.

Variables X_1 through X_5 might be considered as demographic variables since they all involve the size of the city, changes in size, age, or geographic distribution of the population within the city.

Variables X_6 through X_8 include social characteristics of the population such as education, race, or ethnic background. These characteristics can affect expenditure in any of several ways. They may be associated with need for governmental services or with ability to finance governmental services, or they may be related to the political process in some way.

Variables X_9 through X_{13} are tax capacity variables, but they differ considerably in character. Variable X_{11} is not a measure of economic tax capacity but represents an attempt to measure the limits which the state has placed upon municipal utilization of the property tax. Specifically this variable is the sum of the tax limits (expressed in percentage) imposed by the state upon the following funds: corporate, public benefit, library, garbage disposal, fire protection, and street and bridge. The nature of these funds has been spelled out in detail in Chapter 5. The reader should be aware that there may be questions as to the correctness of some of these limits and that several important funds are not subject to rate limitations. Variable X_9 is a direct measure of one of the most important determinants of tax capacity, the assessed value of taxable property in the municipality. Assessed value is, of course, a function of both the true value of property located within the municipality and of assessment practices.

Sales tax yield (variable X_{10}) may be considered a measure of tax *capacity* as well as of yield because all of the municipalities levy it at the maximum permitted rate. Since even administration of the tax lies outside the city, it is permissible to consider this as a *capacity* rather than a performance or effort variable. Variables X_{12} and X_{13} are clearly measures of the wealth or economic well-being of the residents of the municipality. Median income of families is so highly correlated with variable X_{13} that it is not utilized in the analysis.

The first 13 variables are those which are ordinarily used as independent variables unless otherwise indicated in the tables.

Variable X_{14} is the measure of municipal expenditure that was developed in Chapter 2 and will be referred to as general expenditure. The value of this variable for each of the 39 cities was shown in column 2 of Table 14. Since this section is devoted to explaining total expenditure, X_{14} is the principal dependent variable. Variable X_{15} differs from X_{14} in that it includes only current expenditure. Capital expenditure is apt to be more irregular and one would expect that higher coefficients of correlation would be obtained from the use of current expenditure.[3]

Some of these variables are, of course, related to each other. Table A1 shows all of the simple correlation coefficients greater than .50 (positive or negative) among these variables for 39 cities with a population greater than 25,000.

Table A2 shows the results of the first correlation. These results are presented in a standard form which will be followed throughout the appendix. The heading provides information about the dependent variable, indicates which group of cities is involved, and indicates the type of regression equation which is being utilized.

The independent variables are listed in the order in which they entered the stepwise correlation procedure. The coefficient of multiple correlation shown is for the corresponding step in the procedure. Thus in Table A2 the correlation between general expenditure and per capita assessed value is .734. Actually this is a simple correlation coefficient (r) since only two variables are involved. When tax limits is added as an independent variable the multiple correlation (R) is .761. The addition of per cent foreign born as the third dependent variable raises the coefficient to .782. The corresponding standard errors of estimate are shown in parentheses under the correlation coefficient. The regression coefficients and t values shown in the next column are for the final step of the procedure. Thus the regression equation for Table A2 is as follows:

$$Y = -4.94 + .015X_9 + 20.218X_{11} + .930X_7$$

In this equation Y is used to stand for the estimated value of the dependent variable. The equation indicates that per capita general expenditure increases by one and one-half cents for each $1.00 increase in assessed value, by $20.22 for each percentage point increase in tax limits of the six municipal funds and by 93 cents for each percentage point increase in the percentage of foreign-born population.

Since the three independent variables are expressed in different units and have different standard deviations, it is not possible to determine the relative importance of the three variables by comparing regression coefficients. The standardized regression coefficients (betas) shown in the last column are designed to permit such comparison. In this case it is clear that per capita assessed value is by far the most important vari-

[3] For reasons of data availability, the derivation of values for X_{14} and X_{15} differs somewhat for the 107 cities and the 39 cities. For example, U.S. Census figures for highway expenditure are used for the 107 cities while data from the Illinois Division of Highways are used for the 39 cities.

TABLE A1

SIMPLE CORRELATION COEFFICIENTS GREATER THAN .500, INDEPENDENT VARIABLES, 39 CITIES

	X_2 Population per Square Mile	X_3 Per Cent of Population Under 18	X_4 Per Cent of Population Living in Group Quarters	X_5 Per Cent Increase in Population, 1950-60	X_6 Per Cent of Population Nonwhite	X_7 Per Cent of Population Foreign Born	X_8 Median Years of Schooling of Residents	X_9 Per Capita Assessed Value	X_{12} Per Cent of Families with Incomes Under $3,000	X_{13} Median Value of Owner-Occupied Houses
X_2 Population per Square Mile	1.000									
X_3 Per Cent of Population Under 18		1.000								
X_4 Per Cent of Population Living in Group Quarters		−.516	1.000							
X_5 Per Cent Increase in Population, 1950-60		.717		1.000						
X_6 Per Cent of Population Nonwhite					1.000					
X_7 Per Cent of Population Foreign Born	.616					1.000				
X_8 Median Years of Schooling of Residents				.511			1.000			
X_9 Per Capita Assessed Value								1.000		
X_{12} Per Cent of Families with Incomes Under $3,000		−.561			.634	−.513	−.641		1.000	
X_{13} Median Value of Owner-Occupied Houses						.530	.729	.535	−.780	1.000

TABLE A2

COEFFICIENTS OF MULTIPLE CORRELATION AND REGRESSION

Dependent variable: X_{14} — Per capita nonenterprise general expenditure and park and sanitary district levies

Sample size: 39 Mean and standard deviation of dependent variable: 57.23 (14.68)

Statistical model: Linear

Independent Variables[a]	Coefficient of Multiple Correlation[b] (Standard Error)	Regression Coefficient (t)[c]	Standardized Regression Coefficient
X_9 — Per Capita Assessed Value	.734 (10.11)	.015 (6.23)	.703
X_{11} — Tax Limits, Six Municipal Funds	.761 (9.78)	20.218 (1.78)	.191
X_7 — Per Cent of Population Foreign Born	.782 (9.53)	.930 (1.71)	.191
	Y intercept = −4.94		

[a] Listed in order of entry into stepwise program.

[b] Coefficient at corresponding step in analysis. Final figure represents the coefficient at completion of stepwise procedure.

[c] Regression coefficient divided by standard error.

able. It enters first and is obviously of far greater importance whether t values or standardized regression coefficients are utilized as a measure of importance.

None of the three variables which enter the analysis of Table A2 is closely correlated with the other two, hence the problem of multicollinearity is minimized. There are, of course, possible proxy variable problems, and certainly the results raise a number of questions about the decision-making mechanism. For example, one might wonder whether per capita assessed value is important only as an indicator of tax capacity, or whether it functions as an indicator of community wealth, which, in turn, is associated with demand for high quality municipal services. One might also wonder whether per cent of foreign-born population influences expenditure because foreign-born persons and their descendants have a different attitude toward public expenditure, because there are differences in the political processes in communities with a large foreign-born population, or simply because per cent of foreign born is serving as a proxy measure of another characteristic such as community wealth or degree of urbanization. The latter possibility gets some support because there is correlation between per cent foreign born and population per square mile, median values of owner-occupied houses, and per cent of families with incomes under \$3,000. Probably there should be a presumption in favor of accepting the conclusion that per cent of foreign born is important in its own right, since it and not the other variables mentioned enters the stepwise correlation not only when the 39 cities are analyzed but also in problems utilizing data from the 107 cities reported below.

Since tax rates are multiplied by assessed value to determine tax levies, it is possible that a model which involves a multiplicative rather than an additive relationship between these two variables might be appropriate. The results of an attempt to test this hypothesis are shown in Table A3. The modification results in a smaller coefficient of multiple correlation and the combined variable (X_9X_{11}) is not as highly correlated with general expenditure as is assessed value alone.[4]

TABLE A3

COEFFICIENTS OF MULTIPLE CORRELATION AND REGRESSION

Dependent variable: X_{14} — Per capita nonenterprise general expenditure and park and sanitary district levies

Sample size: 39 Mean and standard deviation of dependent variable: 57.23 (14.68)

Statistical model: Linear[a]

Independent Variables	Coefficient of Multiple Correlation (Standard Error)	Regression Coefficient (t)	Standardized Regression Coefficient
X_9X_{11} — Per Capita Assessed Value × Tax Limits, Six Municipal Funds	.569 (12.23)	1.233 (3.53)	.436
X_{13} — Median Value of Owner-Occupied Houses	.678 (11.09)	.001 (3.50)	.430
X_1 — Population of the Municipality	.718 (10.65)	.0002 (2.01)	.247
	Y intercept = 11.93		

[a] The first independent variable entered is the product of variables X_9 (per capita assessed value) and X_{11} (tax limits).

[4] The relationship between assessed value and tax limits is explored more fully below.

TABLE A4

COEFFICIENTS OF MULTIPLE CORRELATION AND REGRESSION

Dependent variable: X_{14} — Per capita nonenterprise general expenditure and park and sanitary district levies

Sample size: 39 Mean and standard deviation of dependent variable: 4.019 (.237)

Statistical model: Log-log transformation[a]

Independent Variables	Coefficient of Multiple Correlation (Standard Error)	Regression Coefficient (t)	Standardized Regression Coefficient
X_9 — Per Capita Assessed Value	.680 (.176)	.666 (.536)	.604
X_{11} — Tax Limits, Six Municipal Funds	.717 (.170)	.234 (2.15)	.246
X_7 — Per Cent of Population Foreign Born	.744 (.165)	.101 (2.21)	.256
X_5 — Per Cent Increase in Population, 1950-60	.765 (.162)	−.074 (−2.97)	−.476
X_3 — Per Cent of Population Under 18	.788 (.157)	.520 (2.07)	.314
X_8 — Median Years of Schooling	.807 (.153)	.481 (1.69)	.215
	Y intercept = −4.113		

[a] All variables (independent and dependent) are taken to log base e and a linear regression equation is employed.

Table A4 reports the results of still another modification of the model. In this case both the dependent and independent variables were transformed by being taken to log base e before being fitted to a linear regression. The resulting regression equation is a multiplicative one of the form:

$$\log Y = -4.113 X_9^{.666} X_{11}^{.717} \ldots$$

Use of this model results in a total of six independent variables entering and produces a slightly higher coefficient of correlation. The first three variables to enter are those which entered the linear model of Table A2 but three additional variables enter. If standardized regression coefficients are utilized as measures of the relative importance of the variable, two of these additional variables are more important than are tax limits and per cent of foreign born.

Although the regression coefficients which have been obtained are relatively high for this type of data, there is still a good deal of unexplained variation. For example, a multiple correlation coefficient of .782 (Table A2) means that only $(.782)^2$ or about 61 per cent of total variation has been statistically "explained." Furthermore, the standard error of $9.53 means that approximately one-third of the per capita expenditure figures "predicted" by the regression equation will be wrong by more than $9.53.

It is sometimes possible to learn more about the forces at work by studying the pattern of differences between the "predicted" and actual expenditure. An analysis of such residuals, computed from the Table A2 regression equation, reveals that the city with the highest positive residual spent $26.29 more than predicted by the regression equation. Looking at the expenditure detail for this city it is observed that more than $13.00 per capita was spent for library capital expenditure in fiscal 1962. This suggests that expenditure for this year may have been unusually high due, in part, to the fact that the city built a new library.

It is also possible to use residuals to determine whether nonquantifiable factors are influencing expenditure in a systematic way. The residuals computed from this linear regression equation were utilized to check the hypothesis that the existence of the city manager form of government affects total expenditure and the possibility that location within one of the SMSA groups would have an influence not reflected in the regression equation. It was found that the 17 manager cities spent an average of five cents less than predicted and that the 22 non–city manager cities spent an average of four and one-half cents more than predicted. This difference is obviously not statistically or practically significant.

The 20 cities within the Chicago SMSA expended 41 cents less per capita than predicted. The 13 cities in downstate SMSA's spent 32 cents less than predicted and the six cities not in a SMSA spent $2.08 more than predicted. In view of the small size of the latter group and the fact that all of the "excess" expenditure occurred in two cities, it is doubtful that any significance should be attached to these variations.

The fact that some of the cities with unusually high residuals are cities which had heavy capital expenditure during fiscal year 1962 suggests that a higher level of correlation might be obtained by modifying the dependent variable so as to exclude capital expenditure.

The results of this are shown in Table A5. The level of correlation has been raised slightly above the level of Table A2 and one additional variable has entered. Another difference is that percentage of population foreign born now appears to be of considerably more importance than tax limits.

TABLE A5

COEFFICIENTS OF MULTIPLE CORRELATION AND REGRESSION

Dependent variable: X_{15} — Per capita current general expenditure and park and sanitary district levies

Sample size: 39 Mean and standard deviation of dependent variable: 46.08 (11.16)

Statistical model: Linear

Independent Variables	Coefficient of Multiple Correlation (Standard Error)	Regression Coefficient (t)	Standardized Regression Coefficient
X_9 — Per Capita Assessed Value	.686 (8.23)	.0100 (5.85)	.635
X_7 — Per Cent of Population Foreign Born	.778 (7.20)	1.4469 (3.70)	.391
X_{11} — Tax Limits, Six Municipal Funds	.801 (6.96)	14.2039 (1.75)	.176
X_6 — Per Cent of Population Nonwhite	.817 (6.81)	.2282 (1.61)	.167
	Y intercept = −2.200		

Because of the importance of per capita assessed value, this variable was deleted from the independent variables and used as a dependent variable. The results are shown in Table A6. Interestingly, none of the independent variables which entered Table A2 entered Table A6. The most important variable in explaining the size of per capita assessed value is median value of owner-occupied houses. This is not an unexpected result, since houses make up a very substantial part of the assessed value in most Illinois municipalities. The positive correlation of assessed value and retail sales tax collections probably reflects the role of commercial property in the tax base. Unfortunately, it has not been possible to develop data that reflect the presence of manufacturing and industrial property in the base. If such a variable were available, it would probably be of equal or greater importance than sales tax collections.

Figure A1 is a diagrammatic representation of the results shown in Tables A1, A2, and A6. All of these are based upon linear correlation of data for the 39 cities. The solid lines connect the significant independent variables to the dependent variables. The beta value on the solid lines indicates the relative importance of the independent vari-

TABLE A6

COEFFICIENTS OF MULTIPLE CORRELATION AND REGRESSION

Dependent variable: X_9 — Per capita assessed value
Sample size: 39 Mean and standard deviation of dependent variable: 3217.68 (709.91)
Statistical model: Linear

Independent Variables	Coefficient of Multiple Correlation (Standard Error)	Regression Coefficient (t)	Standardized Regression Coefficient
X_{13} — Median Value of Owner-Occupied Houses	.535 (607.91)	.0869 (5.37)	.748
X_{10} — Per Capita Sales Tax Collections	.659 (548.40)	95.0835 (1.85)	.248
X_1 — Population of the Municipality	.688 (536.91)	.0083 (1.97)	.248
X_2 — Population Per Square Mile	.715 (524.60)	−.0677 (−1.96)	−.246
X_5 — Per Cent Increase in Population, 1950-60	.740 (512.71)	−2.2340 (−1.61)	−.221
	Y intercept = 1160.30		

ables. The broken lines indicate simple correlations of more than .500 among variables which did not enter the multiple correlation process.

Figure A1 indicates clearly the complicated interconnections among the various variables and suggests the danger of drawing quick generalizations about the nature of the forces which may affect the level of municipal expenditure in Illinois. Fortunately, some positive generalizations can be drawn. It is clear that the level of expenditure in a municipality is very closely related to the economic well-being or affluence of the community. Not only is assessed valuation the most important "determinant" of expenditure but median value of owner-occupied houses is the most important variable when assessed value is used as the dependent variable. Furthermore, median value of owner-occupied houses is closely related to several other measures of the affluence of the community shown in the chart.

Much statistical theory is based upon the idea of drawing a sample from a much larger universe. If certain conditions such as the randomness of the sample are met, tests of statistical significance are available for determining the probability that various characteristics of the sample are also characteristic of the total universe.

FIGURE A1

DIAGRAMMATIC REPRESENTATION OF MULTIPLE AND SIMPLE CORRELATIONS

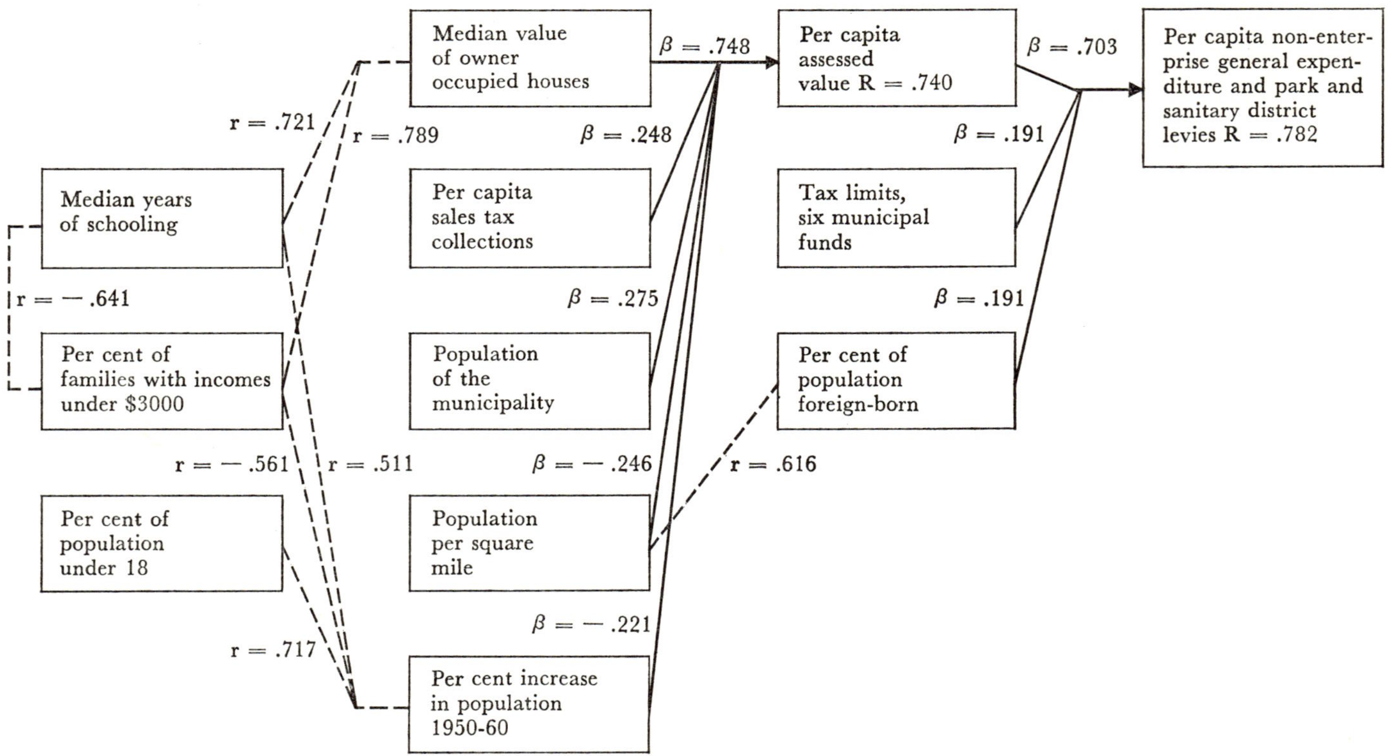

SOURCE: Tables A1, A2, A6

TABLE A7

COEFFICIENTS OF MULTIPLE CORRELATION AND REGRESSION

Dependent variable: X_{14} — Per capita nonenterprise general expenditure and park and sanitary district levies

Sample size: 107 Mean and standard deviation of dependent variable: 41.63 (19.74)

Statistical model: Linear

Independent Variables	Coefficient of Multiple Correlation (Standard Error)	Regression Coefficient (t)	Standardized Regression Coefficient
X_9 — Per Capita Assessed Value	.648 (15.10)	.011 (7.48)	.544
X_{11} — Tax Limits, Six Municipal Funds	.701 (14.21)	37.319 (4.96)	.349
X_7 — Per Cent of Population Foreign Born	.735 (13.58)	2.307 (3.54)	.260
X_4 — Per Cent of Population in Group Quarters	.747 (13.38)	−.434 (−2.03)	−.142
	Y intercept = −8.129		

Clearly, the 39 cities do not constitute such a sample, and statistical methods do little to help determine how far findings can be generalized to municipalities in other states or to smaller municipalities in Illinois. For this reason, the analyses of Tables A2, A5, and A6 have been repeated utilizing data from the 107 cities in the 5,000 to 25,000 population group. The results are shown in Tables A7, A8, and A9.

In general the results are similar to those obtained from the 39 cities. Assessed value, tax limits, and foreign-born population are the principal "determinants" of expenditures in both groups. The major differences occur when per capita assessed value is designated as the dependent variable. Median value of houses is the most important independent variable for both size groups but there is considerable difference in those that enter later. The reasons for some of the differences are obvious. For example, the entry of per cent of population in group quarters undoubtedly reflects the great variation in the importance of institutional population in smaller cities. There are a number of smaller cities in which college students or residents of hospitals or prisons make up a substantial part of the population. Since these persons often live in tax-exempt property, the per cent of population living

TABLE A8

COEFFICIENTS OF MULTIPLE CORRELATION AND REGRESSION

Dependent variable: X_{15} — Per capita current general expenditure and park and sanitary district levies

Sample size: 107 Mean and standard deviation of dependent variable: 33.83 (13.77)

Statistical model: Linear

Independent Variables	Coefficient of Multiple Correlation (Standard Error)	Regression Coefficient (t)	Standardized Regression Coefficient
X_9 — Per Capita Assessed Value	.650 (10.52)	.0067 (7.13)	.475
X_{11} — Tax Limits, Six Municipal Funds	.700 (9.92)	21.3668 (4.71)	.286
X_7 — Per Cent Population Foreign Born	.760 (9.09)	2.0973 (5.13)	.338
X_{10} — Per Capita Sales Tax Collections	.799 (8.45)	1.3519 (4.14)	.254
	Y intercept = −8.249		

in group quarters is negatively correlated with both assessed value and expenditure. Some of the differences are not so easy to explain, but the general impression left by examining the determinants of assessed value for both groups of cities is that per capita assessed value is closely correlated with a number of economic and demographic features of the community which are, in turn, often intercorrelated with each other. Perhaps additional light would be shed on the problem if better data concerning the composition of the tax base by type of property were available.

AN ANALYSIS OF REVENUE BY SOURCE

Since the influence which tax limits have upon total expenditure can operate only through tax rates, it is not surprising to find (Tables A10 and A11) that tax limits are by far the most important determinant of tax rates for both the 39-city group and the 107-city group. An additional independent variable, the total tax rate of all overlapping (non-municipal) governments, was utilized in this analysis, but did not enter the stepwise correlation process.

In view of the importance of tax limits, it becomes important to know

TABLE A9

COEFFICIENTS OF MULTIPLE CORRELATION AND REGRESSION

Dependent variable: X_9 — Per capita assessed value

Sample size: 107 Mean and standard deviation of dependent variable: 2680.17 (975.50)

Statistical model: Linear

Independent Variables	Coefficient of Multiple Correlation (Standard Error)	Regression Coefficient (t)	Standardized Regression Coefficient
X_{13} — Median Value of Owner-Occupied Houses	.657 (738.75)	.1127 (6.65)	.644
X_3 — Per Cent of Population Under 18	.714 (689.50)	−95.9347 (−6.54)	−.562
X_4 — Per Cent of Population Living in Group Quarters	.772 (629.05)	−56.5544 (−5.42)	−.375
X_{12} — Per Cent of Families with Incomes Under $3,000	.786 (614.78)	−41.7839 (−3.42)	−.386
X_2 — Population Per Square Mile	.801 (598.33)	−.1052 (−2.71)	−.171
X_{11} — Tax Limits, Six Municipal Funds	.807 (593.44)	574.2903 (1.64)	.109
	Y intercept = 5588.20		

TABLE A10

COEFFICIENTS OF MULTIPLE CORRELATION AND REGRESSION

Dependent variable: X_{18} — Total municipal tax rate

Sample size: 39 Mean and standard deviation of dependent variable: .710 (.165)

Statistical model: Linear

Independent Variables	Coefficient of Multiple Correlation (Standard Error)	Regression Coefficient (t)	Standardized Regression Coefficient
X_{11} — Tax Limits, Six Municipal Funds	.679 (.122)	.6759 (5.16)	.569
X_{12} — Per Cent of Families with Incomes Under $3,000	.772 (.107)	.0113 (3.48)	.384
	Y intercept = .233		

TABLE A11

COEFFICIENTS OF MULTIPLE CORRELATION AND REGRESSION

Dependent variable: X_{18} — Total municipal tax rates
Sample size: 107 Mean and standard deviation of dependent variable: .559 (.221)
Statistical model: Linear

Independent Variables	Coefficient of Multiple Correlation (Standard Error)	Regression Coefficient (t)	Standardized Regression Coefficient
X_{11} — Tax Limits, Six Municipal Funds	.654 (.168)	.74367 (8.18)	.619
X_3 — Per Cent of Population Under 18	.684 (.163)	−.01209 (−3.82)	−.312
X_7 — Per Cent of Population Foreign Born	.697 (.161)	.01865 (2.39)	.187
X_9 — Per Capita Assessed Value	.707 (.160)	−.00003 (−2.00)	−.152
X_4 — Per Cent of Population in Group Quarters	.716 (.158)	−.00624 (−2.17)	−.182
X_1 — Population of the Municipality	.726 (.157)	.00001 (1.71)	.131
	Y intercept = .691		

whether or not they are, in turn, correlated with other variables. Tables A12 and A13 indicate that some correlation exists but it is not very high.

Analyses of the tax rates of some overlapping governments were made. Although several of these correlations were higher than obtained for the municipalities, there seemed to be little similarity in the factors which affect tax rates. For example, per cent of families with incomes under $3,000 was the most important factor affecting school tax rates in the 39 cities (negative correlation). It should be noted, however, that school tax limits were not available so the analysis is not strictly comparable with the analysis of municipal tax rates.

The factors which are related to assessed value were shown in Tables A6 and A7. It will be noted that a number of independent variables which appear in these tables also appear in Tables A10, A11, A12, and A13. This suggests that to the extent that the independent variables are "causes" of the level of expenditure, they may be operating through *both* assessed value and tax rates.

TABLE A12

COEFFICIENTS OF MULTIPLE CORRELATION AND REGRESSION

Dependent variable: X_{11} — Tax limits, six municipal funds

Sample size: 39 Mean and standard deviation of dependent variable: .529 (.139)

Statistical model: Linear

Independent Variables	Coefficient of Multiple Correlation (Standard Error)	Regression Coefficient (t)	Standardized Regression Coefficient
X_3 — Per Cent of Population Under 18	.376 (.130)	−.01293 (−2.97)	−.451
X_{10} — Per Capita Sales Tax Collections	.472 (.126)	−.02207 (−1.94)	−.295
		Y intercept = 1.137	

TABLE A13

COEFFICIENTS OF MULTIPLE CORRELATION AND REGRESSION

Dependent variable: X_{11} — Tax limits, six municipal funds

Sample size: 107 Mean and standard deviation of dependent variable: .385 (.184)

Statistical model: Linear

Independent Variables	Coefficient of Multiple Correlation (Standard Error)	Regression Coefficient (t)	Standardized Regression Coefficient
X_4 — Per Cent of Population Living in Group Quarters	—[a]	.00861 (3.38)	.302
X_{11} — Per Cent of Families with Incomes Under $3,000	—[a]	.00844 (4.09)	.413
X_9 — Per Capita Assessed Value	.470 (.165)	.00004 (1.84)	.187
		Y intercept = .144	

[a] Variables X_3 (per cent of population under 18) and X_6 (per cent of population nonwhite) entered the program but were later removed.

A multiple correlation analysis of nonproperty tax revenue produced correlation coefficients of .744 for the 39-city group and .497 for the 107-city group. In each case six independent variables entered but the six were not identical and the order of importance as measured by standardized regression coefficients differed considerably.

Attempts to analyze intercity variation in revenue from nonproperty tax sources produced very low coefficients of correlation which were of little significance.

SUMMARY

The multiple correlation analysis reported in this appendix indicates clearly that variations in per capita expenditure are associated with measurable demographic and social conditions and with measures of economic conditions and tax capacity. It is not possible to make a simple definite statement as to the way in which these conditions influence the financial decisions which are made. In some cases it appears likely that the variables utilized are measures of need for a particular kind of governmental service and that this need has created demands which have been transmitted through the political process. The variables which are most important, however, are measures of tax capacity. One of these, per capita assessed value, is, in part, a measure of the wealth of the community and may be related to the demand for governmental services as well as to the availability of revenue. The other, tax limits, is the result of legislative, judicial, and voter decisions made at some past time, and the value of this variable is not closely related to any of the measurable variables utilized in the analysis.

APPENDIX B
A NOTE ON DATA SOURCES

U.S. Census Bureau statistics on local government finance are the basic source of statistical data utilized in this volume. These data are compiled according to a uniform system of classification which is utilized for all local governments in the United States. The modifications of Census data reported in Chapter 2 are designed to facilitate comparison among Illinois cities and to take account of particular features of Illinois municipal finance.

Property tax rate and assessed value data were obtained from compilation made by the Illinois Department of Revenue and directly from the offices of county clerks throughout the state. During visits to county clerks' offices the persons interviewed were asked to provide the tax rate limits which apply to the funds of all municipalities of over 2,500 population. Information was also obtained which made it possible to estimate the rate of all taxes imposed upon property in the municipality by all units of government. In making these estimates, the total taxes imposed upon each tax rate district in the municipality were added and the total was divided by total assessed value to obtain the "average" rate for the municipality as a whole. In cases where more than 90 per cent of the municipality's assessed value was within a single tax rate district, the rate for this district was utilized. In those cases where assessed values for each tax district were not available (usually smaller municipalities), the county clerk's judgment as to which rate was the predominant rate was accepted.

Population figures utilized in computing per capita data were estimated by using straight line interpolations or extrapolations for those years in which no regular or special census was taken after adjusting for those larger annexations which are reported in the *Municipal Year-*

book. April, 1961, population estimates were used with fiscal 1962 financial data since that date is near the beginning of the fiscal year for most municipalities.

Although the time required to collect, compile, and analyze data from hundreds of units of local government means that the statistics in a study of local government are apt to be several years old, the general pattern ordinarily changes slowly. As this is written much of the data in this manuscript is four years old. In this four-year period both revenue and expenditure of Illinois cities have risen and there have been changes in the emphasis which some cities place on expenditure for particular purposes. Several cities have adopted the utility tax or have levied for an additional fund. On the other hand, the statewide picture of revenue and expenditure patterns has changed little.

APPENDIX C

TABLE C1

ESTIMATED PER CAPITA EXPENDITURE, CITIES OVER 25,000 POPULATION, 1962 FISCAL YEAR

	Nonenterprise General Expenditure									
	Police[a]	Fire[a]	Streets[b]	Sewerage	Other Sanitation	Libraries	Health	Parks and Recreation	Financial Administration, General Control and Public Building	Miscellaneous General Expenditure
Municipalities Outside Chicago SMSA										
Alton	$ 7.49	$ 8.54	$ 9.17	$ 1.32	$ 3.34	$ 1.30	$ .03	$ 3.84	$ 3.82	$ .55
Belleville	6.67	6.31	6.87	4.47	3.52	1.69	—	3.05	2.31	2.71
Bloomington	9.37	9.95	10.63	1.70	2.90	2.26	—	3.65	4.51	7.29
Champaign	7.66	6.25	7.72	4.58	.67	1.36	.01	1.56	2.80	5.78
Danville	5.70	8.05	9.15	1.07	2.81	2.40	.68	3.53	2.27	2.09
Decatur	6.83	8.58	12.11	.45	.56	3.26	.79	1.38	3.49	1.25
East St. Louis	9.82	9.23	6.76	4.15	1.70	2.34	—	—	3.39	5.62
Freeport	6.18	8.92	9.70	3.15	2.00	2.58	.22	1.11	2.47	2.92
Galesburg	5.79	5.65	11.09	—	2.23	5.38	.15	2.72	2.88	5.53
Granite City	6.59	6.93	9.43	12.37	4.07	2.11	—	—	3.47	2.66
Kankakee	6.98	9.74	9.29	17.46	4.08	1.19	.29	—	2.77	4.43
Moline	7.19	9.72	14.31	7.01	2.73	3.50	.54	4.34	4.05	9.13
Pekin	6.30	17.78	9.09	1.20	3.74	3.18	.05	.27	3.24	1.93
Peoria	11.72	10.46	7.65	.73	6.07	4.76	2.67	2.61	3.44	3.43
Quincy	6.66	7.81	8.68	35.31	1.89	2.39	—	—	2.21	3.13
Rockford	8.97	9.03	14.19	1.55	3.61	4.81	.76	3.36	2.66	14.33
Rock Island	8.17	8.23	15.35	6.83	2.56	2.32	.89	4.25	3.78	6.48
Springfield	8.76	9.02	8.97	13.53	6.32	3.20	1.86	2.45	6.91	4.70
Urbana	5.87	5.46	22.32	—	1.14	1.93	—	.01	1.98	3.61
Average	7.51	8.72	10.66	6.15	2.94	2.73	.47	2.01	3.29	4.61
Municipalities in Chicago SMSA										
Arlington Hgts.	8.77	2.80	9.77	—	—	1.91	.44	—	6.58	4.37
Aurora	8.44	8.61	12.63	1.22	4.52	3.61	.59	4.37	3.61	2.40
Berwyn	11.15	6.22	8.65	—	2.62	6.45	—	2.73	1.77	1.24
Calumet City	8.28	5.20	12.25	1.01	1.91	1.01	.84	—	5.31	1.59
Chicago Hgts.	9.89	8.18	8.23	2.49	4.73	2.29	.54	.31	4.60	5.20

TABLE C1 (continued)

ESTIMATED PER CAPITA EXPENDITURE, CITIES OVER 25,000 POPULATION, 1962 FISCAL YEAR

	Nonenterprise General Expenditure									
	Police[a]	Fire[a]	Streets[b]	Sewerage	Other Sanitation	Libraries	Health	Parks and Recreation	Financial Administration, General Control and Public Building	Miscellaneous General Expenditure
Cicero	$ 13.78	$ 9.93	$ 7.66	$ 2.59	$ 9.01	$ 1.32	$ 1.12	$ —	$ 3.50	$ 4.13
Des Plaines	9.16	6.08	7.30	1.40	4.27	2.57	.33	—	3.54	2.13
Elgin	8.75	6.63	7.66	—	2.34	—	.35	2.71	2.61	3.03
Elmhurst	8.54	3.46	6.57	7.69	4.18	2.07	.40	—	2.93	1.69
Evanston	14.36	9.80	8.35	.71	6.68	3.39	2.37	7.51	5.46	5.56
Harvey	8.02	6.49	9.34	1.46	2.60	1.30	.12	—	3.67	1.83
Highland Park	24.59	7.83	21.48	3.16	3.14	10.10	.01	3.34	7.93	12.80
Joliet	8.47	9.41	8.12	—	2.90	2.06	—	.35	3.02	3.46
Maywood	10.50	7.83	5.82	—	3.86	2.30	.30	2.14	4.49	2.40
Oak Lawn	8.08	2.99	8.57	1.47	3.70	1.47	—	—	3.11	2.60
Oak Park	11.64	9.83	9.59	.70	4.62	16.18	1.87	4.74	5.32	7.42
Park Forest	7.11	5.06	12.18	.81	.68	8.68	1.22	3.33	3.42	.98
Park Ridge	7.91	3.39	8.23	1.25	2.90	2.68	.22	—	4.92	4.43
Skokie	10.49	8.39	8.18	.22	4.71	3.28	.59	—	8.33	5.58
Waukegan	11.46	9.04	11.27	1.02	3.05	3.01	.47	1.35	5.58	5.20
Wilmette	8.37	8.49	7.37	.74	8.60	3.50	.78	4.45	6.54	3.63
Average	10.37	6.94	9.49	1.33	3.86	3.77	.60	1.78	4.58	3.89
Chicago	25.08	9.65	12.71	4.39	10.10	2.03	2.04	1.57	7.84	9.35

TABLE C1 (continued)

ESTIMATED PER CAPITA EXPENDITURE, CITIES OVER 25,000 POPULATION, 1962 FISCAL YEAR

	Sanitary District Levy[c]	Park District Levy[c]	Semi-Commercial Enterprises				Interest on General Debt	Utility Expenditure		Grand Total
			Parking	Airport	Housing and Urban Renewal	Hospital		Water	Other Utilities	
Municipalities Outside Chicago SMSA										
Alton	$ —	$ —	$ .94	$ —	$ —	$ —	$4.66	$ —	$ —	$44.99
Belleville	—	—	.78	—	—	—	2.67	—	—	41.04
Bloomington	2.71	—	1.27	.13	.56	—	3.05	9.67	5.00	74.66
Champaign	6.26	3.02	1.81	—	—	34.78	1.99	—	—	86.26
Danville	4.94	—	2.14	—	—	—	.95	—	—	45.81
Decatur	6.00	4.59	2.60	—	.19	—	2.08	8.25	—	62.42
East St. Louis	8.92	5.04	.39	—	—	—	9.61	—	—	66.98
Freeport	—	6.02	.77	.23	—	—	1.25	8.93	—	56.45
Galesburg	3.77	—	1.76	1.01	—	—	.80	9.30	—	58.05
Granite City	13.93	4.47	.66	—	—	—	1.02	—	—	67.70
Kankakee	—	5.18	1.32	—	—	—	3.96	—	—	66.70
Moline	—	—	2.27	—	—	56.17	3.29	15.20	—	139.45
Pekin	—	2.99	.97	—	—	—	1.46	—	2.86	55.07
Peoria	4.65	5.08	.21	—	—	2.39	.49	—	—	66.36
Quincy	—	3.07	1.42	—	—	—	5.85	11.48	—	89.91
Rockford	3.98	4.14	2.86	—	—	3.29	1.21	13.49	—	92.27
Rock Island	—	—	1.08	—	1.34	—	5.47	9.59	—	76.35
Springfield	4.05	2.31	.19	—	—	—	3.99	15.22	60.83	152.32
Urbana	4.97	3.36	—	—	—	—	2.70	—	—	53.34
Average	3.38	2.59	1.23	.07	.11	5.09	2.97	5.32	3.62	73.48
Municipalities in Chicago SMSA										
Arlington Hgts.	8.17	6.56	1.55	—	—	—	1.20	13.52	—	65.63
Aurora	4.92	3.62	1.70	.10	—	—	1.34	7.89	—	69.58
Berwyn	8.75	—	.81	—	—	—	.74	11.11	—	62.23
Calumet City	6.90	3.25	.38	—	—	—	1.14	12.97	—	62.04
Chicago Hgts.	6.48	3.09	1.79	—	—	—	.70	18.31	—	76.84

TABLE C1 (continued)

ESTIMATED PER CAPITA EXPENDITURE, CITIES OVER 25,000 POPULATION, 1962 FISCAL YEAR

	Sanitary District Levy[c]	Park District Levy[c]	Semi-Commercial Enterprises				Interest on General Debt	Utility Expenditure		Grand Total
			Parking	Airport	Housing and Urban Renewal	Hospi-tal		Water	Other Utilities	
Cicero	$12.88	$ 5.95	$ .95	$ —	$ —	$ —	$3.67	$20.42	$ —	$ 96.91
Des Plaines	9.78	5.64	1.06	—	—	—	.84	13.14	—	67.24
Elgin	9.28	—	.82	—	1.20	—	.90	6.37	—	52.63
Elmhurst	—	4.94	.58	—	—	—	.57	7.53	—	51.14
Evanston	12.31	.36	1.38	—	—	—	1.71	6.65	—	86.61
Harvey	8.65	1.88	1.43	—	—	—	2.48	28.62	—	77.89
Highland Park	10.04	4.72	1.51	—	—	—	6.89	9.60	—	127.12
Joliet	—	—	1.99	—	2.05	—	.26	12.60	—	54.70
Maywood	9.88	.41	.40	—	17.82	—	.66	14.59	—	83.39
Oak Lawn	8.57	2.52	—	—	—	—	3.13	12.26	—	58.49
Oak Park	11.68	3.23	2.56	—	—	—	1.59	21.96	—	112.94
Park Forest	4.78	—	.21	.14	—	—	.85	8.90	—	58.36
Park Ridge	12.10	6.90	1.31	—	—	—	2.67	18.40	—	77.31
Skokie	15.10	7.55	.24	—	—	—	1.49	11.94	—	86.08
Waukegan	7.21	2.57	.26	—	.06	.29	.19	5.93	—	67.98
Wilmette	14.35	5.40	.62	—	—	—	.71	5.24	—	78.79
Average	8.66	3.27	1.03	.01	1.01	.01	1.61	12.76	—	74.95
Chicago	10.01	11.36	.91	8.99	4.91	2.77	6.31	14.23	—	144.26

[a] Police and fire expenditure include estimated normal cost of pension funds. See text of Chapter 2.

[b] Street expenditure is three-year average maintenance and construction expenditure as reported by the Illinois Division of Highways.

[c] Park and sanitary district levies are estimated levies imposed upon property within the municipality by park and sanitary districts.

SOURCE All data from U.S. Bureau of the Census, unpublished worksheets for the 1962 Census of Governments, except for modifications indicated in footnotes a, b, c.

INDEX